The Religious Life

The Religious Life

The Insights of William James

Donald Capps

CASCADE Books • Eugene, Oregon

THE RELIGIOUS LIFE
The Insights of William James

Copyright © 2015 Donald Capps. All rights reserved. Except for brief quotations in critical publications or reviews, no part of this book may be reproduced in any manner without prior written permission from the publisher. Write: Permissions, Wipf and Stock Publishers, 199 W. 8th Ave., Suite 3, Eugene, OR 97401.

Cascade Books
An Imprint of Wipf and Stock Publishers
199 W. 8th Ave., Suite 3
Eugene, OR 97401

www.wipfandstock.com

ISBN 978-1-4982-1994-5

Cataloguing-in-Publication data:

Capps, Donald

    The religious life : the insights of William James / Donald Capps.

    xiv + 248 p. ; 23 cm. Includes bibliographical references.

    ISBN 978-1-4982-1994-5

    1. James, William (1842–1910)—Criticism and interpretation. 2. James, William (1842–1910)—Varieties of Religious Experience. 3. Experience—Religion. 4. Psychology (Religious). 5. Religion. 6. Conversion. I. Title.

BL53 J363 C50 2015

Manufactured in the U.S.A.   10/22/2015

Terry Bard, editor of *The Journal of Pastoral Care and Counseling*, has granted permission for the use of the author's article, "The Letting Loose of Hope: Where Psychology of Religion and Pastoral Care Converge," *The Journal of Pastoral Care* 51 (1997) 139–49.
Springer Publications has granted permission for the use of the author's article, "A Spiritual Person," *Journal of Religion and Health* 50 (2011) 313–20.

Scripture quotations marked (NRSV) come from the New Revised Standard Version Bible, copyright 1989, Division of Christian Education of the National Council of the Churches of Christ in the United States of America. Used by permission. All rights reserved.
Scripture quotations marked (KJV) come from the King James Version Bible.

Contents

Acknowledgments | vii
Introduction | ix

Part I: Varieties of Religious Experience

1. The Book and Its Author | 3
2. Personal Religious Experience | 23
3. The Healthy Mind | 47
4. The Sick Soul | 61
5. The Divided Self and the Process of Its Unification | 91
6. The Psychology of Religious Conversion | 116
7. The Saintly Character | 154
8. The Prayerful Consciousness | 184

Part II: Living In Hope

9. A Troubled Man: The Case of Ansel Bourne | 207
10. A Spiritual Person: The Example of Phillips Brooks | 216
11. The Letting Loose of Hope | 226

References | 237
Index of Names | 245

Acknowledgments

I want to express my appreciation to the editorial team at Cascade Books, especially K. C. Hanson, editor-in-chief; Jim Tedrick, managing editor; and Brian Palmer, editorial administrator; and to James Stock, marketing director; and Jeremy Funk, copy editor.

In the course of writing this book, I have been reminded again and again of the insightfulness of William James. The dictionary defines *insight* as "the ability to see and understand clearly the inner nature of things, especially by intuition," and it defines *intuition* as "the direct knowing or immediate understanding of something without the conscious use of reasoning."[1] As I consider the fact that I have dedicated my life, vocationally speaking, to the religious life, I am deeply grateful for William James's ability to see and understand the inner nature of the religious life, and for his capacity to express this understanding in a way that confirms that a life dedicated to the religious life is well worth living.

—Donald Capps

My dad was proof-reading this book the morning of the day he died, suddenly, after a car accident. This is a book about hope. It's a book about finding relief and comfort in a world where, in the end, the odds are stacked against us.

I need to thank Ian Creeger, Jeremy Funk, and K.C. Hanson for helping me finish the proof-reading. I also want to thank Evelyn Brister, Nathan Carlin, and Bob Dykstra, among others, for their thoughtful words that helped bring other sides of my father into focus.

1. Agnes, *Webster's New World*, 739, 750

My dad talks about a life worth living in his acknowledgements, above. He ends the book with a poignant description of the death of William James's toddler son, Herman. In between is an insightful study of James's *Varieties* that argues for the importance of a certain kind of religious experience that is hopeful, to be sure, but also realistic. These experiences point to a Jamesian "more" but are also grounded in our actual lives and relationships to others. I think my dad's own religious experiences came in listening to others, in offering words of sympathy and encouragement, in giving wise advice, and in proposing strategies that were sometimes pure lunacy—but that also brought more realistic solutions into focus. If that was my father's religious life then this book is his fitting last word.

—John Capps

Introduction

WILLIAM JAMES (1842–1910) BEGAN teaching philosophy at Harvard College in 1879. He was appointed assistant professor of philosophy in 1880 and promoted to professor of philosophy in 1885. He was also appointed professor of psychology in 1889. He resigned his professorships in 1907. George Herbert Palmer, who was appointed instructor in philosophy in 1872, wrote a tribute to James in 1920 on the occasion of the publication of James's letters. Palmer had this to say about him:

> Though he called his philosophy "Radical Empiricism" and liked to try how complete a world might be constructed by ingenious manipulation of material elements, yet to the last he kept ample room in his empiric universe for spiritual forces. Man is free. An approachable God exists, reverence for whom is the beginning of wisdom, and religion the most urgent of human concerns. He himself was a peculiarly devout man, and though living at a distance, liked to begin his day with the service at Appleton Chapel.[1]

This is a book on William James's understanding of the religious life. It focuses especially on his classic text *The Varieties of Religious Experience*, which was originally published in 1902.[2] But several lesser known essays are also drawn upon in order to expand on central themes in *The Varieties*. In this book I emphasize James's claim that *The Varieties* is, according to its subtitle, "a study in human nature," and that for James a fundamental feature of human nature is that we possess a conscious and a subconscious mind and that the subconscious mind is deeply implicated in the religious life.

We tend to associate the subconscious mind with Sigmund Freud and the psychoanalytic tradition, but James also emphasized the influence of

---

1. Simon, *William James Remembered*, 35. Appleton Chapel is Harvard University's chapel.
2. James, *The Varieties of Religious Experience*.

our subconscious mind on our mental and emotional processes. He thought of the conscious mind as the center of the mind, and the subconscious mind as the mind's outer margins. The image that expresses what he had in mind is a circle within a larger circle. He also viewed the subconscious mind as the place or locus where religious ideas and emotions incubate and then, when circumstances permit, gain entrance into the conscious mind. In effect, the subconscious region of the mind is the soil in which religious ideas and emotions germinate.

As Palmer indicates, James kept ample room in his empiric universe for spiritual forces. He did so by suggesting that there is a spiritual world that exists outside the mind but that informs and even invades the mind, typically by gaining entry into the subconscious mind at least initially. He begins lecture 3 of *The Varieties*—"The Reality of the Unseen"—with this observation:

> Were one asked to characterize the life of religion in the broadest and most general terms possible, one might say that it consists of the belief that there is an unseen order, and that our supreme good lies in harmoniously adjusting ourselves thereto. This belief and this adjustment are the religious attitude in the soul.[3]

James notes that "all of our attitudes, moral, practical, or emotional, as well as religious, are due to the 'objects' of our consciousness, the things which we believe to exist, whether really or ideally, along with ourselves."[4] These "objects" may be present to our senses or only to our thought, but in either case they elicit from us a reaction, and our reaction may be as strong or stronger when the object is only in our thought and not available to our sense perceptions. In general, the more concrete objects of most persons' religion—the God or gods in which they believe—are known to them only in idea. Although some persons have testified to their having seen the object of their belief—face-to-face, as it were—religion is primarily based on the belief or conviction that an unseen world exists outside the human mind, both individually and collectively. And although this belief or conviction can take the form of an abstract idea, it is more likely to manifest "a sense of reality, a feeling of objective presence, a perception of what we may call 'something there.'"[5]

In his concluding lecture in *The Varieties* James speaks of this sense of reality and feeling of objective presence as something "more," which is

---

3. Ibid., 53.
4. Ibid.
5. Ibid., 58.

INTRODUCTION   xi

operative in the universe outside of oneself. James proposes as a hypothesis "that whatever it may be on its *farther* side, the 'more' with which in religious experience we feel ourselves connected is on its *hither* side the subconscious continuation of our conscious life."[6] Clearly, the "more" exists independently of our own thoughts and emotions, but the very purpose of religion is to enable us to feel ourselves "connected" with it. As Palmer notes, for James "an approachable God exists." Moreover, an approachable God exists for James because he understands God to be the initiator as well as the object of approach. The religious life then is one in which we "keep in working touch" with the spiritual world that surrounds and embraces us.

Now, a word about the contents of this book: Chapter 1 provides a brief summary of the contents of *The Varieties of Religious Experience* and a biography of its author focusing primarily on his professional career. Chapter 2 is concerned with James's emphasis in *The Varieties of Religious Experience* on personal not institutional forms and expressions of religion. It cites several examples of the religious experiences of individuals whom James either knows or has read about to illustrate what he means by personal religion. Chapter 3 focuses on James's chapter called "The Religion of Healthy-Mindedness," which emphasizes the growing influence of the mind-cure movement especially in the United States. Chapter 4 is concerned with James's chapter on "The Sick Soul." It takes particular note of James's view that melancholy is the worst form of soul-sickness and considers his own experience of melancholy, which he presents anonymously in the chapter. Chapter 5 introduces James's view of religion as implicated in the experience of division within oneself but also as a resource in the resolution of this sense of inner division. Chapter 6 is concerned with James's lecture on religious conversion and his use of psychological theories to understand the inner workings of conversion. Chapter 7, on the saintly character, draws on three of James's lectures on saintliness and focuses on his suggestion that the saintly character is a person for whom spiritual emotions are the habitual center of one's personal energy, and that there is "a certain composite photograph of universal saintliness, the same in all religions, of which the features can easily be traced."[7] Chapter 8 concerns James's lecture on other characteristics of religion and his emphasis in this lecture on prayer, or what he calls "the prayerful consciousness." The chapter shows that James placed particular emphasis on prayer as the religious experience that facili-

---

6. Ibid., 508, 512. In his answers to a questionnaire prepared by James Bissett Pratt, James said that "Religion means primarily a universe of spiritual relations surrounding the earthly practical ones, not merely relations of 'value,' but agencies and their activities." James, *Writings 1902–1910*, 1183.

7. Ibid., 271.

tates the connection between the human mind and the spiritual world that surrounds us.

The three relatively brief chapters in Part 2 pick up on several prominent themes in *The Varieties of Religious Experience*. Chapter 9 focuses on James's interest in the clergyman Ansel Bourne, who experienced himself as two different persons, and on James's efforts to help him via hypnosis to reconcile his dual selves. This case has clear associations with James's discussion in *The Varieties* of the divided self and of the role of religion in the process of unification. Chapter 10 centers on James's identification of the clergyman Phillips Brooks as exemplary of a "spiritual person" and suggests that what James recognized and celebrated in Brooks was his emphasis on the inner resources that are available to us in our personal and collective struggles with the difficulties and problems of life. Finally, chapter 11 concerns James's suggestion in *Pragmatism* that what fundamentally distinguishes the religious view of life from the views expressed in materialism and in narrow understandings of science is that life on this earth is fundamentally hopeful.[8] This chapter suggests that the death of James's son Herman played an important role in James's own assurance of the truth of the religious life.

This book does not cover all the topics that James discusses in *The Varieties of Religious Experience*. The topics of mysticism (to which he devoted two lectures) is not discussed, and philosophy (to which he devoted a single lecture) is considered only as it impinges on other topics. Also, the chapter on the saintly character deals with his first chapter on saintliness but not the second. His final chapter—"Conclusions"—and postscript are not discussed either.

Thus, the book does not present *The Varieties of Religious Experience* in a comprehensive way. However, my hope is that it provides the reader with a clear and compelling sense of James's understanding of the religious life, one that I believe is as relevant today as it was at the turn of the twentieth century. Of course, James's discussion and references reflect the social and cultural realities of his own day, and he uses theories and concepts, especially psychological, that were current at the time. But the manner in which he addresses and explores the religious life and especially what makes a person religious is as insightful today as it was in his own day. *The Varieties of Religious Experience* is considered a classic in the broad field of religious studies and more focally in the psychological study of religion. What makes a book a classic, I believe, is that it invites its readers to enter into the text in a way that is personally meaningful to them. Moreover, it *remains* a classic

---

8. James, *Pragmatism*, 49.

because its readers over the course of their own lives discover new ways in which the book is personally meaningful to them. It is my hope that this book will serve as an invitation to readers to discover that the book is, in this sense, a classic for them.

PART I

Varieties of Religious Experience

1

The Book and Its Author

In this introductory chapter I will provide a brief summary of William James's *The Varieties of Religious Experience* followed by a brief summary of his life, focusing primarily on his professional career. The summary of his life will provide some useful information about James and his life as a Harvard professor and will also enable readers to appreciate the role that *The Varieties of Religious Experience* played in his professional life.

THE VARIETIES OF RELIGIOUS EXPERIENCE

The Varieties of Religious Experience is based on James's 1901–1902 Gifford Lectures at the University of Edinburgh. It was originally published in 1902 (when James was sixty years old).[1] It consists of twenty lectures, some of which are combined into a single chapter in the book itself, and a postscript. The table of contents includes the titles of the lectures and summaries of the topics and issues covered in each lecture. Thus it is possible for readers to gain an informed understanding of what the lectures are about simply by reading the table of contents. On the other hand, one of the unique features of the book is the fact that in each lecture James uses personal testimonies to illustrate the points that he is making. There are approximately 150 testimonies in the book, and they are drawn from a variety of sources, including autobiographies, diaries, letters, sermons, books on the religious life, and theological writings.

---

1. James, *The Varieties of Religious Experience*.

The first three chapters (lectures 1–3) on "Religion and Neurology," "Circumscription of the Topic," and "The Reality of the Unseen," describe the general focus of the lectures. The fourth and fifth chapters (which comprise lectures 4–7) focus on the distinction that James makes between the religion of healthy-mindedness and the religion of morbid-mindedness (or the sick soul). Chapter 6 (based on lecture 8) is concerned with the divided self and the process of its unification; and chapters 7 and 8 (based on lectures 9 and 10) focus on conversion, which, as James shows, is the means by which the unification of the self is realized. These chapters make up ten or half of the twenty lectures.

Two chapters on saintliness come next. They comprise five of the original lectures (lectures 11–15) in the second series of the Gifford Lectures. Chapter 9 focuses on the characteristics of saintliness, and chapter 10 is concerned with the value of saintliness, especially for the person who exemplifies saintly qualities, but it is also concerned with the beneficial role of saintliness in society. Chapter 11 on mysticism (which comprises lectures 16 and 17) follows, and it covers a wide variety of topics, most notably the role that mystical states play in affording a sense of union with the Absolute. Chapter 12 on philosophy (which comprises lecture 18) introduces pragmatism as a test of the value of religious conceptions and the role that philosophy can play in the development of a science of religions. Chapter 13 (which comprises lecture 19) is titled "Other Characteristics" and covers a variety of topics but especially significant is the fact that it emphasizes the role that prayer plays in the religious life. Chapter 14 (which comprises lecture 20) is titled "Conclusions." It returns to the theme of personal religious experience and the intermediating role of the subconscious mind between human nature and the "higher region" where God is the supreme reality.

A final "Postscript" identifies the philosophical perspective of the book as a sort of "piecemeal" as opposed to "universalistic" supernaturalism. It suggests that the author does not fit easily within either "popular Christianity" or "scholastic theism," but that he wishes again to emphasize the role of "prayerful communion" as the way one may realize the reality of God and as a result experience regenerative effects that are unattainable in other ways.

With this brief summary of *The Varieties of Religious Experience* in mind, I would now like to provide a brief account of William James's life, focusing especially on his professional career. There are many excellent biographies of James, and this very fact indicates that he was well-known during his lifetime, and that he was very much in contact with others, whether in social situations (as a teacher, lecturer, colleague, and friend) or through written correspondence.² In addition, as we have seen in the case of the Gifford Lectures, his lectures and addresses were transformed into books so that his writings were available to others to read, and these writings often included self-referential comments. In short, James made every effort to be accessible to others.

THE LIFE OF WILLIAM JAMES

Childhood and Adolescence

William James (known as Willy in the family) was born on January 11, 1842, in New York City. He was the first child of Henry and Mary James, both thirty-one years old. They had just purchased a house at 5 Washington Place, but they had returned to the Astor House, the hotel where they had been living, for the lying-in. When William was fifteen months old, his brother Henry (known as Harry) was born. The family went to Europe in October 1843, and remained in England until the summer of 1845 when they returned to the United States. When William was three years old, his brother Garth Wilkinson James (nicknamed Wilky) was born, and a year later his brother Robertson (nicknamed Bob) was born. When William was six years old, his sister Alice was born. The next year his mother suffered a miscarriage after which she had no more children.

As the family grew, they moved around a great deal. William lived in at least eighteen different houses by the time he was sixteen years old, and this does not count their long residences in hotels. His father, who had originally planned to become a minister but withdrew from Princeton Theological Seminary before graduating, was responsible for these relocations.³ He had inherited considerable wealth from his father, and this freed him to write, go to conferences and lectures, and spend a great deal of time with his family. William was taught at home, mostly by young women, until the age of ten. Then, between the ages of ten and sixteen he attended at least

---

2. For the following brief summary of James's life I have drawn extensively on Robert D. Richardson's biography titled *William James: In the Maelstrom of American Modernism*. To make this summary easy to read, I have not used quotation marks and page references. I have also drawn indirectly on other biographies, including Gay Wilson Allen's *William James*; Howard M. Feinstein's *Becoming William James*; Gerald E. Myers's *William James*; Ralph Barton Perry's *The Thought and Character of William James*; and Linda Simon's *Genuine Reality*. Other informative texts are R. W. B. Lewis's *The Jameses: A Family Narrative*; and Alfred Habegger's *The Father*, a biography of James's father Henry James Sr.

3. He met his future wife, Mary Walsh, through her brother Hugh, who was also a student at Princeton Theological Seminary.

nine different schools, with several interludes of homeschooling. Part of this time the family lived in New York City, but there were also periods when they lived in Geneva, Switzerland, and in Paris, France. When William was sixteen years old, the family returned to the United States and lived in Newport, Connecticut. They were essentially settled in Newport from 1858 to 1864 (when William was sixteen to twenty-two years old). He attended the art studio of William Morris Hunt at the beginning of this period and was planning on becoming an artist. Then quite suddenly in 1861 he quit drawing and painting and signed up as a ninety-day recruit in the state militia shortly after the Confederate Army fired on Fort Sumter in April 1861, the event that marked the onset of the Civil War.

College and Medical School

But James did not serve in the state militia. Instead he enrolled in the Lawrence Scientific School in Cambridge in the fall of 1861. Lawrence Scientific School was part of Harvard University but clearly separate from Harvard College. His emphasis was chemistry. In his second year his brother Henry joined him. In his third year he completed the fall term but he did not return for the spring semester. Instead he began a program of reading and note-taking on his own. By early February he was feeling "apathetic and indisposed for work," but he pushed himself by writing notes on everything that he read. At this time his brothers Wilky and Bob were drafted into military service but he was not called up. His brother Henry had recently suffered an accident and was declared unfit to serve.

James returned to Cambridge in September 1863 and shifted his studies from chemistry to anatomy and physiology. He knew he needed to make a professional choice, and although he preferred natural history he was aware that it wouldn't pay much, so he reconciled himself to attending Harvard Medical School. He began attending lectures at the medical school in February 1864. In May the family moved from Newport to Boston. They took up residence in the Beacon Hill area, and James began living at home, as it was a short walk from home to the medical school. He continued attending medical lectures in the fall of 1864 and winter of 1865, but he was having difficulty settling down, so when he was given the opportunity to go on a scientific expedition to Brazil conducted by the natural historian Louis Agassiz, he jumped at the chance. He left medical school abruptly and boarded the steamship *Colorado* in New York on March 29, 1865.

After a twenty-two-day trip, the steamship anchored at Rio de Janeiro. During the voyage the Civil War came to an end and President Lincoln was assassinated. While Agassiz and others explored inland, James was assigned to collect polyps, jellyfish, and other marine life in the bay area of Rio. He came down with a mild form of smallpox that led to his hospitalization, and he made plans to return home, feeling that it was a mistake to have gone in the first place. But his health improved rapidly, and Agassiz put him in charge of a small expedition for collecting fish in two little-known rivers that ran into the Amazon. There were things he enjoyed about the expedition, especially the discovery in himself of new strengths and abilities, but he came to realize that he did not want to become a field naturalist. So when he returned to Boston the following spring, he resumed his medical studies. He also became involved in the social scene and enjoyed the company of young women.

During the summer vacation in 1866 he obtained an appointment as acting house surgeon at Massachusetts General Hospital. His closest friend was Oliver Wendell Holmes Jr., known as Wendell, who was the son of Dr. Oliver Wendell Holmes Sr. Dr. Holmes, who was teaching James microscopy that summer at the medical school, was not only a physician but also a poet, novelist, and editor. Wendell, Dr. Holmes's son, was a student at the medical school, but he was greatly interested in philosophy, and he encouraged James to read philosophy.

In early fall James was beginning to feel that medicine was a professional dead end. While working as acting house surgeon during the summer, he had begun to experience problems with his eyes, his digestion, and sleeplessness. Then in November 1866, his back gave out. It was apparently a sudden episode of acute lower-back pain with muscle spasm brought on by overexertion, strain, trauma, or stress. To James, this was the physical correlate to the breakdown of his career plans. In December he went through the motions of applying for a position in the medical side of the hospital, but he was already thinking of escaping to Europe.

Interest in Physiological Psychology

In April 1867, James sailed for Brest (in what is today Belarus), made his way to Paris and Dresden, and then in September he settled in Berlin. He remained in Germany until November 1868, reading philosophy and attending lectures in physiology at the University of Berlin. He also began reading psychology, which at that time was becoming grounded in physiology, and he informed his father in a letter written in late December 1867 that he was working on the border ground between physiology and psychology. However, in January 1868, he confessed in a letter to Wendell Holmes that he was really down in the dumps, and in the spring of 1868 he was writing about his state of depression and his feelings of being totally demoralized. Yet he read voraciously, and when he returned to the United States in November 1868, he was giving serious thought to pursuing the emerging field of physiological psychology. He also set about the task of completing his medical degree, which would involve writing a thesis.

On May 21, 1869, James handed in his medical thesis on the effects of cold on the human body, and one month later he took his medical exam and passed it. He had successfully completed his medical education, but it was clear that he viewed this achievement as the end and not the beginning of something. He continued to live with his parents and his sister Alice, and during this time he developed a close relationship with Minnie Temple. She was three years younger and a first cousin (the daughter of his father's sister). It was a complicated relationship because James had strong feelings about the appropriateness of first-cousin marriages, she was seriously ill, and he was not especially healthy either. But she was the first person he could talk with about his deepest religious and spiritual concerns. They came to an understanding of their relationship—most likely as soulmates who could not be married—and this only increased his unhappiness. In January she wrote him a letter of intimacy and renunciation, and although he would have approved of the tone of renunciation in the letter, it left him feeling emptier than ever. On February 1, 1870, James wrote in his diary that today "I about touched bottom." Minnie died on March 8. Sometime between her death and the end of April he experienced his worst crisis of all, a crisis which he relates anonymously in *The Varieties of Religious Experience*. I will focus on this crisis in chapter 4.

Beginning of Harvard Teaching Career

For the next several months James struggled to control his despondency and general depression of spirits. The second half of 1870 and most of 1871 he was clearly at a low point in his life. On the other hand, during this time he read a great deal, and somewhere around April 1871 his reading took a more professional turn toward books and articles on physiology, psychology, and philosophy. He was now in continual touch with a friend, Henry Bowditch, who was well on his way toward becoming a leading American physiologist. Also in April 1871 Bowditch was offered a position at Harvard Medical School as assistant professor of physiology, and he told James that he was expecting James to join him in working on experimental physiology. Then when the professor in comparative anatomy and physiology at

Harvard retired in the spring of 1872, Bowditch was approached by the president, Charles Eliot, about taking over the retiring professor's post. Bowditch, however, had his medical school position and laboratory, so he recommended James for the post. As James was working almost every day in Bowditch's laboratory, Eliot quickly agreed to the proposal, and in August 1872 James was appointed instructor in physiology in the college and scheduled to begin teaching in January 1873. He was thirty-one years old.

James's first course was on comparative anatomy and physiology of vertebrates. As he began teaching, his spirits underwent a marked change for the better, and it was clear that his real vocation was teaching. However, the following summer he was not feeling well, and in late August he asked to be excused from teaching so that he could go to Europe. During his sojourn in Europe he experienced a deep sense of homesickness, and when he returned in March he began to feel better physically. He resumed work in Bowditch's lab. In the fall of 1874 he returned to teaching and again taught the course on comparative anatomy and physiology. The following year he repeated the course and also taught a graduate course on the relations between physiology and psychology. Then in early December he proposed a new course in psychology to President Eliot. In his proposal he referred to the broad field of "mental science," which included philosophy, and noted that the four courses that were already being offered in this subject area belonged mainly to the history of philosophy. In February 1876 he was promoted to assistant professor of physiology, and the new course on physiological psychology was offered the next academic year.

Marriage and Transfer to Philosophy Department

In early 1876 a friend invited him to attend a gathering at the home of Reverend John T. Sargent, a Unitarian minister. It was at this gathering that he met Alice Gibbens. After a long and complicated courtship, they were married on July 10, 1878, at Alice's grandmother's home. He was thirty-six, and Alice was twenty-nine years old. At this time he was hoping that he could be transferred from physiology to the philosophy department; a philosophy position would include teaching psychology, as there was no separate psychology department. James was also beginning to publish essays on philosophical topics.[4] Because there were already two professors in the philosophy department, one of whom was George Herbert Palmer (whose

---

4. For example, his essay titled "The Sentiment of Rationality" was published in *Mind* in July 1879. See James, *The Will to Believe and Other Essays in Popular Philosophy*, 63–110.

tribute to James was quoted in the introduction), it was unclear whether there was room for James. However in January, 1879 he had a conversation with President Eliot that left him convinced that he had the inside track on the position held by Francis Bowen if and when Bowen retired. In May Alice gave birth to their son Henry.

In the fall of 1880 James was appointed assistant professor of philosophy. On January 29, 1882, his mother died (she was seventy-one years old), and in June their son William was born. In September James set off by himself for his sabbatical in Europe in hopes of working on his book *The Principles of Psychology*, for which he had signed a contract two years earlier. By November his father's health had declined, but his wife Alice assured him that if he returned he couldn't do anything for his father that wasn't already being done, and she added that his return would disrupt work on his book. His father died on December 18, 1882, and in January 1883 James began working on his book in earnest. It was as if he now felt free to write. He felt, though, that he would make more progress if he were at home and had his personal library and the Harvard library close by, so in late March he returned home.

Later that year his brother Wilky died, and in January 1884 James's third son, Herman, was born. At the same time his brother Bob was having health problems relating to his alcoholism, and he was making frequent trips to Boston, leaving his wife and children in Milwaukee, Wisconsin, and taking rooms nearby. James felt a special responsibility for his younger brother and arranged for him to work as his research assistant. But caring for Bob and being the father of three young boys made it difficult for him to make headway on his psychology book. Also, in 1884 he worked on a book containing his father's writings, and during this time he felt an intimacy with his father he had not enjoyed during his father's lifetime. The book was published in 1885.[5]

Death of Herman and Interest in Parapsychology

Meanwhile, James was promoted to full professor and given an increase in salary. But in early June 1885 his son Herman (nicknamed Humster) came down with a bad case of the whooping cough, and it progressed into pneumonia. He died on July 9. He was only eighteen months old. I will return to his death and its impact on James in chapter 11.

During this time James was becoming interested in parapsychology, viewing it as a legitimate aspect of psychology and as receptive, therefore,

---

5. James, *The Literary Remains of Henry James*.

to the same empirical methods one would use for any other psychological investigation. He attended séances and reported on mediums, which he tended to consider fraudulent. But he was encouraged by a favorable report of the Boston medium Leonora Piper by Richard Hodgson, a member of the London Society for Psychical Research who had traveled to the United States to investigate her. James came to believe that she possessed knowledge that she had not gained by the use of her sense perceptions or normal intelligence. Although he felt he should be spending more time on his psychology book, he was drawn more and more into psychical research, and in March 1886 he was experimentally hypnotizing Harvard students. He began to seek some middle ground between the spiritualist community in Boston and its skeptical debunkers. His wife Alice was also curious about spiritualist matters so this was to be one of the many interests they shared in common.

Appointment as Professor of Psychology

When the school year began in October 1886 James felt he was well on his way to finishing his *The Principles of Psychology*. In late December he read John Dewey's book *Psychology*. Dewey, who was twenty-seven years old at the time, was fresh from doctoral studies at Johns Hopkins University. In James's view Dewey's book was too much influenced by German idealism. But when Dewey read James's *The Principles of Psychology* in the early 1890s, he changed his view of psychology to a more naturalistic approach, and the two of them together became colleagues in the shaping of American psychology and philosophy.

On March 24, 1887, James's daughter Margaret Mary was born, and it was clear from his letter to his mother-in-law announcing her birth that he had fallen immediately in love with baby Margaret. Their son Henry (nicknamed Harry) was now seven years old, and son William (nicknamed Billy) was four. The behavior of children was very much on James's mind as he wrote his chapter on "Instinct" for *The Principles of Psychology*.[6] At this time he also spent some time with Annie Payson Call, a young woman who would soon be a leader in the New Thought or mind-cure movement. Her popular books would be based on his views about the power of habit and he, in turn, learned a great deal about the importance of muscular relaxation from her work.[7]

---

6. James, *The Principles of Psychology*, 2:383–441.

7. See James, "The Gospel of Relaxation," in James, *Talks to Teachers*, 99–112. See also Call, *Power through Repose*; and Call, *As a Matter of Course*; and Capps, "Relaxed

Meanwhile Harvard's department of philosophy was flourishing. Josiah Royce had joined the faculty (on James's recommendation) in 1885, and George Santayana was appointed instructor in philosophy following the completion of his PhD in May 1889. In August 1889 James attended the first International Congress of Physiological Psychology in Paris and experienced the affirmation of European colleagues who had read his essays. In the fall of 1889 President Eliot wanted to appoint him to the professorship in moral philosophy recently vacated due to a retirement and James suggested that Harvard needed to catch up with the times and appoint a professor of psychology. A few weeks later Eliot offered James a professorship in psychology. In May 1890 James finally completed *The Principles of Psychology*. The book was published in September.[8] In December Alice gave birth to a baby boy. When he was three they named him Alexander Robertson James. In the interim James called him Tweedy and Alice called him Francis. He was later known as Aleck.

In March 1891 James wrote a glowing review of Annie Payson Call's *Power through Repose*.[9] With the encouragement of his publisher he also began work on a shortened version of *The Principles of Psychology* that could be used as a textbook. It took him only six weeks to complete and it was published in 1892.[10] By this time his laboratory responsibilities were beginning to weigh him down, especially because he was no longer directly involved in experimental psychology, so he asked for permission to sound out a possible replacement. Hugo Münsterberg, a young German psychologist whom James had met at the Congress on Physiological Psychology in Paris, was appointed to take his place.

In March 1892 James's sister Alice, who had been living with his brother Henry in London, died.[11] Her partner Katherine Loring brought her remains back to the United States, and they were placed in the Cambridge Cemetery lot with the remains of their father and mother. The following academic year James was on sabbatical, and the whole family spent the year in Lausanne, Switzerland.

Bodies."

    8. James, *The Principles of Psychology*.

    9. Call, *Power through Repose*. Her second book, *As a Matter of Course*, was published three years later.

    10. James, *Psychology: The Briefer Course*.

    11. See my discussion of her death in Capps, *Jesus the Village Psychiatrist*, 113–14.

Acquaintance with Sigmund Freud

When the family returned in September 1893, James felt good about resuming his academic responsibilities after a fifteen-month sabbatical but in a few weeks he began to experience what he called a "really awful melancholy." In January 1894 he turned fifty-two and shortly thereafter he suffered his first attack of angina pectoris. His health issues stimulated a renewal of his interest in hysteria, and through his reading of Pierre Janet's *État Mentale des Hystériques* he became acquainted with Josef Breuer and Sigmund Freud's 1893 article on the psychical mechanism of hysterical phenomena.[12] In addition to his review of Janet's book, his brief review of the Breuer and Freud article was published in *Psychological Review*. This was the first published reference to Freud by an American.

James and Freud met fifteen years later in September 1909. Freud, accompanied by C. G. Jung and Sandor Ferenczi, traveled to America for the twentieth anniversary of the founding of Clark University in Worcester, Massachusetts. Twenty-nine lecturers participated in the conference organized by the University president, G. Stanley Hall. Freud delivered five lectures and Jung delivered three. James attended one of Jung's lectures (on word association) and one of Freud's lectures (on dream interpretation). Later that day, James invited Freud to walk with him to the Union Depot, where James would take the train back to Boston. In his autobiographical study Freud describes what happened:

> I shall never forget one little scene that occurred as we were on a walk together. He stopped suddenly, handed me a bag he was carrying and asked me to walk on, saying that he would catch me up as soon as he had gone through an attack of angina pectoris which was just coming on. He died of that disease a year later; and I have always wished that I might be as fearless as he was in the face of approaching death.[13]

---

12. Janet, *État Mentale des Hystériques*. Breuer and Freud's "On the Psychical Mechanism of Hysterical Phenomena (Preliminary Considerations)" became the lead chapter in Breuer and Freud, *Studies on Hysteria*, 3–17. James's reviews of Janet's book and Breuer and Freud's article were published in *Psychological Review* 1 (1894) 195–200. See Taylor, *William James on Exceptional Mental States*, 184–85.

13. Freud, *An Autobiographical study*, 99; see also Rosenzweig, *The Historic Expedition to America*.

Becoming a Popular Lecturer

In late January 1895 James gave a lecture on the effects of alcohol to the Harvard Total Abstinence League. After acknowledging that he took an occasional drink, he suggested that the best way to wean people from intemperance is to fill them with a love of temperance for its own sake. In the fall of 1896 he gave a number of talks to teachers in Boston on psychology and its educational uses. They were published in 1899 together with three talks he had given to students in Boston and at several women's colleges.[14] In February 1897 he gave a set of three lectures in Boston on abnormal states or types of character, and then in the fall of 1897 he enlarged on these lectures in his Lowell Lectures, a popular lecture series established by the Lowell family in 1836.[15]

In the same time frame he gave several lectures that focused on religious themes. One was "The Dilemma of Determinism," which was given to Harvard Divinity students and published in the *Unitarian Review* in September 1884. Another was "Is Life Worth Living?," which was given to the Harvard Young Men's Christian Association in April 1895 and published in the *International Journal of Ethics* in October 1895. A third was "The Will to Believe," which was given to the philosophical club at Yale University in April 1896 and published in *New World* in June 1896. These lectures were republished in December 1896 along with seven other articles and addresses under the title *The Will to Believe and Other Essays in Popular Philosophy*.[16]

---

14. James, *Talks to Teachers*. The talks to teachers consists of fifteen chapters on such topics as the stream of consciousness, the child as a behaving organism, education and behavior, the laws of habit, the acquisition of ideas, and the will. The three talks to students are titled "The Gospel of Relaxation," "On a Certain Blindness in Human Beings," and "What Makes a Life Significant?" James refers to Freud in "The Gospel of Relaxation," noting that "a Viennese neurologist of considerable reputation has recently written about the *Binnenleben*, as he terms it, or buried life of human beings. No doctor, this writer says, can get into really profitable relations with a nervous patient until he gets some sense of what the patient's *Binnenleben* is, of the sort of unuttered inner atmosphere in which his consciousness dwells alone with the secrets of its prison-house" (100–101).

15. These lectures, which were not published, have been reconstructed from James's notes in Eugene Taylor, *William James on Exceptional Mental States*. There were eight lectures on the following topics: dreams and hypnotism, automatism, hysteria, multiple personality, demoniacal possession, witchcraft, degeneration, and genius. I will refer in chapter 9 to one of the cases he discusses in his lecture on the multiple personality.

16. James, *The Will to Believe and Other Essays in Popular Philosophy*. The others include "The Sentiment of Rationality," "Reflex Action and Theism," "The Moral Philosopher and the Moral Life," "Great Men and Their Environment," "The Importance of Individuals," "On Some Hegelisms," and "What Psychical Research Has Accomplished." In the concluding essay, James makes a strong case for the existence of a "subliminal

Invited to Give the Gifford Lectures

At fifty-five years of age, James was a very busy man. In addition to his teaching responsibilities at Harvard he taught an extra course at Radcliffe and lectured in the Harvard summer school. He was also heavily involved in departmental politics and was in great demand as a speaker and reviewer. Then he received a letter from the University of Aberdeen in Scotland inquiring whether he would be interested in giving the Gifford Lectures there in 1898–1899 and 1899–1900. Lord Gifford had endowed two two-year lectureships, one at Aberdeen and the other at Edinburgh, and James would have preferred the Edinburgh lectureships because he had friends there and Edinburgh University carried more prestige. As he had already been nominated for an honorary degree at Edinburgh, he turned down the Aberdeen invitation. In January 1898 Edinburgh asked him to give the Gifford Lectures for 1899–1900 and 1900–1901, and he immediately accepted. Meanwhile, he gave the Ingersoll Lecture at Harvard on "A Future Life." It was titled "Human Immortality" in the 1898 published version.[17]

Trip to California

In August 1898 James traveled by rail to California to deliver a lecture to the Philosophical Union at Berkeley. He spoke on the topic "Philosophical Conceptions and Practical Results." There were eight hundred people in the audience. This talk is known as the beginning of the pragmatist movement. The word *pragmatism* was coined by Charles Sanders Peirce, whose articles began appearing in the *Journal of Speculative Philosophy* in 1868.[18] In the address James explained the fundamental principle of pragmatism by noting that the effective meaning of any philosophical proposition always comes down to some particular consequence in our future practical experience. If there is a dispute about, say, how many angels can dance on the head of a pin, and no possible answer can make any imaginable difference in any of our lives, then the dispute and the question are meaningless. James applied

---

self," or "what may be called an ultra-marginal consciousness" (ibid., 315).

17. James, *Human Immortality*.

18. See Peirce, *Selected Writings*. Peirce graduated from Harvard in 1859 with a master's degree in chemistry. His only teaching position was that of an instructor in logic at Johns Hopkins University from 1879 to 1884. He was not reappointed, due largely to low enrollments. James tried to get him appointed at Harvard, but his efforts were unsuccessful, in part because Peirce had divorced a New England woman from a clerical family and subsequently married a young French woman. He lived with his French wife in extreme poverty. Born in 1839, he died in 1914 at the age of seventy-five.

this principle to conceptions of God and suggested that these conceptions need to be understood in terms of their practical application. If they are merely abstract definitions, then they have nothing to offer as far as the religious life itself is concerned.

The lecture was popular, and as James himself realized, it was a rehearsal for his forthcoming Gifford Lectures. He had a couple weeks to spend in California before returning home in mid-September, so he visited Stanford University and spent a good deal of time with Edwin Starbuck, who had received an MA from Harvard Divinity School in 1895 and was deeply invested in the psychology of religion. Starbuck viewed this field as the inductive study of the phenomenon of religion in individual experience and had begun to put together a collection of statements about personal religious development based on personal interviews. He gave James a great deal of this material for his forthcoming lectures. James also presented his teachers' talks in Berkeley.

Begins Work on the Gifford Lectures

In the summer of 1899 James began experiencing severe chest pains, and in July he, Alice, and their daughter Margaret (nicknamed Peggy) went to Bad Nauheim, a spa in Germany that specialized in treating heart problems. In September James was feeling better and began working on his Gifford lectures. But then he experienced another thoracic collapse, and he requested the postponement of his lectures for a year. A doctor whom he consulted did not find any heart abnormalities and suggested that he might be suffering from a neurosis possibly due to the prospect of preparing twenty lectures. In a few weeks his health improved and he and Alice went to Switzerland and then visited his brother Henry in London.

In the spring of 1900 his health was much improved and by April he had written the first three lectures. Then, however, his health worsened again, and he and Alice returned to Bad Nauheim where he received more baths, but the first few treatments made him so much worse that he left. In mid-July they went to Lucerne and he finally began work on lecture 4, "The Religion of Healthy-Mindedness." Now his strategy for presenting the material was clearly established. For each point he would provide examples, primarily extensive quotations from personal accounts such as letters, diaries, and autobiographical writings. In August he was ordered by his physician to return to Bad Nauheim, but the baths did not help him.

Nevertheless, he was able to finish lecture 5, on the sick soul, by mid-November, and by the end of November he felt he had written enough to cover the first set of ten lectures. In effect, the lecture on the divided self would introduce the topic of conversion, and conversion would take up two lectures. It was also evident that the topics of saintliness and mysticism would need to be addressed in the second set of lectures, and this meant that he would not be able to devote as much time to the philosophy of religion, which in his original outline was to be the whole focus of the second set of lectures.

In the spring of 1901 he wrote to a correspondent that he looked forward to regaining his equilibrium "after the Edinburgh nightmare is over." He and Alice had been in Europe for nearly two years, and he was feeling more and more like an exile.

Delivers the Gifford Lectures

In May 1901 James's son Henry arrived from the United States, and James, together with Alice and Harry, went to Edinburgh where he delivered the first set of lectures in the space of a month. The audience for his first lecture, some 250 persons, was larger than expected, and it was also exceedingly sympathetic. James delivered the last of the ten lectures on June 17 to an audience of some 300 persons, and he felt both triumphant and relieved. As he began the fall semester back at Harvard, he also set to work on his second set of lectures, and by the end of December he had completed two-thirds of them. The first five, on saintliness, were, in effect, a concrete illustration of the pragmatic principle James had enunciated in Berkeley in 1898. Between January and March he completed the remaining lectures on mysticism, philosophy (which was largely based on his Berkeley lecture), on other characteristics of religious experience, and conclusions.

On April 1, 1902, he and Alice sailed for Liverpool, then rushed to Edinburgh where James was to accept his honorary degree on April 11. On May 13 he began the second set of lectures. The audience was smaller than the previous year, and after the great excitement of the previous year the experience this year seemed a little flat. But on the final day the audience erupted in applause, and the students broke into cheers and sang "For He's a Jolly Good Fellow." Eight days later William and Alice were home again. *The Varieties of Religious Experience* was published later that year and 11,500 copies were sold the first year. James confided to a correspondent that the book had made him a wealthy man. Having struggled throughout his life with financial difficulties he found the success of the book a very welcome surprise.

In 1903 James gave a short address at the centennial celebration of Ralph Waldo Emerson's birth in Concord, Massachusetts, and the experience led him to feel that from now on he should devote himself to his own vocation and leave such other matters as university business to others. He wanted to write another book that would be more contemplative. In December 1903 he wrote a letter of resignation to President Eliot, but Eliot refused to consider it, explaining that he did not want Harvard's name separated from James's in the public mind. However, throughout following academic year James continued to think about resigning.

Writings on Radical Empiricism and Pragmatism

James's plan for the summer of 1903 was to write a new book. He wrote two essays, "Does Consciousness Exist?" and "A World of Pure Experience." They enunciated his philosophy of radical empiricism that in turn provided the foundation for his own understanding of pragmatism. His *Essays in Radical Empiricism*, a collection of twelve previously published essays, was brought together by his student and friend Ralph Barton Perry several years after James's death.[19] He was also working on a book on pragmatism, and his Wellesley College lectures in February and March 1904 on "Characteristics of an Individualistic Philosophy" were, in effect, a first draft of *Pragmatism*, which was published in 1907. He also reworked his Wellesley College lectures for an engagement at the University of Chicago in June. He expected an audience of fifty, but seven hundred fifty came to hear his first lecture and the audience never fell below five hundred.

In December 1905 he again traveled to California where he was scheduled to teach at Stanford University in the second semester. He taught a general introduction to philosophy course. Four hundred students signed up for it. On February 5 he addressed the Pacific Coast Unitarian Club on reason and faith. In the address he focused on Martin Luther and the way that Luther understood the psychology of conversion. He noted that, as with Luther, mind-cure and evangelical forms of Christianity reveal the new ranges of life that succeed our most despairing moments.

In April Alice came out to be with him for the remainder of the semester, and on April 18 San Francisco suffered the Great Earthquake. James accompanied a colleague, psychology professor Lillian Martin, into San Francisco to search for her sister, whom she succeeded in finding. He wrote an article published in *The Youth's Companion* in June 1906 on the outpouring of humanitarian actions and the spirit of cheerfulness and fortitude that

---

19. James, *Essays in Radical Empiricism*.

he witnessed that day and on his return trip to San Francisco eight days later.[20]

When he and Alice returned home in May, the positive feelings that he had gained from witnessing the earthquake and its aftermath began to fade, and during the summer he was feeling physically drained. He was scheduled to teach his introduction to philosophy course one last time in the fall semester, but he wanted President Eliot to be prepared to appoint a substitute instructor in case he was unable to complete the course. Yet, in November and early December he presented the Lowell Lectures on pragmatism, and on December 28, 1906 he delivered his presidential address to the American Philosophical Association at Columbia University on "The Energies of Men."[21]

Harvard Retirement

On January 22, 1907, James gave his final lecture in his philosophy course and he received a huge ovation. A group of students came down the aisle and presented him with a loving cup and a silver-mounted inkwell. Technically, he was now retired, but a week later he went to Columbia University to repeat his pragmatism lectures. The first lecture, scheduled for a room that held two hundred fifty persons, was moved to the eleven-hundred-seat chapel at Teacher's College, and it was almost filled. The philosophy department made an effort to get John Dewey to come to Harvard to take James's faculty position, but they were informed by the president that there was no money available to replace James.

In March 1907 James had his *Pragmatism* book ready for the printer, and it was published in June. It was a very popular book, but the philosophical community, apart from Dewey and a few others, was quite critical of it. James came to feel that the word *pragmatism* was an unfortunate choice as it seemed to support all sorts of practical interests and to exclude logical arguments. But as time went on, a more generous view of what he had written began to emerge, and it was not long before pragmatism became viewed as a legitimate philosophical orientation, one that represented the true America.

---

20. James, "On Some Mental Effects of the Earthquake," in James, *Writings 1902–1910*, 1215–22.

21. James, "The Energies of Men," in James, *Writings, 1902–1910*, 1223–41. See also my "Relaxed Bodies, Emancipated Minds, and Dominant Calm."

Lectures at Oxford

In November 1907 James received an invitation to give a set of lectures in Oxford in May 1908. The invitation was from Manchester College, which at that time was not yet a part of Oxford University. Manchester was a Unitarian college, and it published a leading liberal periodical, the *Hibbert Journal*. James was asked to speak on the religious aspect of his philosophy. He accepted the invitation and sailed to England on April 21, 1908, to deliver the eight lectures. His lectures attracted such a large crowd (five hundred) that they were moved from the Manchester College library to a large examination room in the center of town. James's fourth lecture, on the German physicist-philosopher Gustav Fechner, was especially significant for James himself because Fechner portrays the world as "thick," as vivid and pulsating with life.[22] The audiences remained large throughout the series and James was extremely satisfied with how they had turned out. He remained in Europe through the summer and early fall, traveling and working on the four lectures which he had promised as articles for the *Hibbert Journal*. The book titled *A Pluralistic Universe* was scheduled for publication in April 1909 so that the articles could appear in the journal first.

After returning home he repeated the lectures in Cambridge, but the initial audience of six hundred declined to two hundred, and James found the experience rather dispiriting. In the early months of 1909 he devoted himself to writing a sequel to *Pragmatism* titled *The Meaning of Truth*. Several of the chapters were transferred from the book he had been writing on radical empiricism, and other chapters were based on articles he had published between 1907 and 1909.[23] The final chapter, newly written for the book, consists of an imaginary dialogue between a pragmatist and an antipragmatist.[24] The book was published in October 1909.

---

22. See Capps, *At Home in the World*, 153–56. When Fechner's *Büchlein vom Leben nach dem Tode* was published in English translation in the United States in 1904, James accepted the invitation of the translator, Mary C. Wadsworth, to write an introduction for it. See Fechner, *Life after Death*, 13–20. In the introduction James explained the "general background" of Fechner's treatise on life after death: "Once grasp the idealistic notion that inner experience is the reality, and that matter is but a form in which inner experiences may appear to one another when they affect each other from the outside: and it is easy to believe that consciousness or inner experience never originated, or developed, out of the unconscious, but that it and the physical universe are co-eternal aspects of one self-same reality, much as concave and convex are aspects of one curve" (ibid., 16).

23. James, *The Meaning of Truth*, in James, *Writings, 1902–1910*, 821–978.

24. Ibid., 969–74.

Physical Incapacity and Death

James turned sixty-eight on January 11, 1910, and although he was increasingly limited physically, he was keeping up an extensive correspondence and finishing and sending off several articles, one of which was "The Moral Equivalent of War," an article that took up the argument that military service instills in younger persons qualities or virtues of discipline, courage, loyalty, and the like. Although James was a pacifist, he did not reject or minimize these positive effects of military service, but he argued that the same qualities may be instilled in younger persons by conscripting them for service at home in coal and iron mines, foundries, road building, tunnel making, and other forms of service.[25]

In May 1910 James returned to Bad Nauheim with Alice and their son Henry, who was suffering from severe depression at the time. James wrote to his mother-in-law that he was unable and Henry was unwilling to do anything but sit and watch the time pass. Alice wrote in her diary, "William cannot walk and Henry cannot smile." By the end of June Henry was beginning to emerge from his depression, but William was having increasingly bad nights. On July 3 James's brother Bob died in his sleep in Concord, Massachusetts. James wrote out some instructions to the student who was editing his book *Some Problems in Philosophy* and then, on August 11, he, Alice, and Henry returned to America, and they arrived at their summer home in Chocorua, New Hampshire, on August 19. William James died on August 26. Alice noted in her diary that the autopsy showed acute enlargement of the heart. It might be said that this diagnosis also applied to the spirit of William James.

CONCLUSION

In the introduction I quoted a passage from James's colleague George Herbert Palmer's personal testimony to James on the occasion of the publication of James's letters ten years after his death.[26] Here is how Palmer began his testimony:

> In view of the publication of the letters of William James, I am asked to state how he appeared to his colleagues in the daily course of his work as a Harvard professor. In brief he showed

---

25. James, "The Moral Equivalent of War," in James, *Writings, 1902–1910*, 1281–93. His proposal may well have served as an inspiration for the Peace Corps, inaugurated in 1961 by executive order of President John F. Kennedy.

26. Henry James, ed., *The Letters of William James*.

among us the same surprising, rich, brilliant, and profitable variety of speech and act which appeared in his home, his books, and his championship of an unpopular cause. His nature was so abundant and original that it never became standardized or usual. We, who met him most intimately, found in him every day something fresh to wonder at and admire.[27]

Palmer went on to note that James "had a delicate consideration of others, an observant tactfulness in putting all at ease" and that "few persons are habitually so kind."[28]

I would like to conclude this chapter with a passage from another testimonial, written by Theodor Flournoy, who taught psychology at the University of Geneva. Flournoy writes:

> William James was an artist by virtue of an originality and perfection of literary style which made him one of the most brilliant writers of his own country. But above all he was an artist in his extraordinarily vivid and delicate feeling for concrete realities, his penetrating vision in the realm of the particular, and his aptitude for seizing on that which was characteristic and unique in everything that he met. I do not here refer to external and material realities (although it is true that James appreciated as few do the beauties of nature, and having a remarkable facility for drawing, he entertained for a time the idea of becoming a painter), for in the life of the soul he saw a still more mysterious and fascinating spectacle, and it is to the observation of this that he resolved to devote himself.[29]

James's devotion to the observation of the life of the soul is especially evident in *The Varieties of Religious Experience*, and his observations in this regard clearly reflect his "artistic temperament."[30] As noted earlier, James was planning to become an artist when he was sixteen years old and living in Newport, Connecticut. It is unclear whether his father's gift of a microscope that year came in response to his desire to study science or as an attempt to lure him away from art, but what *is* clear is that his father was not in favor of his becoming an artist.[31] And yet, what is also abundantly clear is that, as Flournoy observes, William James was an artist of the life of the soul. In this regard *The Varieties of Religious Experience* was his masterpiece.

27. In Simon, *William James Remembered*, 30.
28. Ibid., 31.
29. Ibid., 84.
30. Ibid.
31. Simon, *Genuine Reality*, 81.

2

Personal Religious Experience

THE FIRST THREE CHAPTERS of *The Varieties of Religious Experience* describe the general focus of the lectures. They are titled "Religion and Neurology," "Circumscription of the Topic," and "The Reality of the Unseen." I will begin this chapter with James's explanation in the first two chapters of how he intends to address the subject of religion and the rationale he offers for his decision to focus on personal religious experiences. Then I will take up the third chapter and cite several of the personal religious experiences he presents in support of his view that a fundamental aspect of personal religious experience is the sense of the presence of God.

THE PSYCHOLOGICAL STUDY AND EVALUATION OF RELIGIOUS PROPENSITIES

James begins the first chapter of *The Varieties of Religious Experience*—"Religion and Neurology"—with the confession that it is "with no small amount of trepidation that I take my place behind this desk, and face this learned audience," for "to us Americans, the experience of receiving instruction from the living voice as well as from the books of European scholars, is very familiar."[1] He suggests that the natural thing for Americans is to listen while the Europeans talk and the contrary habit of talking while Europeans listen is not one that Americans have yet acquired. Yet he expresses the hope that as years go by, many of his own countrymen will be asked, as he has been asked, to lecture in the Scottish Universities of Aberdeen and

1. James, *The Varieties of Religious Experience*, 1.

Edinburgh so that "our people may become in all these higher matters even as one people; and that the peculiar philosophic temperament, as well as the peculiar political temperament, that goes with our English speech may more and more pervade and influence the world."[2]

As for the manner in which he will administer the lectureship, he acknowledges that he is "neither a theologian, nor a scholar learned in the history of religion, nor an anthropologist."[3] In fact, "Psychology is the only branch of learning in which I am particular versed."[4] But this is no reason for avoiding the subject of religion. In fact, "to the psychologist the religious propensities must be at least as interesting as any other of the facts pertaining to his mental constitution. It would seem, therefore, that, as a psychologist, the natural thing for me would be to invite you to a descriptive survey of these religious propensities."[5] If, however, "the inquiry be psychological," then "not religious institutions, but rather religious feelings and religious impulses must be its subject, and I must confine myself to those more developed subjective phenomena recorded in literature produced by articulate and fully self-conscious men, in works of piety and autobiography."[6]

He notes that if he were a historian or anthropologist of religion, it is likely that he would pay greater attention to the origins of the religious propensities of man, but the very fact that he is a psychologist means that he needs to take a different approach, one that may be equally interesting if not more so. For "interesting as the origins and early stages of a subject always are, yet when one seeks earnestly for its full significance, one must always look to its more completely evolved and perfect forms. It follows from this that the documents that will most concern us will be those of the men who were most accomplished in the religious life and best able to give an intelligible account of their ideas and motives. These men, of course, are either comparatively modern writers, or else such earlier ones as have become religious classics."[7]

This does not mean, however, that he will be focusing on learned theological texts. On the contrary, "the *documents humains* which we shall find most instructive need not then be sought for in the haunts of special erudition—they lie along the beaten highway; and this circumstance, which flows so naturally from the character of our problem, suits admirably also

---

2. Ibid., 2.
3. Ibid.
4. Ibid.
5. Ibid, 2–3.
6. Ibid., 3.
7. Ibid.

your lecturer's lack of special theological training. I may take my citations, my sentences and paragraphs of personal confession, from books that most of you at some time will have had already in your hands, and yet this will be no detriment to the value of my conclusions."[8]

But what, after all, are the religious propensities? And what is their significance? These, he believes, are two distinct questions, and it is important that we recognize this. The first question seeks to get at the nature of the thing and this usually involves learning about how it came into existence, its origin, and its history. The second question seeks to understand its importance, meaning, significance, or value. The latter, he notes, cannot be deduced from the former, and in any case it is vital that we give appropriate attention to the latter, for the existential facts are insufficient in themselves for determining the value of a religious expression or experience. In effect, determining their value is a spiritual problem and is one that calls for spiritual judgment. On the other hand, James is fully aware of the fact that because his listeners know that he is a psychologist they will suspect that he will treat the value question from a narrow biological or psychological perspective and view religious experiences as if they are mere curious factors of individual history.

James wants to assure his listeners that it is not his intent "to discredit the religious side of life," that, in fact, such a result is "absolutely alien" to his intentions. This being the case, he feels that he needs to say something more about this suspicion, especially because he will be focusing in these lectures on those persons whose pursuit of the religious life is such that it often becomes not only exceptional but also eccentric. James is not speaking here of the ordinary religious believer who follows the conventional observances of his religious tradition, whether Buddhist, Christian, Islamic, Hindu, etc. Rather, he has in mind those who have been "pattern-setters," individuals "for whom religion exists not as a dull habit but as an acute fever," and they have often shown signs of nervous instability. Frequently, they "have been subject to abnormal psychical visitations" and have "led a discordant inner life, and had melancholy during a part of their career."[9] Also, they have "been liable to obsessions and fixed ideas" and "have fallen into trances, heard voices, seen visions, and presented all sorts of peculiarities which are ordinarily classed as pathological." Moreover, "these pathological features in their career have often helped to give them their religious authority and influence."[10]

---

8. Ibid. See also Allport, *The Use of Personal Documents in Psychological Science.*
9. James, *The Varieties of Religious Experience*, 6–7.
10. Ibid., 7.

For a concrete example, James cites the case of George Fox, founder of the Quaker religion. He notes that in a day of shams this "was a religion of veracity rooted in spiritual inwardness, and a return to something more like the original gospel truth than men had ever known in England."[11] Also, "no one can pretend for a moment that in point of spiritual sagacity and capacity, Fox's mind was unsound."[12] In fact, everyone who confronted him personally, from Oliver Cromwell to county magistrates and jailers, seems to have acknowledged his superior power. And yet, "from the point of view of his nervous constitution, George Fox was a psychopath or *détraqué* of the deepest dye."[13] James cites in this regard a passage in Fox's journal in which he tells about how the Lord commanded him to remove his shoes, enter the city of Lichfield, and cry with a loud voice, "Woe to the bloody city of Lichfield!" Fox continued walking, and as he entered the marketplace, there seemed to him to be a channel of blood running down the streets. Later, he learned that under the Emperor Diocletian a thousand Christians were martyred in Lichfield and that by walking barefoot through the channel of their blood he had raised up the memorial of their blood.[14]

James notes that because we are studying religions' existential conditions, "we cannot possibly ignore these pathological aspects of the subject. We must describe and name them just as if they occurred in non-religious men."[15] To be sure, there is something offensive about the association of Fox's religious experience with what we know to be pathological experiences, especially because "any object that is infinitely important to us and awakens our devotion feels to us also as if it must be *sui generis* and unique," and "probably a crab would be filled with a sense of personal outrage if it could hear us class it without ado or apology as a crustacean, and thus dispose of it. 'I am no such thing,' it would say; 'I am MYSELF, MYSELF

---

11. Ibid.

12. Ibid.

13. Ibid.

14. Ibid., 7–8. Throughout the book, I will be treating James's use of material from the autobiographical writings of other authors as case material (similar to what one finds in psychotherapeutic texts) because in many cases the quoted material from these personal documents is several pages in length. Therefore, despite the fact that this material appears in *The Varieties of Religious Experience*, I will not represent it as quotations by James himself. This eliminates the need to present this material within single quotation marks. On the other hand, the footnotes will indicate the page numbers on which this material appears in *The Varieties* and the title and author of the original text. In most cases, the case material as presented here will be substantially reduced and much of it will be rewritten in the interests of brevity.

15. Ibid., 9.

alone."[16] On the other hand, James is necessarily engaged here in an intellectual enterprise, and the first thing the intellect does with an object is to class it along with something else, and this, it would seem, is unavoidable. However, he wants to assure his listeners that in demonstrating the association of a religious experience like the one that George Fox describes in his journal to a pathological state, his intention is not to discredit it. Instead, he will be concerned with the question of the meaning, significance, and value of these religious experiences.

James goes on to note that another way that the intellect tends to discredit a religious experience "is to lay bare the causes in which the thing originates."[17] To explain how this works he cites the French literary critic and historian Hippolyte Taine's statement in the introduction to his history of English literature: "'Whether facts be moral or physical, it makes no matter. They always have their causes. There are causes for ambition, courage, veracity, just as there are for digestion, muscular movement, animal heat.'"[18] James notes that where religion is concerned, those who are religious or have positive feelings toward religion tend to resent this procedure because they feel that spiritual value is undone if its origins are identified.

Common examples of this approach are the comments that unsentimental people make about the religious interests and perspectives of their more sentimental acquaintances. They say that "Alfred believes in immortality so strongly because his temperament is so emotional. Fanny's extraordinary conscientiousness is merely a matter of over-instigated nerves. William's melancholy about the universe is due to bad digestion—probably his liver is torpid. Eliza's delight in her church is a symptom of her hysterical condition. Peter would be less troubled about his soul if he would take more exercise in the open air, etc." [19] James adds that a more fully developed

16. Ibid.
17. Ibid.
18. Ibid.

19. Ibid., 10. It is noteworthy that James uses his own name—William—in the example of a person whose melancholy about the universe is attributed to bad digestion due to the sluggish functioning of the liver. As we saw in chapter 1, and will discuss in more detail in chapter 4, James had a debilitating experience of melancholy when he was in his late twenties. He does not, of course, endorse the idea that his melancholy was due to poor digestion due to torpidity of the liver, but it is worth noting that in his article "The Liver as the Seat of the Soul" Morris Jastrow Jr. discusses the ancients' (including the early Israelites') belief that the soul is located in the liver. Jastrow notes that the liver was also considered the organ through which the gods spoke, a belief that supported divination practices: e.g., priests cutting open the belly of a sheep or goat and reading the markings on the animal's liver. However, Richard Selzer points out in *Mortal Lessons* that with "the separation of medicine from the apron strings of religion and the rise of anatomy as a study in itself, the liver was toppled from its central role

example of the same kind of reasoning is the fashion, quite common these days, of criticizing the religious emotions by showing a connection between them and the sexual life: "Conversion is a crisis of puberty and adolescence," and "the macerations of saints, and the devotion of missionaries, are only instances of the parental instinct of self-sacrifice gone astray," and for the hysterical nun who is starving for natural life "Christ is but an imaginary substitute for a more earthly object of affection."[20] We are "all familiar in a general way with this method of discrediting states of mind for which we have an antipathy," and we all "use it to some degree in criticizing persons whose states of mind we regard as overstrained."[21] But when other people criticize "our own more exalted soul-flights by calling them 'nothing but' expressions of our organic disposition, we feel outraged and hurt, for we know that whatever be our organism's peculiarities, our mental states have their substantive value as revelations of the living truth."[22]

Suggesting that "medical materialism" is a good term for the simple-minded thinking that these examples illustrate, James notes that "medical materialism finishes up Saint Paul by calling his vision on the road to Damascus a discharging lesion of the occipital cortex, he being an epileptic. It snuffs out Saint Teresa as a hysteric, Saint Francis of Assisi as a hereditary degenerate. George Fox's discontent with the shams of his age, and his pining for spiritual veracity it treats as a symptom of a disordered colon."[23] In its supposition that all such mental overtensions are mere affairs of diathesis (auto-intoxications most probably) due to the perverted action of various glands which physiology will yet discover, such an employment of medical materialism would lead to the claim that the spiritual authority of all

---

and the heart was elevated" (65). Selzer notes that from its beginnings Christianity was a religion of the heart. Moreover, it transformed the earlier barbaric rituals—such as eating the slain enemy's heart as a means of taking upon oneself his strength, valor and skill—into a more spiritualized form, such as the adoration of the heart of a saint. In Capps, *A Time to Laugh* I note that the belief that the soul is in the liver was based on the fact that the liver is self-regenerative, and I cite Selzer's reference to the case of Prometheus and the liver transplants carried out in the 1990s in which the liver adapted itself to the recipient's body; the liver's return to its normal size following cessation of alcohol abuse is another example of the liver's ability to adapt. I also proposed a psychophysical model of the human person (ibid. 103–12), composed of the soul (located in the liver), the spirit (located in the heart), and the self (located in the brain). The rationale for locating the self in the brain is that the self has to do with identity, and identity is based on memory. To illumine the spirit/soul distinction, I drew on Hillman, *Revisioning Psychology*, 68-69; and Hillman, "Peaks and Vales."

20. James, *The Varieties of Religious Experience*.
21. Ibid., 10–11.
22. Ibid., 11–12.
23. Ibid., 13.

such personages has been successfully undermined.[24] Moreover, modern psychology, assuming that the dependence of mental states on bodily conditions is thoroughgoing and complete, might not endorse this application of medical materialism in every detail yet agree that its claims are true in a general sort of way.

But for James this raises the critical question: "How can such an existential account of facts of mental history decide in one way or another on their spiritual significance?"[25] After all, a general postulate of psychology is that there is not a single one of our states of mind, high or low, healthy or morbid, that has not some organic process as its condition, and this means that all of our states of mind are "equally organically founded, be they of religious or non-religious content."[26] Thus, "to plead the organic causation of a religious state of mind, then, in refutation of its claim to possess superior spiritual value, is quite illogical and arbitrary."[27] In fact, to be consistent, one would also have to conclude that "none of our thoughts and feelings, not even our scientific doctrines, not even our *dis*beliefs, could retain any value as revelations of the truth, for every one of them without exception flows from the state of their possessor's body at the time."[28]

James adds, however, that in point of fact medical materialism does not draw such a sweeping, skeptical conclusion, for it "is sure, just as every simple man is sure, that some states of mind are inwardly superior to others, and reveal to us more truth, and in this it simply makes use of an ordinary spiritual judgment."[29] On the other hand, there have been instances in which medical materialism has attempted to "discredit the states which it dislikes by vaguely associating them with nerves and liver, and connecting them with names connoting bodily affliction."[30] In doing so, medical materialism has been "altogether illogical and inconsistent."[31]

Thus, James makes clear that he will not engage in any effort to discredit personal religious experiences, ideas, or claims on physiological grounds. In

---

24. Ibid. James cites an article by Charles Binet-Sanglé as a "first-rate example" of this type of reasoning; Binet-Sanglé's *La Folie de Jésus*, in which he argued that Jesus experienced hallucinations, was his most controversial work. *Diathesis* means "a predisposition to certain diseases," and antointoxications are toxic substances generated within the body. See Agnes, *Webster's New World*, 399, 96.

25. James, *The Varieties of Religious Experience*, 14.

26. Ibid.

27. Ibid.

28. Ibid.

29. Ibid., 14–15.

30. Ibid., 15.

31. Ibid.

fact, he suggests that persons who engage in this kind of argument are likely to have formed a dislike for these religious expressions on other grounds and are merely invoking the physiological argument to support their previously formed opinions. James notes, however, that in the natural sciences and industrial arts "it never occurs to anyone to try to refute opinions by showing up their author's neurotic constitution."[32] Instead, opinions are invariably tested by logic and experiment no matter what their author's neurological type may be, and it "should be no otherwise with religious opinions."[33] These too should be judged exclusively on their value, and this "can only be ascertained by spiritual judgments directly passed upon them, judgments based on our own immediate feeling primarily; and secondarily on what we can ascertain of their experiential relations to our moral needs and to the rest of what we hold as true."[34]

In his view, the only available criteria for judging their value are *immediate luminousness, philosophical reasonableness,* and *moral helpfulness.* He observes in this connection that Saint Teresa might have had the nervous system of the most placid cow, but this would not have saved her theology if it did not meet these basic criteria. Conversely, if her theology can stand these other tests, "it will make no difference how hysterical or nervously off her balance Saint Teresa may have been when she was with us here below."[35]

PERSONAL AND INSTITUTIONAL RELIGION

In chapter 2 of *The Varieties*—"Circumscription of the Topic"—James says that because "the field of religion is as wide as it is, it is manifestly impossible that I should pretend to cover it."[36] Therefore, his lectures "must be limited to a fraction of the subject."[37] He also notes that it would be foolish to set up an abstract definition of *religion* and then attempt to defend it against all comers. On the other hand, this should not prevent him from taking his own narrow point of view of religion *"for the purpose of these lectures,* or, out of the many meanings of the word, from choosing the one meaning in which I wish to interest you particularly, and proclaiming arbitrarily that when I say 'religion' I mean *that.*"[38]

32. Ibid., 17.
33. Ibid., 17–18.
34. Ibid., 18.
35. Ibid.
36. Ibid., 28.
37. Ibid.
38. Ibid.

One useful way to do this is to indicate what aspects of religion he intends to consider and what aspects he intends to leave out. He notes that there is one "great partition that divides the religious field," the *institutional* and the *personal*.[39] Central to the former are "worship and sacrifice, procedures for working on the dispositions of the deity, theology and ceremony and ecclesiastical organization"; and central to the latter are "the inner dispositions of man himself," including "his conscience, his deserts, his helplessness, his incompleteness."[40] In the former, gaining the favor of the deity is central. In the latter, the favor of the deity "is an essential feature of the story, and theology plays a vital part therein, yet the acts to which this sort of religion prompts are personal not ritual acts, the individual transacts the business by himself alone, and the ecclesiastical organization, with its priests and sacraments and other go-betweens, sinks to an altogether secondary place. The relation goes direct from heart to heart, from soul to soul, between man and his maker."[41]

Thus, James proposes to "ignore the institutional branch entirely, to say nothing of the ecclesiastical organization, to consider as little as possible the systematic theology and the ideas about the gods themselves, and to confine myself as far as I can to personal religion."[42] He acknowledges that to some listeners "personal religion, thus nakedly considered, will no doubt seem too incomplete a thing to wear the general name," and that it doesn't even warrant the name "religion," for in their view "the name 'religion' should be reserved for the fully organized system of feeling, thought, and institution, for the Church, in short, of which this personal religion so called, is but a fractional element."[43] His response to this point is that it simply illustrates the fact that "the question of definition tends to become a dispute about names,"[44] and rather than prolong the dispute he is willing to accept almost any name for the personal religion that he intends to discuss in these lectures. If his listeners would prefer to call it conscience or morality, this is acceptable to him for it is no less worthy of study under these names. On the other hand, the word *morality* does not convey all of what he intends to speak about in these lectures, so he will employ the word "religion," and then, in the final concluding lecture, he will say something about the relations between personal religion as discussed in the lectures

39. Ibid.
40. Ibid., 29.
41. Ibid.
42. Ibid.
43. Ibid.
44. Ibid., 30.

and "the theologies and ecclesiasticisms" that he will not be discussing in these lectures.[45]

Next, he invokes the origins procedure in support of his decision to focus on personal religion, noting that in one sense "personal religion will prove itself more fundamental than either theology or ecclesiasticism."[46] This is because churches once established "live at second-hand upon tradition," whereas "the *founders* of every church owed their power originally to the fact of their direct communication with the divine."[47] This, however, is not only true of the founders of the major historical religions but also of the founders of Christian sects. Thus even to those who consider it incomplete, "personal religion" is still "the primordial thing."[48]

This discussion leads him to propose the definition of *religion* that will inform his lectures: "Religion, therefore, as I now ask you arbitrarily to take it, shall mean for us *the feelings, acts, and experiences of individual men in their solitude, so far as they apprehend themselves to stand in relation to whatever they may consider the divine.*"[49] He adds that inasmuch as the relation to whatever one considers the divine "may be either moral, physical, or ritual, it is evident that out of religion in the sense in which we take it, theologies, philosophies, and ecclesiastical organizations may secondarily grow."[50] However, as he has already said, in these lectures, "the immediate personal experiences will amply fill our time, and we shall hardly consider theology or ecclesiasticisms at all."[51]

James goes on to suggest that there are understandings of religious experience incompatible with what he has in mind here, and he notes in particular that he accepts the view of common men that religious experience

---

45. Ibid.
46. Ibid.
47. Ibid.
48. Ibid. James acknowledges that other things in religion are chronologically more primordial than personal religion, such as fetishism and magic, and this would mean "that personal religion in the inward sense and the genuinely spiritual ecclesiasticisms which it founds are phenomena of secondary or even tertiary order" (ibid.). However, he notes that many anthropologists distinguish "magic" from "religion," and that "the whole system of thought which leads to magic, fetishism, and the lower superstitions may just as well be called primitive science as called primitive religion" (ibid., 31). But this simply introduces another potential dispute about names. Also "our knowledge of all these early stages of thought and feeling is in any case so conjectural and imperfect that farther discussion would not be worthwhile" (ibid.).
49. Ibid., 31 (italics original).
50. Ibid.
51. Ibid.

signifies "a *serious* state of mind."[52] Thus it precludes vain chatter, smart wit, and even light irony. On the other hand, it excludes heavy grumbling and complaint. Thus:

> There must be something solemn, serious, and tender about any attitude which we denominate religious. If glad, it must not grin or snicker; if sad, it must not scream or curse. It is precisely as being *solemn* experiences that I wish to interest you in religious experiences. So I propose—arbitrarily again, if you please—to narrow our definition once more by saying that the word "divine," as employed therein, shall mean for us not merely the primal and enveloping and real, for that meaning if taken without restriction might well prove too broad. The divine shall mean for us only such a primal reality as the individual feels impelled to respond to solemnly and gravely, and neither by a curse nor a jest.[53]

He recognizes, however, that there could be some controversy over the word *divine*, especially if we take it in too narrow a sense. He notes for example that Buddhism is considered religious even though it does not positively assume a God, and he cites Ralph Waldo Emerson's view of the universe as having "a divine soul of order, which soul is moral, being also the soul within the soul of man."[54] But whether this soul of the universe is a mere quality like the eye's brilliancy or the skin's softness, or whether it is a self-conscious life like the eye's seeing or the skin's feeling "is a decision that never unmistakably appears in Emerson's pages."[55] Rather, "it quivers on the boundary of these things, sometimes leaning one way, sometimes the other, to suit the literary rather than the philosophical need."[56]

But since these religious expressions have the same appeal and response found in Christianity and other religious faiths, there is no reason to exclude them from the definition of religion that he is employing here. Rather, "when in our definition of religion we speak of the individual's relation to 'what he considers the divine,' we must interpret the term 'divine' very broadly, as denoting any object that is god*like*, whether it be a concrete deity or not."[57]

---

52. Ibid., 37.

53. Ibid., 38.

54. Ibid., 33. Emerson, *Miscellanies*, 120; and Emerson, *Lectures and Biographical Sketches*, 186.

55. James, *The Varieties of Religious Experience*, 33.

56. Ibid.

57. Ibid., 34.

It is clear from the foregoing that James intends his definition of *religion* to be a working definition for the purpose of the lectures. The question of course is whether personal religion can be "thus nakedly considered."[58] One way of answering this question is to read what James has written and to make a judgment as to whether he succeeded in this endeavor. Some readers of his text have pointed out that the very language that individuals use to describe their experiences of apprehending God is itself derived from the ecclesiastical and theological traditions, which he has "arbitrarily" excluded, and they note that the religious experiences recorded in *The Varieties* illustrate this very fact.

For example, the conversion account by Stephen H. Bradley, which comes at the very beginning of James's initial lecture on "Conversion" is replete with Christian theological terms (*Savior*, *Holy Spirit*, and the like) and is understood by Bradley himself to be similar to the experiences of the first apostles on the Day of Pentecost. Furthermore, while Bradley's personal religious experience occurred in solitude, it was triggered by his having attended church earlier that evening. Thus for Bradley the experience derives its meaning from a specific theological and ecclesiastical context and cannot be understood apart from it. If James separates the personal and the institutional branches of religion, many of the individuals who populate his text do not. For them, absent the institutional branch, they have no way of attributing meaning or significance to their religious experiences. There is no other way to authenticate these experiences.

What are we to make of this objection to James's whole project? I suggest that we may do one of two things: On the one hand, we may take the view that what James has tried to keep separate—the personal and the institutional—cannot be treated separately. In taking this view we may actually claim James's own ostensible support for it as he himself says that his division of the two aspects of religion is an arbitrary one for the purpose of these lectures only.

On the other hand, we may take the view that James seems to have taken in his own life, that an individual may be able to be "religious" in the purely personal sense of the term and to do so without the assistance of the institutional branch of religion. In his discussion of Saint Teresa in his lecture on the value of saintliness he notes that she "had a powerful intellect," wrote "admirable descriptive psychology," possessed a will "equal to any emergency," had "a great talent for politics and business, a buoyant disposition, and a first-rate literary style."[59] He adds that others have been

---

58. Ibid., 29.
59. Ibid., 346.

moved by the fact that she "put her whole life at the service of her religious ideals."[60] And yet, he cannot avoid the feeling that it was a pity "that so much vitality of soul should have found such poor employment," i.e., in her life in the convent.[61] Later, he cites Saint Teresa's mystical experiences in his lectures on mysticism, and here it is clear that he has a deep respect for her own account of how such experiences contribute to "the formation of a new center of spiritual energy."[62] Thus, although he recognizes that some mystical experiences may not be authentic, his uneasiness regarding Saint Teresa's religious "employments" do not apply to her personal religious experiences but to her dedication to the institutional branch of religion. He clearly believes that her religious life exemplified the very priority that he is giving in these lectures to the personal over the institutional branch of religion.

On the other hand, as noted, he recognizes that others may not have similar feelings to his own about her dedication to the convent, and it is clear that he is not trying to change their minds in this regard. Rather, his primary concern is to make a case for the value and validity of personal religion—that is, the religious experiences of the individual—and not to treat them as inferior to the institutional forms and expressions of religion. Thus, in his concluding lecture he challenges the view so common to the sciences of his day that the experiences of individuals are of no concern, that only the aggregate matters. As he points out:

> Religion makes no such blunder. The individual's religion may be egotistic, and those private realities which it keeps in touch with may be narrow enough; but at any rate it always remains infinitely less hollow and abstract, as far as it goes, than a science which prides itself on taking no account of anything private at all . . . By being religious we establish ourselves in possession of ultimate reality as the only points at which reality is given us to guard. Our responsible concern is with our private destiny, after all.[63]

To be "privately religious" assumes that one may not be a regular participant in rituals and other group activities and therefore that one's personal religious experiences may have minimal if any connection to any ecclesiastical context. It also means that one may not use theological language or the language of any established religious tradition to describe and interpret the personal experiences that one takes to be "religious." The question, then, is

60. Ibid.
61. Ibid., 346–47.
62. Ibid., 414.
63. Ibid., 500–501.

whether religion may in fact be an entirely individual matter, unrelated to and disconnected from any and all religious traditions?

The illustrations that he employs in *The Varieties* seem to provide overwhelming evidence against this idea. Virtually every account of personal religious experience included in his book appears to support the counter thesis that there is no purely personal religious experience, that all religious experiences are related in one way or another to religious traditions, drawing on their systems of ideas and beliefs, their social and communal aspects, or both. In fact, as we will see in chapter 3, James's own experience of melancholy (which is reported anonymously in *The Varieties*) draws on the religious tradition in which he was raised. On the other hand, it does so in a way that supports his own view that one may have a purely personal religious experience, an experience that is essentially disconnected—in the mind of the person who has this experience—from theological and ecclesiastical systems and from social and communal aspects of religion. In other words, the experience is not mediated by or through these other influences and channels. All this is to say that some personal religious experiences are so personal that one does not perceive them to be related, other than in an incidental way, to the religious institutions and the theologies that these institutions embrace and promote. To be sure, the connections between these personal experiences and their institutional influences can be teased out and demonstrated, but doing so is likely to obscure the very fact that the experiences occur to individuals "in their solitude, so far as they apprehend themselves to stand in relation to whatever they may consider the divine."[64]

James's response to a questionnaire on religious experience helps to clarify the distinction that I am suggesting here. In 1904, two years after the publication of *The Varieties*, he filled out a questionnaire sent out by Professor James B. Pratt of Williams College.[65] Pratt, who had been a student of James's at Harvard, went on to write several books in the psychology of religion.[66] In a brief paragraph at the top of the questionnaire, Pratt explains its purpose:

> It is being realized as never before that religion, as one of the most important things in the life both of the community and of the individual, deserves close and extended study. Such study

64. Ibid., 31.

65. James, *Writings, 1902–1910*, 1183–85. Originally published in Henry James, *The Letters of William James*.

66. Pratt, *The Psychology of Religious Belief*; Pratt, *What Pragmatism Means*; Pratt, *The Religious Consciousness*; and Pratt, *Matter and Spirit*. See also Myers, *Self, Religion, and Metaphysics*, which includes a biographical sketch of Pratt and a bibliography of his publications.

can be of value only if based upon the personal experiences of many individuals. If you are in sympathy with such study and are willing to assist in it, will you kindly write out the answers to the following questions and return them with this questionnaire, as soon as you conveniently can, to James B. Pratt, 20 Shepard Street, Cambridge, Mass. Please answer the questions at length and in detail. Do not give philosophical generalizations, but your own personal experience.[67]

There were ten questions: What does religion mean to you personally? What do you mean by God? Why do you believe in God? Or do you not so much *believe* in God as want to *use* him? Is God very real to you, as real as an earthly friend, though different? Do you pray, and if so, why? What do you mean by "spirituality"? Do you believe in personal immortality? Do you accept the Bible as *authority* in religious matters? What do you mean by a "religious experience"?[68] Several of these questions also had subquestions designed to elicit a more nuanced response.

In response to the question, "Is God very real to you, as real as an earthly friend, though different?" James replied, "Dimly (real); not (as an earthly friend)." When asked, "Do you feel that you have experienced his presence? If so, please describe what you mean by such an experience," James simply wrote, "Never." Addressing those respondents who answered this question in the negative, Pratt asked whether they "accept the testimony of others who claim to have felt God's presence directly?" James answered affirmatively, "Yes! The whole line of testimony on this point is so strong that I am unable to pooh-pooh it away. No doubt there is a germ in me of something similar that makes response." To Pratt's open-ended question, "What do you mean by a 'religious experience'?" he replied, "Any moment of life that brings the reality of spiritual things more 'home' to one."[69]

If we take James's responses to these questions at face value, we would have to conclude that he does not feel that he has experienced the presence of God, although he says that there is a germ in him of something similar that responds to what others have experienced. Moreover, he is sympathetic toward the testimony of others who say that they have felt God's presence directly. This sympathy is elaborated in his response to the question, "What do you mean by God?" That question offers several options: "Is he a person? Or is He only a Force? Or is God an attitude of the Universe toward you?" In response to the general question James replied: "A combination

---

67. James, *Writings, 1902–1910*, 1183.
68. Ibid., 1183–85.
69. I will discuss this response in greater detail in chapter 8.

of Ideality and (final) efficacy." Then in response to the first option—"Is he a person?"—he wrote: "He must be cognizant and responsive in some way"; and in response to the second option—"Or is He only a Force?"—he answered, "He must do." His answer to the third option—"Or is God an attitude of the Universe toward you?"—is the one that elaborates on his sympathy with the testimony of others:

> Yes but more conscious. "God" to me, is not the only spiritual reality to believe in. Religion means primarily a universe of spiritual realities surrounding the earthly practical ones, not merely relations of "value," but agencies and their activities. I suppose that the chief premise for my hospitality towards the religious testimony of others is my conviction that "normal" or "sane" consciousness is so small a part of actual experience. What e'er be true, it is not true exclusively, as philistine scientific opinion assumes. The other kinds of consciousness bear witness to a much wider universe of experiences, from which our belief selects and emphasizes such parts as best satisfy our needs.[70]

If he has not "experienced" the presence of God in a direct and immediate way, does this mean that he does not believe in God? The answer is no. In response to Pratt's question "Why do you believe in God?" for which he offers a list of possible *why*'s, James indicates that his belief is not based on any rational or intellectual argument for the existence of God ("Emphatically, no") or on personal experience or authority, such as that of the Bible or of some prophetic person. However, he adds to his negative response to the "personal experience" option that he believes "because I need it so that it 'must' be true" and to his negative response to the "authority" option he adds that he does make "admiring response" to "the whole tradition of religious people." Finally, given the option of adding any other reasons he writes, "Only for the social reasons." This comment suggests that he would be reluctant to take a position over against "the whole tradition of religious people."

In this response to Pratt's questionnaire, James comes across as one who takes personal religious experiences seriously despite the fact that he cannot claim to belong to the ranks of those who have experienced the presence of God in some immediate or palpable way. To say that one makes "admiring response" to those who claim personal experiences of God is to present oneself as a sympathetic observer, as one who feels he has an understanding of what they have experienced despite the fact that he doesn't feel that he has had this experience himself. James also seems to convey that

70. James, *Writings, 1902–1910*, 1183–84.

he has had experiences that are similar to their experiences. In any case, he does not associate himself with the scientific community that studies religion as if it were any other object of study, for religion involves forms of consciousness that are not met with in ordinary human experience.

James's sympathies with those who have had an experience of the sense or presence of God may perhaps be illustrated by an experience of his brother Henry. Unlike their younger brothers Wilky and Bob, William and Henry were not called up for active duty in the Civil War. Yet Henry viewed his experience of being psychologically immobilized as a result of his having fought a fire in his hometown of Newport as an imaginative identification of himself as "a member of the elect company of the experienced."[71] In a similar way William James cannot claim to be numbered among those who have experienced the palpable presence of God and yet there is an imaginative identification with them based on his awareness of "a universe of spiritual relations surrounding the early practical ones" and of the "kinds of consciousness [that] bear witness to a much wider universe of experiences" than that of "'normal' or 'sane' consciousness."[72] The very fact that James responded to Pratt's questionnaire in such a thoughtful way is itself an indication that he has no desire to "pooh-pooh . . . away" the religious experiences of others. And as we will see in chapter 3, James includes his own experience of religious melancholy in *The Varieties of Religious Experience*. Thus, if there had been a group portrait of some 150 persons whose testimonials are included in *The Varieties*, he would be somewhere in the picture—not, of course, in the middle of the first row but present nonetheless.[73]

THE REALITY OF THE UNSEEN

James begins chapter 3—"The Reality of the Unseen"—with the observation that if one were asked "to characterize the life of religion in the broadest and most general terms possible, one might say that it consists of the belief that there is an unseen order, and that our supreme good lies in harmoniously adjusting ourselves thereto."[74] Noting that this belief and this adjustment "are the religious attitude in the soul," he indicates that he will be calling

---

71. Eakin, "Henry James and the Autobiographical Act," 125.

72. James, *Writings, 1902–1910*, 1183–84.

73. The approximate figure of 150 is based on my own count. It includes some 90 persons who are named and some 60 persons who are anonymous. Ten of those who are named are women. Approximately 25 of the personal testimonials are from George Starbuck's collection (and many of these are identified by age). James identifies several of the unnamed persons as his personal friends.

74. James, *The Varieties of Religious Experience*, 53.

attention "to some of the psychological peculiarities of such an attitude as this, or belief in an object which we cannot see."[75]

He acknowledges that in a certain sense there isn't anything unique about this attitude. After all, all of our attitudes, whether moral, practical, emotional, or religious are due to the "objects" of our consciousness, and these objects may or may not be present to our senses, for they may just as well be present only to our thoughts, and their presence in our thoughts may be stronger than their presence to our senses. For example, "the memory of an insult may make us angrier than the insult did when we received it."[76]

In the case of religion, the concrete objects of most people's religion—the deities which they worship—are known to them as ideas, not as sensible realities. For example, very few Christian believers have had a sensible vision of their Savior, and the whole force of the Christian religion is in general exerted by the instrumentality of pure ideas, of which nothing in one's past experience directly serves as a model. He notes there have been enough sensible appearances of these religious objects to merit our attention, and that later in the chapter he will provide examples of this phenomenon, but it is striking that ideas have played such a prominent role in religion, that religion "is full of abstract objects," and that these abstract objects have power equal to the objects that are present to one's senses. There are, for example, ideas concerning the attributes of God such as holiness, omniscience, mercy, infinity, and tri-unity. Moreover, the mystical authorities in all religions insist that the very absence of definite sensible images is critical for the contemplation of higher divine truths. He cites philosophers Immanuel Kant and Plato and their insistence that abstract ideas have a power that sensible images lack. He also reminds his listeners that in the lecture preceding this one he referred to Ralph Waldo Emerson's emphasis on "the abstract divineness of things," and that in churches that view themselves as ethical societies there is "a similar worship of the abstract divine" and of "the moral law believed in as an ultimate object."[77]

This, however, leads James to focus on the role that the senses may play in making these abstract ideas more real to us. He suggests that the Greek gods were originally only half-metaphoric personifications of these great spheres of abstract law and order, and he compares this process of personification to the ways in which we today "speak of the smile of the morning, the kiss of the breeze, or the bite of the cold, without really meaning that

---

75. Ibid.
76. Ibid.
77. Ibid., 57.

these phenomena of nature actually wear a human face."[78] Yet, he feels that there is a sense that is deeper than the particular senses of sight, hearing, touch and smell, as if "there were in human consciousness a *sense of reality, a feeling of objective presence, a perception* of what we may call 'something there,' more deep and more general than any of the special and particular 'senses' by which the current psychology supposes existent realities to be originally revealed."[79] If there is such a sense, we might assume that the role of the particular senses of sight, hearing, touch, and smell is to awaken our attitudes and conduct by exciting this sense of reality; but anything else, any idea, for example, might also excite it, and insofar "as religious conceptions were able to touch this reality-feeling, they would be believed in despite criticism, even though they might be so vague and remote as to be almost unimaginable."[80]

James goes on to suggest that the most curious proofs of the existence of such an undifferentiated sense of reality are found in hallucinatory experiences because "it often happens that an hallucination is imperfectly developed: the person affected will feel a 'presence' in the room, definitely localized, facing in one particular way, real in the most emphatic sense of the word, often coming suddenly, and as suddenly gone; and yet neither seen, heard, touched, nor cognized in any of the usual 'sensible' ways." [81] To illustrate this hallucinatory sense of a "presence" in the room he cites the case of an "intimate friend of mine, one of the keenest intellects I know," who "has had several experiences of this sort."[82] This is what the friend wrote in response to his inquiries: "I have several times within the past few years felt the so-called 'consciousness of a presence.' The experiences which I have in mind are clearly distinguishable from another kind of experience which I have had very frequently, and which I fancy many persons would also call the 'consciousness of a presence.' But the difference for me between the two sets of experience is as great as the difference between feeling a slight warmth originating I know not where, and standing in the midst of a conflagration with all the ordinary senses alert."[83]

James's friend went on to describe the first of these experiences:

> It was about September, 1884, when I had the first experience. On the previous night I had had, after getting into bed at my

78. Ibid., 58.
79. Ibid.
80. Ibid.
81. Ibid., 58–59.
82. Ibid., 59.
83. Ibid.

> rooms in College, a vivid tactile hallucination of being grasped by the arm, which made me get up and search the room for an intruder; but the sense of presence so called came on the next night. After I had got into bed and blown out the candle, I lay awake awhile thinking on the previous night's experience, when suddenly I *felt* something come into the room and stay close to my bed. It remained only a minute or two. I did not recognize it by any ordinary sense, and yet there was a horribly unpleasant "sensation" connected with it. It stirred something more at the roots of my being than any ordinary perception. The feeling had something of the quality of a very large tearing vital pain spreading chiefly over the chest, but within the organism—and yet the feeling was not *pain* so much as *abhorrence*. At all events, something was present with me, and I knew its presence far more surely than I have ever known the presence of any fleshly living creature. I was conscious of its departure as of its coming; an almost instantaneously swift going through the door, and the "horrible sensation" disappeared.[84]

Continuing his account of the experience, he described what happened the following night:

> On the third night when I retired my mind was absorbed in some lectures which I was preparing, and I was still absorbed in these when I became aware of the actual presence (though not of the *coming*) of the thing that was there the night before, and of the "horrible sensation.." I then mentally concentrated all my effort to charge this "thing," if it was evil, to depart, if it was *not* evil, to tell me who or what it was, and if it could not explain itself, to go, and that I would compel it to go. It went as on the previous night, and my body quickly recovered its normal state.[85]

He added that on two other occasions he has had exactly the same "horrible sensation," and one time it lasted a full quarter of an hour. In all three instances he experienced the certainty that *something* was standing there and that it was indescribably *stronger* than the ordinary certainty of companionship that we experience when we are in the close presence of ordinary living people. He added, "The something seemed close to me, and intensely more real than any ordinary perception. Although I felt it to be like unto myself,

---

84. Ibid., 59–60.
85. Ibid., 60 (italics original).

so to speak, or finite, small, and distressful, as it were, I didn't recognize it as any individual being or person."[86]

James adds that on other occasions the same friend has "had the sense of presence developed with equal intensity and abruptness, only then it was filled with a quality of joy."[87] On these occasions it was not "a mere consciousness of something there, but fused in the central happiness of it, a startling awareness of some ineffable good."[88] Nor was it a vague feeling like the emotional effect of a poem or of music. Rather, he had "the sure knowledge of the close presence of a sort of mighty person," and after it left the memory persisted as the perception of reality, not a dream.[89] James notes that his friend does not interpret these latter experiences theistically, as signifying the presence of God, but "it would clearly not have been unnatural to interpret them as a revelation of the deity's existence."[90]

Acknowledging that the oddity of this account might be disconcerting to his listeners, James goes on to cite a couple of similar narratives to show that such experiences are quite common. These accounts include the sense that a friend is standing nearby, that there is a spiritual presence in the room, and that a man has squeezed himself under the crack of the door and moved across the room. James concludes that these cases "prove the existence in our mental machinery of a sense of present reality more diffused and general than that which our special senses yield."[91] How to explain them in organic terms would, he suggests, present the psychologist with a "pretty problem," although it is natural to relate them to some muscular sense "with the feeling that our muscles were innervating themselves for action."[92]

But what especially interests him here is the similarity between these accounts and accounts in the pages of religious biography of the believer's direct perception of a living God's existence. He cites in this regard a brief memorandum by James Russell Lowell, who, when he was at a small gathering at a friend's house, happened to say something about "the presence of spirits (of whom, I said, I was often dimly aware)."[93] Whereupon "Mr. [James] Putnam entered into an argument with me on spiritual matters,"

86. Ibid.
87. Ibid.
88. Ibid.
89. Ibid., 60–61.
90. Ibid., 61. I have discussed the possibility that the "intimate friend" was James himself in Capps, *Men, Religion, and Melancholia*, 37–42.
91. James, *The Varieties of Religious Experience*, 63.
92. Ibid.
93. Ibid., 66.

and "as I was speaking, the whole system rose up before me like a vague destiny looming from the Abyss."[94] Lowell continues: "I never before so clearly felt the Spirit of God in me and around me. The whole room seemed to me full of God. The air seemed to waver to and fro with the presence of Something I know not what. I spoke with the calmness and clearness of a prophet."[95] He adds that he cannot say "what this revelation was" because he has "not yet studied it enough," but "I shall perfect it one day, and then you shall hear it and acknowledge its grandeur."[96]

James cites another example, this one from George Starbuck's manuscript collection, in which a clergyman felt the presence of God when he was standing on a hilltop. The clergyman writes: "I did not seek Him, but felt the perfect unison of my spirit with Him. The ordinary sense of things around me faded. For the moment nothing but an ineffable joy and exultation remained."[97] Noting the impossibility of describing the experience fully, he compared it to the effect of some great orchestra "when all the separate notes have melted into one swelling harmony that leaves the listener conscious of nothing save that his soul is being wafted upwards, and almost bursting with its own emotion."[98] He added that the "perfect stillness of the night was thrilled by a more solemn silence," and that "the darkness held a presence that was all the more felt because it was not seen. I could not any more have doubted that *He* was there than that I was. Indeed, I felt myself to be, if possible, the less real of the two."[99]

James cites several more cases in which the writer notes that during these experiences the presence of God was so palpable that God was, if anything, more real than oneself. In some of these cases the person would also hear a passage from Scripture—for example, "My grace is sufficient for thee"—and in one instance a boy who was seventeen years old experienced God sitting beside him at church and singing and reading the Psalms with him. James concludes from these accounts: "Such is the human ontological imagination, and such is the convincingness of what it brings to birth.

---

94. Ibid.
95. Ibid.
96. Ibid.
97. Ibid. The statement in footnote 14 of chapter 2 about James's use of material from the autobiographical writings of other authors also applies to his use of material from Starbuck's manuscript collection. Thus, this material is not presented here as quotations from *The Varieties* but as quotations from the original unpublished manuscripts. However, the page numbers in the footnotes are the pages on which this material is located in *The Varieties*.
98. Ibid.
99. Ibid., 66–67.

Unpicturable beings are realized, and realized with an intensity almost like that of an hallucination. They determine our vital attitude as decisively as the vital attitude of lovers is determined by the habitual sense, by which each is haunted, of the other being in the world."[100]

As for the fact that they are so convincing, James suggests that they are proof that the part of the mental life of which rationalism can give an account is relatively superficial: "If you have intuitions at all, they come from a deeper level of your nature than the loquacious level which rationalism inhabits. Your whole subconscious life, your impulses, your faiths, your needs, your divinations, have prepared the premises, of which your consciousness now feels the weight of the result; and something in you *absolutely* knows that the result must be truer than any logic-chopping rationalistic talk, however clever, that may contradict it."[101] Also, it is typically the case that our intuitions precede their articulation in the form of reason, that the "unreasoned and immediate assurance is the deep thing in us" while "the reasoned argument is but a surface exhibition."[102] If, then, "a person feels the presence of a living God after the fashion shown by my quotations, your critical comments, be they never so superior, will vainly set themselves to change his faith."[103] It is noteworthy in this connection that James Russell Lowell's experience of the Spirit of God all around him occurred in the midst of an argument he was having with his friend James Putnam on spiritual matters.

James adds that he is not, at least for the moment, suggesting that it is better that the subconscious mind *should* hold primacy in the religious realm. He is only noting that this is in fact the case. He concludes the chapter with a brief discussion of the attitudes that the sense of the reality of religious objects characteristically awaken, and he notes that he has already proposed in the second lecture that they should be *solemn*. But he also notes that the testimonies he has presented suggest that *joy* is often experienced, especially in cases of self-surrender. To be sure, a review of the literature on personal religious experiences would suggest that sadness and gladness have both been emphasized, and James sees no reason to exclude either one, for they, no doubt, are a reflection of the constitution or temperament of the person who has the experience. But most important, the solemnity of the experience gives the sense of joy a depth greater than ordinary animal joys; in fact, it suggests a deeper sense of inner peace.

---

100. Ibid., 72.
101. Ibid., 73.
102. Ibid., 74.
103. Ibid.

Finally, James reminds his listeners that in his preceding lecture he had quoted the English psychologist Havelock Ellis's opinion "that laughter of any sort may be considered a religious exercise, for it bears witness to the soul's emancipation," and that he had quoted Ellis's opinion "in order to deny its adequacy."[104] Now, however, it is necessary to "settle our scores more carefully with this whole optimistic way of thinking" for it is "far too complex to be decided off-hand."[105] Therefore, religious optimism will be the theme of the next two lectures.

---

104. Ibid., 77.

105. Ibid. Ellis, *The New Spirit*, 232. Ellis was especially noted for his writings on sexuality. See Ellis, *Erotic Symbolism*; Ellis, *Sexual Inversion*; and Ellis, *Sex in Relation to Society*.

3

THE HEALTHY MIND

IN THE FIRST SET of Gifford Lectures James devoted lectures 4 and 5 to "The Religion of Healthy-Mindedness" and lectures 6 and 7 to "The Sick Soul." It could be argued that these four lectures were the centerpiece of the first set of lectures, and that he anticipated that listeners would be especially likely to recall that he, in effect, identified two religious expressions, one fundamentally optimistic and the other tending to be rather morbid. I will focus in this chapter on the religion of healthy-mindedness. We will see in the course of this chapter that the mind-cure movement in the United States was very much on James's mind as he prepared his lectures on healthy-mindedness.

THE DESIRE FOR HAPPINESS

James begins his lectures on the religion of healthy-mindedness with the observation that if we were to ask "What is human life's chief concern?" one of the answers we would likely receive is that "It is happiness."[1] Indeed, "How to gain, how to keep, how to recover happiness, is in fact for most men at all times the secret motive of all they do, and of all they are willing to endure."[2] James notes that the hedonistic school in ethics bases the moral life wholly on the experiences of happiness and unhappiness that different kinds of conduct bring, and that "even more in the religious life than in the

---

1. James, *The Varieties of Religious Experience*, 78.
2. Ibid.

moral life, happiness and unhappiness seem to be the poles around which the interest revolves."³

But what does this association of religion and happiness really mean? James continues:

> We need not go so far as to say with the author whom I lately quoted [he is referring to Havelock Ellis] that any persistent enthusiasm is, as such, religion, nor need we call mere laughter a religious exercise; but we must admit that any persistent enjoyment may *produce* the sort of religion which consists in a grateful admiration of the gift of so happy an existence; and we must also acknowledge that the more complex ways of experiencing religion are new manners of producing happiness, wonderful inner paths to a supernatural kind of happiness, when the first gift of natural existence is unhappy, as it so often proves to be.⁴

In the first of the two lectures on the religion of healthy-mindedness James focuses on what he calls "the simpler kinds of religious happiness," and in the second he deals with "the more complex sorts."⁵ As far as its simpler kinds are concerned, he notes that in many persons, happiness is congenital, and this applies not only to persons who are "animally happy" but also to "those who, when unhappiness is offered or proposed to them, positively refuse to feel it, as if it were something mean or wrong."⁶ He observes that we find "such persons in every age, passionately flinging themselves upon their sense of the goodness of life, in spite of the hardships of their own condition, and in spite of the sinister theologies into which they may be born."⁷ James adds his hope that "we all have some friend, perhaps more often feminine than masculine, and young than old, whose soul is of this sky-blue tint, whose affinities are rather with the flowers and birds and all enchanting innocencies than with dark human passions, who can think no ill of man or God, and in whom religious gladness, being in possession from the outset, needs no deliverance from any antecedent burden."⁸

He goes on to cite Francis W. Newman's suggestion that God has two families of children on this earth—the once-born and the twice-born—and quotes Newman's description of the once-born:

---

3. Ibid.
4. Ibid., 78.
5. Ibid., 79.
6. Ibid.
7. Ibid.
8. Ibid., 80.

They see God, not as a strict Judge, not as a Glorious Potentate; but as the animating spirit of a beautiful harmonious world, Beneficent and Kind, Merciful as well as Pure. The same characters generally have no metaphysical tendencies: they do not look back into themselves. Hence they are not distressed by their own imperfections: yet it would be absurd to call them self-righteous; for they hardly think of themselves *at all*. This childlike quality of their nature makes the opening of religion very happy to them: for they no more shrink from God, than a child from an emperor, before whom the parent trembles: in fact, they have no vivid conception of *any* of the qualities in which the severer Majesty of God consists.[9]

James adds in a footnote that he "once heard a lady describe the pleasure it gave her to think that she 'could always cuddle up to God.'"[10]

James also quotes the Unitarian preacher and writer Dr. Edward Everett Hale's observation that he was born into a family in which the religion was simple and rational, and he had no knowledge or awareness of the religious struggles that are presented in many autobiographies and are portrayed as virtually essential to the formation of the author. He says that "I always knew God loved me, and I was always grateful to him for the world he placed me in. I always liked to tell him so, and was always glad to receive his suggestions to me," and he recalls "that when I was coming to manhood, the half-philosophical novels of the time had a [great] deal to say about the young men and maidens who were facing the 'problem of life.' I had no idea whatever what the problem of life was. To live with all my might seemed to me easy; to learn where there was so much to learn seemed pleasant and almost of course; to lend a hand, if one had a chance, natural; and if one did this, why, he enjoyed life because he could not help it, and without proving to himself that he ought to enjoy it."[11] James observes that one "can but recognize in such writers as these the presence of a temperament organically weighted on the side of cheer and fatally forbidden to linger, as those

---

9. Ibid., 80–81. F. W. Newman, *The Soul*, 89, 91. Newman relates his religious odyssey in *Phases of Faith, or Passages from the History of My Creed*. He was professor of Latin at University College, London for most of his professional career and the younger brother of John Henry Newman, who converted from the Church of England to the Roman Catholic Church in his mid-forties. See J. H. Newman, *Apologia Pro Vita Sua*; see also Capps, *Young Clergy*, chapters 4 and 7; and Capps, "The 'Reversal of Generations' Phenomenon."

10. James, *The Varieties of Religious Experience*, 81.

11. Ibid., 82–83. Hale's statement is quoted in Starbuck, *The Psychology of Religion*, 305–6.

of opposite temperament linger, over the darker aspects of the universe."[12] James adds, however, that in some individuals such "optimism may become quasi-pathological," that the "capacity for even a transient sadness or a momentary humility seems cut off from them as by a kind of congenital anesthesia."[13]

THE INABILITY TO FEEL EVIL

James goes on to discuss the American poet Walt Whitman, who, he suggests, is the "supreme contemporary example of such an inability to feel evil."[14] He points out that the only sentiments that Whitman allowed himself to express "were of the expansive order," and he did so in the first person, "not as your mere monstrously conceited individual might so express them, but vicariously for all men, so that a passionate and mystic ontological emotion suffuses his words, and ends by persuading the reader that men and women, life and death, and all things are divinely good."[15] He adds that many persons today regard Whitman "as the restorer of the eternal natural religion," and that Whitman "has infected them with his own love of comrades, with his own gladness that he and they exist."[16]

James disagrees with those who suggest that Whitman lacks an awareness of evil, but he feels that Whitman's optimism is "too voluntary and defiant," and that his gospel "has a touch of bravado and an affected twist" that "diminishes its effect on many readers who yet are well disposed towards optimism."[17] If, therefore, "we give the name of healthy-mindedness to the tendency which looks on all things and sees that they are good, we find that we must distinguish between a more involuntary and a more voluntary or systematic way of being healthy-minded. In its involuntary variety, healthy-mindedness is a way of feeling happy about things immediately. In its systematical variety, it is an abstract way of conceiving things as good."[18]

In systematic healthy-mindedness good is viewed as the essential and universal aspect of being, and evil is deliberately excluded from its field of vision. Some may view this procedure as insincere, but in James's view the

---

12. James, *The Varieties of Religious Experience*, 83.
13. Ibid.
14. Ibid., 84.
15. Ibid., 85. He has reference here to Whitman's epic poem *Song of Myself;* see Whitman, *Selected Poems*, 15–84.
16. James, *The Varieties of Religious Experience*, 85.
17. Ibid., 87.
18. Ibid., 87–88.

issue is more complex than this; for happiness, "like every other emotional state, has blindness and insensibility to opposing facts given it as its instinctive weapon for self-protection against disturbance."[19] Thus, "when happiness is actually in possession, the thought of evil can no more acquire the feeling of reality than the thought of good can gain reality when melancholy rules. To the man actively happy, from whatever cause, evil simply cannot then and there be believed in. He must ignore it; and to the bystander he may then seem perversely to shut his eyes to it and hush it up."[20] Moreover, the hushing of it up may grow into a deliberate religious policy, a refusal to recognize or acknowledge the bad things that seem so self-evident to others, for the ruling of your thoughts is your principal concern.

James suggests that such a deliberate religious policy is not to be disparaged. After all, the attitude of unhappiness is not only painful to oneself, but it also tends to be injurious to others because it "fastens and perpetuates the trouble which occasioned it, and increases the total evil of the situation."[21] In contrast, the deliberate attitude of happiness tends to expand beyond the subjective sphere of the one who adopts it, and therefore "our resolution not to indulge in misery, beginning at a comparatively small point within ourselves, may not stop until it has brought the entire frame of reality under a systematic conception optimistic enough to be congenial with its needs."[22] The systematic cultivation of healthy-mindedness as a religious attitude "is consonant therefore with important currents in human nature, and is anything but absurd. In fact, we all do cultivate it more or less, even when our professed theology should in consistency forbid it."[23] In this connection, "the advance of liberalism, so-called, in Christianity, during the past fifty years, may fairly be called a victory of healthy-mindedness within the church over the morbidness with which the old hell-fire theology was more harmoniously related."[24] There are congregations now whose preachers, rather than magnifying our consciousness of sin, tend to make little of it: "They ignore, or even deny, eternal punishment, and insist on the dignity rather than the depravity of man," and they "look at the continual preoccupation of the old-fashioned Christian with the salvation of his soul as something sickly and reprehensible rather than admirable."[25] James says he

19. Ibid., 88.
20. Ibid.
21. Ibid., 89.
22. Ibid.
23. Ibid., 90.
24. Ibid., 91.
25. Ibid.

is not asking whether or not these preachers and congregations are right, that he is only pointing out the change.

THE MIND-CURE MOVEMENT

James notes that in addition to these developments in liberal Christianity, the "mind-cure movement" or "New Thought" seems to be gathering force every day. He observes that there are differences among the various groups that make up the "mind-cure movement" but their agreements are so profound that he feels justified in neglecting their differences for the purposes of his discussion of healthy-mindedness. What they share in common is a "deliberately optimistic scheme of life, with both a speculative and a practical side."[26] Mind-cure is informed by various sources, traditional and more contemporary, but the most characteristic feature of the mind-cure movement is "the intuitive belief in the all-saving power of healthy-minded attitudes as such, in the conquering efficacy of courage, hope, and trust, and a correlative contempt for doubt, fear, worry, and all nervously precautionary states of mind."[27]

James suggests that this belief in the all-saving power of healthy-minded attitudes has been corroborated by the practical experience of their disciples, for in a very practical way "the blind have been made to see, the halt to walk," and "lifelong invalids have had their health restored."[28] Its moral fruits have been equally remarkable. The deliberate adoption of a healthy-minded attitude has proved possible to many who never supposed they had it in them, regeneration of character has taken place on an extensive scale, and cheerfulness has been restored to countless homes. Even complaints about the weather are forbidden in many households, and more and more people are recognizing that it is bad form to speak of disagreeable sensations or to make an issue of the ordinary inconveniences and ailments of life.[29]

To be sure, innumerable failures and self-deceptions have been mixed in with the successes, and quite a lot of the mind-cure literature is "so moonstruck with optimism and so vaguely expressed that an academically trained intellect finds it almost impossible to read it at all."[30] And yet, the spread of the movement has been due to its practical fruits, and it is noteworthy that

26. Ibid, 94.
27. Ibid., 94–95.
28. Ibid., 95.
29. Ibid.
30. Ibid., 96.

the practical nature of the American people should be so intimately connected with its "concrete therapeutics."[31]

James goes on to note that mind-cure shares with traditional forms of Christianity the belief that man has a dual nature, a shallower and a profounder sphere, but whereas Christian theology has always considered the essential vice of the shallower sphere to be its stubborn, uncontrollable willfulness, mind-cure believes that fear is the fundamental problem. James cites Horace Fletcher's observation that fear had its uses in the evolutionary process but that much of the fear that humans experience today is unnecessary,[32] and he cites Henry Wood's observation that man "often has fear stamped upon him before his entrance into the outer world; he is reared in fear; all his life is passed in bondage to fear of disease and death, and thus his whole mentality becomes cramped, limited, and depressed, and his body follows its shrunken pattern and specification."[33]

James also notes that mind-cure uses a greater variety of words and phrases to describe the profounder sphere than is found in traditional Christianity, but he notes that some of this language is prefigured in Christian mysticism while other expressions reflect the modern psychology of the subliminal self. Central to its understanding of the profounder sphere of the human person, however, is the idea that this deeper sphere is continuous with the infinite life and power of God.[34]

James goes on to quote rather extensively from the personal accounts of persons who identify with the mind-cure movement, including two unnamed women who are personal friends of his. Suggesting that the "underlying cause of all sickness, weakness or depression is the *human sense of separateness* from that Divine Energy which we call God," the first correspondent went on to declare that the "possibility of annulling forever the law of fatigue has been abundantly proven in my own case; for my earlier life bears a record of many, many years of bedridden invalidism, with spine and lower limbs paralyzed."[35] She says that her former "belief in the necessity of illness was dense and unenlightened; but since my resurrection in the flesh, I have worked as a healer unceasingly for fourteen years without a vacation, and can truthfully assert that I have never known a moment of fatigue or

---

31. Ibid.
32. Fletcher, *Happiness as Found in Forethought minus Fearthought*, 21–22.
33. Wood, *Ideal Suggestion through Mental Photography*, 54.
34. James, *The Varieties of Religious Experience*, 100–101.
35. Ibid., 102.

pain, although coming in touch constantly with excessive weakness, illness, and disease of all kinds."[36]

The second correspondent observes that there was a time in her life when she "was always breaking down, and had several attacks of what is called nervous prostration, with terrible insomnia, being on the verge of insanity; besides having many other troubles, especially of the digestive organs."[37] She adds that she had been sent away from home in charge of doctors, had taken all the narcotics, and stopped all work, and knew all the doctors within reach, but she never recovered permanently till this New Thought took possession of her. What impressed her most about the New Thought "was learning the fact that we must be in absolutely constant relation or mental touch (this word is to me very expressive) with that essence of life which permeates all and which we call God."[38] She goes on to note that the meaning of this new attitude for bodily health is "an incidental result," as it simply "comes of itself," without "any special mental act or desire to have it."[39] In fact, she considers the acquisition of bodily health to be among "the outer things we are all so wildly seeking," such as "success in business, fame as an author or artist, physician or lawyer, or renown in philanthropic undertakings."[40] Such things, she says, "should be results, not objects, for what is essential is turning "inward to the light within you" and living "in the presence of God or your divine self."[41]

Following these personal accounts, James observes that it is impossible *not* to view mind-cure as primarily a religious movement. Moreover, its doctrine of the oneness of our life with God's life is indistinguishable from interpretations of Christ's message which have been expressed in previous Gifford lectures by renowned religious philosophers. If there is a difference between them it is perhaps in the fact that mind-curers, while aware of the reality of evil, do not offer an explanation for it. Instead, they choose not to worry about it as a "mystery" or "problem" and simply focus their thoughts on that which is good and positive. In effect, they have a doctrine that thoughts are "forces," and "the great point in the conduct of life is to get the heavenly forces on one's side by opening one's own mind to their influx."[42]

---

36. Ibid.
37. Ibid.
38. Ibid., 102–3.
39. Ibid., 103.
40. Ibid.
41. Ibid.
42. Ibid., 107.

James concludes his discussion of the mind-cure movement by noting the psychological similarity between it and the Lutheran and Wesleyan movements, both of which responded to the anxious query, "what must I do to be saved?" with the answer, "You are saved now, if you would but believe it." To be sure, the wording is different as the word "salvation" has lost its meaning for those attracted to mind-cure, but they labor under the same eternal human difficulty. Things are wrong with them, and the form of their question is, "What shall I do to be clear, right, sound, whole, well?" And the answer is "You are well, sound, and clear already, if you did but know it." As one of the mind-cure authors puts it, "God is well, and so are you. You must awaken to the knowledge of your real being."[43]

At this point in the lecture James anticipates that some members of this academic audience may be feeling that "such contemporary vagaries" should not "take so large a place in dignified Gifford lectures."[44] And yet, it is his hope that these lectures will impress upon his listeners "the enormous diversities which the spiritual lives of different men exhibit":

> Their wants, their susceptibilities, and their capacities all vary and must be classed under different heads. The result is that we have really different types of religious experience; and, seeking in these lectures closer acquaintance with the healthy-minded type, we must take it where we find it in [its] most radical form. The psychology of individual types of character has hardly begun even to be sketched as yet—our lectures may possibly serve as a crumb-like contribution to the structure. [But] the first thing to bear in mind . . . is that nothing can be more stupid than to bar out phenomena from our notice, merely because we are incapable of taking part in anything like them ourselves.[45]

The lecture continues with several more allusions to the fact that mind-cure may be viewed as continuous with the history of Lutheran salvation by faith and of Methodist conversions. These are followed by a reference to a story that revivalist preachers often tell about a man who one night slipped down the side of a precipice: "At last he caught a branch which stopped his fall, and remained clinging to it in misery for hours. But finally his fingers had to loose their hold, and with a despairing farewell to life, he let himself drop. He fell just six inches. If he had given up the struggle earlier, his agony would have been spared. As the mother earth received him, so, the preachers tell us, will the everlasting arms receive *us* if we confide absolutely in

---

43. Ibid., 108.
44. Ibid., 108–9.
45. Ibid., 109.

them, and give up the hereditary habit of relying on our personal strength, with its precautions that cannot shelter and safeguards that never save."[46] In James's view, the mind-curers have given the widest scope to this sort of experience: "They have demonstrated that a form of regeneration by relaxing, by letting go, psychologically indistinguishable from the Lutheran justification by faith and the Wesleyan acceptance of free grace, is within the reach of persons who have no conviction of sin and care nothing for the Lutheran theology. It is but giving your little private convulsive self a rest, and finding that a greater Self is there."[47] Furthermore, "the results, slow or sudden, or great or small, of the combined optimism and expectancy, the regenerative phenomena which ensue on the abandonment of effort, remain firm facts of human nature, no matter whether we adopt a theistic, a pantheistic-idealistic, or a medical-materialistic view of their causal explanation."[48]

James adds in a footnote that the theistic explanation is that of divine grace, which creates a new nature within a person once the old nature is sincerely given up. The pantheistic explanation, which is that of most mind-curers, is that by the merging of the narrower private self into the wider or greater self (or the spirit of the universe that is your own subconscious self), the isolating barriers of mistrust and anxiety are removed. The medical-materialistic explanation is that simpler cerebral processes act more freely where they are left to act automatically by the shunting-out of physiologically "higher" ones, which, seeking to regulate the cerebral processes, only succeed in inhibiting results. James notes that whether in a psychophysical account of the universe the third explanation might be combined with either of the others is, at least for the moment, an open question.

James indicates that he now wants to say a brief word about the mind-curer's methods. He observes that these methods essentially draw upon the power of suggestion. Since the suggestive influence of the environment plays an enormous part in all spiritual education, he believes that we should not make too much of an issue of the fact that mind-cure makes conscious and deliberate use of suggestion in its methods. After all, suggestion is only another name for the power of ideas insofar as they prove efficacious over belief and conduct. Moreover, "ideas efficacious at some times and in some human surroundings are not so at other times and elsewhere. The ideas of Christian churches are not efficacious in the therapeutic direction today, whatever they may have been in earlier centuries; and when the whole

---

46. Ibid., 111. His essay "The Gospel of Relaxation," one of his talks to students, is relevant here. See James, *Talks to Teachers*, 99–112.

47. James, *The Varieties of Religious Experience*, 111 .

48. Ibid.

question is as to why the salt has lost its savor here or gained it there, the mere blank waving of the word 'suggestion' as if it were a banner gives no light."[49]

James cites a psychological essay by Henry Herbert Goddard on faith cures that ascribes these cures to nothing but ordinary suggestion. Goddard argues that there is nothing extraordinary about the suggestions that are used by mind-curers. After all, religion in all its various forms possesses "all there is in mental therapeutics, and has it in its best form," so living up to our religious ideas, whatever their sources may be, "will do anything for us that can be done."[50] However, James believes that popular Christianity was largely ineffective in this regard until mind-cure came to its rescue. In any event, the important point is that for an idea to be genuinely suggestive it "must come to the individual with the force of a revelation" and "mind-cure with its gospel of healthy-mindedness has come as a revelation to many whose hearts the church Christianity had left hardened. It has let loose their springs of higher life. In what can the originality of any religious movement consist save in finding a channel, until then sealed up, through which these springs may be set free in some group of human beings?"[51] James adds that "the force of personal faith, enthusiasm, and example, and above all the force of novelty, are always the prime suggestive agency in this kind of success," and this means that if mind-cure should ever "become official, respectable, and entrenched, these elements of suggestive efficacy will be lost."[52] This, James notes, the church knows well enough, as it has always been engaged in "an inner struggle of the acute religion of the few against the chronic religion of the many," the latter of whom often exhibit an obstructive disposition "worse than that which irreligion opposes to the moving of the Spirit."[53]

James concludes that in addition to its promotion of ideas that have come to many individuals with the force of a revelation, the success of the mind-cure movement is the apparent existence, in large numbers, of individuals who "unite healthy-mindedness with readiness for regeneration by letting go."[54] In this regard, Protestantism has been too pessimistic, and Catholicism has been too legalistic and moralistic, to appeal in any generous

---

49. Ibid., 112.
50. Ibid.; see Goddard, "The Effects of Mind on Body as Evidenced by Faith Cures."
51. James, *The Varieties of Religious Experience*, 113–14.
52. Ibid., 114.
53. Ibid.
54. Ibid.

way to the type of character to which mind-cure makes its appeal.[55] This readiness for regeneration by letting go is especially reflected in the fact that mind-cure has made an "unprecedentedly great use of the subconscious life."[56] In addition to their reasoned advice and dogmatic assertions, its founders have added systematic exercise of passive relaxation, concentration, meditation, and even the use of something like hypnotic practice. James cites the following passages from writings by Horatio W. Dresser:

> The value, the potency of ideals is the great practical truth on which the New Thought most strongly insists—the development namely from within outward, from small to great. Consequently one's thought should be centered on the ideal outcome, even though this trust be literally like a step in the dark . . . To attain the ability thus effectively to direct the mind, the New Thought advises the practice of concentration, or in other words, the attainment of self-control. One is to learn to marshal the tendencies of the mind, so that they may be held together as a unit by the chosen ideal. To this end, one should set apart times for silent meditation, by one's self, preferably in a room where the surroundings are favorable to spiritual thought. In New Thought terms, this is called "entering the silence."[57]

James suggests that these and other exercises advocated by the mind-curers do not differ in any intrinsic way from the contemplative practices of Catholic discipline.

RELIGION AND SCIENCE

In the closing paragraphs of his chapter on healthy-mindedness James notes that mind-cure has implications for the question of the relation of religion to science but that he will defer this discussion to a later lecture. For now, however, he wants to take note of the fact that there are plenty of persons today

> who will tell you that religion is a mere survival [or] atavistic reversion to a type of consciousness which humanity in its more enlightened examples has long since left behind and outgrown. If you ask them to explain themselves more fully, they will probably say that for primitive thought everything is conceived of

---

55. Ibid.
56. Ibid., 115.
57. Ibid.; see Dresser, *Living by the Spirit,* 58; Dresser, *Voices of Freedom,* 53.

under the form of personality. The savage thinks that things operate by personal forces, and for the sake of individual ends. For him, even external nature obeys individual needs and claims, just as if these were so many elementary powers. Now science, on the other hand, these positivists say, has proved that personality, so far from being an elementary force in nature, is but a passive resultant of the really elementary forces, physical, chemical, physiological, and psycho-physical, which are all impersonal and general in character. Nothing individual accomplishes anything in the universe save in so far as it obeys and exemplifies some universal law.[58]

Thus, these persons would argue that if you follow science's conceptions practically by ignoring personality altogether, you will always be corroborated, for nature's forces are impersonal and universal.

But then, James notes, along comes mind-cure with her diametrically opposite philosophy based, however, on an exactly identical claim: "Live as if I were true, she says, and every day will practically prove you right. That the controlling energies of nature are personal, that your own personal thoughts are forces, that the powers of the universe will directly respond to your individual appeals and needs, are propositions which your whole bodily and mental experience will verify."[59] The fact that experience largely verifies these primeval religious ideas is proved by the fact that the mind-cure movement spreads as it does, not simply by proclamation and assertion but by palpable experiential results. Thus, here, "in the very heyday of science's authority, it carries on an aggressive warfare against the scientific philosophy, and succeeds by using science's own peculiar methods and weapons. Believing that a higher power will take care of us in certain ways better than we can take care of ourselves, if we only genuinely throw ourselves upon it and consent to use it, it finds the belief, not only not impugned, but corroborated by its observation."[60] Thus, like science, it makes its appeal to the method of experimental verification, and comes to the opposite conclusion.

58. James, *The Varieties of Religious Experience*, 118–19.
59. Ibid., 119.
60. Ibid., 119–20. James uses the terms "higher power" and "higher powers" several times in *The Varieties of Religious Experience*, e.g., 228, 243, 273, 311, and 465. As the "higher power" is commonly associated with Alcoholics Anonymous, it is noteworthy that, as Robert D. Richardson points out in *William James*, "*The Varieties of Religious Experience* is . . . the acknowledged inspiration for the founding of Alcoholics Anonymous. It is James's understanding of conversion that AA has found especially helpful" (6). In a footnote Richardson recommends Nan Robertson's *Getting Better* for an account of James's influence on Bill W. (William Griffith Wilson), one of the founders of Alcoholics Anonymous. Richardson also cites Wilson's comment that AA "has made

However, in James's view, it is unnecessary to choose between a scientific frame of reference and a religious one. Why, he asks,

> need we assume that only one such system of ideas can be true? The obvious outcome of our total experience is that the world can be handled according to many systems of ideas, and is so handled by different men, and will each time give some characteristic kind of profit, for which he cares, to the handler, while at the same time some other kind of profit has to be omitted or postponed. Science gives to all of us telegraphy, electric lighting, and diagnosis, and succeeds in preventing and curing a certain amount of disease. Religion in the shape of mind-cure gives to some of us serenity, moral poise, and happiness, and prevents certain forms of disease as well as science does, or even better in a certain class of persons. Evidently, then, the science and the religion are both of them genuine keys for unlocking the world's treasure-house to him who can use either of them practically. Just as evidently neither is exhaustive or exclusive of the other's simultaneous use.[61]

Thus, if we consider the fact that the world is so complex as to consist of many interpenetrating spheres of reality, then it stands to reason that we may use different conceptions and assume different attitudes in an alternating sort of way even as mathematicians handle the same numerical and spatial facts by geometry, algebra and calculus: "On this view, religion and science, each verified in its own way from hour to hour and from life to life, would be co-eternal. Primitive thought, with its belief in individualized personal forces, seems at any rate as far as ever from being driven by science from the field today. Numbers of educated people still find it the [most direct] experimental channel by which to carry on their intercourse with reality."[62]

James ends the lecture by acknowledging that the case of mind-cure was so close at hand that he could not resist the temptation of using it to bring these last truths to his audience's attention. But he notes that he will give much more explicit attention to the relations of religion both to science and to primitive thought in a later lecture.

---

conversion experiences—nearly every variety reported by James—available on an almost wholesale basis," and his later comment that "James, though long in his grave, had been a founder of Alcoholics Anonymous" (ibid., 531).

61. James, *The Varieties of Religious Experience*, 122.
62. Ibid., 123.

4

The Sick Soul

James begins his lectures on the sick soul with a brief reference to the preceding lectures on the healthy-minded temperament, "the temperament which has a constitutional incapacity for prolonged suffering and in which the tendency to see things optimistically is like a water of crystallization in which the individual's character is set."[1] James notes that these two lectures showed that "this temperament may become the basis for a peculiar type of religion, a religion in which good, even the good of this world's life,

---

1. James, *The Varieties of Religious Experience*, 127. It is noteworthy that he uses the word "temperament" here, and that in the lectures on the sick soul he will be viewing the sick soul as a contrasting temperament. The dictionary defines *temperament* as "one's customary frame of mind or natural disposition" (Agnes, *Webster's New World*, 1473). It also notes that in medieval physiology, temperament is any of the four conditions of body or mind, the *sanguine, phlegmatic, choleric* (or *bilious*), and *melancholic temperaments*, attributed to an excess of one of the four corresponding humors" (Ibid.). It defines *humor* as "any of the four fluids . . . considered responsible for one's health and disposition" (ibid., 696). In "The Persistence of the Four Temperaments" John Doody and John Immerwahr discuss the remarkable durability of the four temperaments concept by citing texts that implicitly employ the medieval construct of four identifiable temperaments. They cite, for example, James David Barber's *The Presidential Character*, a study of American presidents; Robert R. Blake and Jane S. Mouton's *The Managerial Grid*, a study of management styles; and Thomas Harris's *I'm OK, You're OK*, a popular version of transactional analysis, a form of psychotherapy based largely on the work of Eric Berne. See Berne, *Transactional Analysis in Psychotherapy*; also Berne, *Games People Play*. According to Doody and Immerwhar, the four temperaments and their primary features are *sanguine* (joyful, courageous); *phlegmatic* (insipid, cowardly); *choleric* (irritable, angry); and *melancholic* (solitary, unsociable). In effect, James focuses on the *sanguine* (healthy-minded) and *melancholic* (sick-soul) temperaments in *The Varieties of Religious Experience*.

is regarded as the essential thing for a rational being to attend to."[2] Thus, the religion it inspires directs a person to settle his scores "with the more evil aspects of the universe by declining to lay them to heart or make much of them, by ignoring them in his reflective calculations, or even, on occasion, by denying outright that they exist."[3] After all, "evil is a disease; and worry over disease is itself an additional form of disease, which only adds to the original complaint."[4]

This means that even repentance and remorse "may be but sickly and relaxing impulses," and that the "best repentance is to up and act for righteousness, and forget that you ever had relations with sin."[5] James points out that Baruch Spinoza's philosophy "has this sort of healthy-mindedness woven into the heart of it, and this has been one secret of its fascination."[6] For Spinoza, knowledge of evil is inadequate knowledge, fit only for slavish minds, so he categorically condemns repentance. Spinoza says that when men make mistakes, one might expect the gnawing of conscience and repentance to help restore them to the right path, and might therefore conclude that these affections are good things. Yet, "when we look at the matter closely, we shall find that not only are they not good, but on the contrary deleterious and evil passions."[7] After all, "it is manifest that we can always get along better by reason and love of truth than by worry of conscience and remorse."[8]

James suggests that within the Christian body repentance of sins has been the critical religious act, but that healthy-mindedness has always come forward with its milder interpretation, for, according to healthy-minded Christians, repentance means "*getting away from* the sin, not groaning and writhing over its commission."[9] In fact, the Catholic practice of confession and absolution is a way of keeping healthy-mindedness on top, for by this practice a person's "accounts with evil are periodically squared and audited, so that he may start the clean page with no old debts inscribed."[10]

---

2. James, *The Varieties of Religious Experience*, 127.

3. Ibid.

4. Ibid.

5. Ibid.

6. Ibid.

7. Ibid., 128. James indicates that he is quoting here from Spinoza's *Tract on God, Man, and Happiness*, book 2, chapter 10. See Spinoza, *The Philosophy of Spinoza*.

8. James, *The Varieties of Religious Experience*, 128.

9. Ibid. (italics original).

10. Ibid.

Moreover, although Martin Luther did not belong to the healthy-minded type in the radical sense, he did have some very healthy-minded things to say about repentance, and these were due primarily to the largeness of his conception of God. In his commentary on Paul's Letter to the Galatians (from which James provides a lengthy quotation), Luther notes that those who truly believe in God trust that God is favorable and merciful to them for Christ's sake, and they "look unto Christ their reconciler, who gave his life for their sins" so they "know that the remnant of sin which is in their flesh is not laid to their charge, but freely pardoned."[11] In James's view, there is something healthy-minded in this way of viewing one's sinful nature.

James suggests that this also was true of Miguel Molinos, the founder of Quietism, who, due to the influence of the Jesuits, was condemned for his healthy-minded opinion of repentance. Molinos pointed out in his spiritual guide that when you do something wrong, Satan will cause you to believe that you are out of God's favor, will try to make you distrust the grace of God, and will put it "into thy head that every day thy soul grows worse instead of better."[12] Employing the analogy of a footrace, he says that one would be a mere fool if after falling he were to lie weeping on the ground and afflict himself with discourses upon his fall. Instead he should "lose no time, get up and take the course again, for he that rises again quickly and continues his race is as if he had never fallen."[13] So, if you have fallen once or even a thousand times, you should "make use of the remedy I have given thee, that is, a loving confidence in divine mercy."[14] Thus, one finds in traditional Christianity much evidence of the healthy-minded spirit that is presented in a more radical form in contemporary mind-cure and New Thought.

THE MAXIMIZATION OF EVIL

But now, James says, it is time to introduce "a radically opposite view, a way of maximizing evil, if you please to call it, based on the persuasion that the evil aspects of our life are of its very essence and that the world's meaning

---

11. Ibid., 129.

12. Ibid., 130. See Molinos, *The Spiritual Guide Which Disentangles the Soul.* James indicates that he is quoting from chapters 17–18; chapter 17 is titled "How the Soul is to Carry Itself" and chapter 18 is a continuation of the same topic.

13. Ibid.

14. Ibid.

most comes home to us when we lay them most to heart."[15] This will involve turning toward "those persons who cannot so swiftly throw off the burden of the consciousness of evil, but are congenitally fated to suffer from its presence."[16] To understand their difficulty in this regard James introduces the word "threshold," noting that it is being used in recent psychology as a symbolic designation for the point at which one state of mind passes into another. He notes that individuals have different threshold levels. For example, in reacting to outer stimuli, "one with a high threshold will doze through an amount of racket by which one with a low threshold would be immediately waked."[17]

The same holds true for individuals' misery threshold: "The sanguine and healthy-minded live habitually on the sunny side of their misery line [while] the depressed and melancholy live beyond it, in darkness and apprehension."[18] Or, to put it another way, there are those "who seem to have started in life with a bottle or two of champagne inscribed to their credit; whilst others seem to have been born close to the pain-threshold, which the slightest irritants fatally send them over."[19] This being the case, "does it not appear as if one who lived more habitually on one side of the pain-threshold might need a different sort of religion from one who habitually lived on the other?"[20]

James notes that this question "of the relativity of different types of religion to different types of need" invites further consideration, but before we can do this, "we must address ourselves to the unpleasant task of hearing what the sick souls, as we may call them in contrast to the healthy-minded, have to say of the secrets of their prison-house, their own peculiar form of consciousness."[21] He suggests that the way to embark on this unpleasant task is to ask, "How *can* things so insecure as the successful experiences of this world afford a stable anchorage? A chain is no stronger than its weakest link, and life is after all a chain."[22] This means that even in the healthiest and most prosperous existence there are inevitably links of illness, danger, and disaster, and from the bottom of every fountain of pleasure "something bitter rises up: a touch of nausea, a falling dead of the delight, a whiff of

15. Ibid., 130–31.
16. Ibid., 133–34.
17. Ibid., 135.
18. Ibid.
19. Ibid.
20. Ibid.
21. Ibid.
22. Ibid., 136.

melancholy, things that sound a knell, for fugitive as they may be, they bring a feeling of coming from a deeper region and often have an appalling convincingness."[23] Even a person who is "so packed with healthy-mindedness to have never experienced any of these sobering intervals" must, if he is a reflective person, "generalize and class his own lot with that of others; and, doing so, he must see that his escape is just a lucky chance and no essential difference."[24]

James provides several illustrations of persons who would identify themselves as sick souls. For example, there is the German poet and dramatist Johann Wolfgang von Goethe, an eminently successful man, who declared that, at bottom, his existence "has been nothing but pain and burden, and I can affirm that during the whole of my seventy-five years, I have not had four weeks of genuine well-being."[25] James also cites the case of Martin Luther, another successful man, "who looked back on his life as if it were an absolute failure," and who responded to a woman who wished that he might live another forty years, "Madam, rather than live forty years more, I would give up my chance of Paradise."[26] James exclaims:

> Failure, then, failure! So the world stamps us at every turn. We strew it with our blunders, our misdeeds, our lost opportunities, with all the memorials of our inadequacy to our vocation. And with what a damning emphasis does it then blot us out! No easy fine, no mere apology or formal expiation, will satisfy the world's demands, but every pound of flesh exacted is soaked with all its blood. The subtlest forms of suffering known to man are connected with the poisonous humiliations incidental to these results. And they are pivotal human experiences. A process so ubiquitous and everlasting is evidently an integral part of life.[27]

If, then, our very nature is rooted in failure, James asks, "Is it any wonder that theologians should have held it to be essential, and thought that only through the personal experience of humiliation which it engenders the deeper sense of life's significance is reached?"[28] James cites several verses from the book of Ecclesiastes: e.g., "What profit hath a man of all his labor which he taketh under the sun? I looked on all the works that my hands had

23. Ibid.
24. Ibid.
25. Ibid., 137.
26. Ibid., 137–38.
27. Ibid., 138.
28. Ibid.

wrought, and behold, all was vanity and vexation of spirit" (1:3, 2:11, KJV); and he points out that although the early Greeks have been held up to us "as models of the healthy-minded joyousness which the religion of nature may engender," they became "unmitigated pessimists" when they "grew systematically pensive and thought of ultimates."[29] Thus, Epicureanism advocates the effort to escape unhappiness rather than the search for happiness, and Stoicism advises that the only genuine good that life can yield is the free possession of one's own soul; all other goods are lies.[30] If we take these witnesses seriously, we cannot avoid concluding that the "securest way to the rapturous sorts of happiness of which the twice-born make report has as an historic matter of fact been through a more radical pessimism than anything that we have yet considered."[31]

PATHOLOGICAL MELANCHOLY

And this, James suggests, is where melancholy enters the picture. For "there is a pitch of unhappiness so great that the goods of nature may be entirely forgotten, and all sentiment of their existence vanishes from the mental field,"[32] and

> for this extremity of pessimism to be reached, something more is needed than observation of life and reflection upon death. The individual must in his own person become the prey of a pathological melancholy. As the healthy-minded enthusiast succeeds in ignoring evil's very existence, so the subject of melancholy is forced in spite of himself to ignore that of all good whatever: for him it may no longer have the least reality. Such sensitiveness and susceptibility to mental pain is a rare occurrence where the nervous constitution is entirely normal; one seldom finds it in a healthy subject even where he is the victim of the most atrocious cruelties of outward fortune.[33]

And so, the neurotic condition of which he said so much in his first lecture makes "its active entrance on our scene" and is "destined to play a part in much that follows."[34] And given the fact that

29. Ibid., 142.
30. Ibid., 143.
31. Ibid., 144.
32. Ibid.
33. Ibid., 145.
34. Ibid.

these experiences of melancholy are in the first instance absolutely private and individual, I can now help myself out with personal documents. Painful indeed they will be to listen to, and there is almost an indecency in handling them in public. Yet they lie right in the middle of our path; and if we are to touch the psychology of religion at all seriously, we must be willing to forget conventionalities, and dive below the smooth and lying official conversational surface.[35]

To set the stage for this discussion of pathological melancholy, it will be useful to take a brief look at James's earlier reflections on melancholy in his chapter "The Perception of Reality" in *The Principles of Psychology*. He indicates in a footnote that this chapter is an expansion of an article published in the philosophical journal *Mind* in 1869.[36] It is noteworthy that James was twenty-seven years old at the time and thus in the period of his life when he was in the throes of his own struggle with pathological melancholy.[37] The chapter begins with a consideration of the nature of belief and specifically with the assertion that belief is the "sense of the reality" of that which is believed. This means that doubt and inquiry, not disbelief, are the true opposites of belief because in doubt and inquiry the "content of our mind is in unrest"—we do not yet know whether the object is real or not—whereas in disbelief we have settled the issue by declaring to ourselves that the object does not exist in the real world. He notes, however, that belief, on the one hand, and doubt and inquiry, on the other, are emotions that may be "pathologically exalted."[38] Belief, for example, is typically exalted in states of drunkenness, and doubt is pathologically exalted in the "questioning mania" which is found, for example, in some forms of philosophy ("why is a glass a glass, a chair a chair?" and so forth).[39]

But James notes that there is another pathological state as far removed from doubt as from belief: "the feeling that everything is hollow, unreal, dead," and he indicates that he will speak of this state later in the chapter.[40] This is melancholy, and he introduces it by noting that "those things which

---

35. Ibid.
36. James, *The Principles of Psychology*, 2:283.
37. Ibid., 283. James does not provide a citation for this article (and I have been unable to find it), but in light of the fact that he changed this chapter title from "The Psychology of Belief" to "The Perception of Reality" in the course of writing *The Principles*, it is likely that the original article was titled "The Psychology of Belief." On the title change itself, see Richardson, *William James*, 289.
38. Ibid., 284.
39. Ibid.
40. Ibid., 285.

have an intimate connection with my life are things whose reality I cannot doubt," but things that "fail to establish this connection are things which are practically no better for me than if they existed not at all."[41] To illustrate the latter experience, James points out that "In certain forms of melancholic perversion of the sensibilities and reactive powers, nothing touches us intimately, rouses us, or wakens natural feeling,"[42] and he adds: "The consequence is the complaint so often heard from melancholic patients, that nothing is believed in by them as it used to be, and that all sense of reality is fled from life. They are sheathed in India-rubber; nothing penetrates to the quick or draws blood, as it were."[43] James cites in this connection Wilhelm Griesinger's observation that patients suffering from melancholia will say, "I see, I hear, but the objects do not reach me, it is as if there were a wall between me and the outer world!"[44] He also cites Griesinger's observation that alterations in our psychic relations to the outer world are brought about by advancing age, on the one hand, and emotions and passions on the other. Griesinger writes:

> In childhood, we feel ourselves to be closer to the world of sensible phenomena, we live immediately with them and in them; an intimately vital tie binds us and them together. But with the ripening of reflection this tie is loosened, the warmth of our interest cools, things look differently to us, and we act more as foreigners to the outer world, even though we know it a great deal better. Joy and expansive emotions in general draw it nearer to us again. Everything makes a more lively impression, and with the quick immediate return of this warm reciptivity for sense impressions, joy makes us feel young again. In depressing emotions it is other way. Outer things, whether living or inorganic, suddenly grow cold and foreign to us, and even our favorite objects of interest feel as if they belonged to us no more. Under

---

41. Ibid., 298.
42. Ibid.
43. Ibid.
44. Ibid. See Greisinger, *Mental Pathology and Therapeutics*, 50. See also Stanley W. Jackson's discussion of Greisinger's *Mental Pathology and Therapeutics* in *Melancholia and Depression*, 160–66. Jackson notes that Greisinger attributed melancholy to various causes, especially to painful emotional states (anger, grief, and so forth) and to disappointed ambitions, regrets, unrequited love, forced sojourn in inadequate circumstances, and the like. Greisinger also mentions "mixed" causes (physical and psychological combined, such as drunkenness, masturbation, and sexual deprivation). As for therapeutic interventions, he recommends careful regulation of diet, rest and activity, fresh air, and exercise, and he advises family members and friends to distract the sufferer from his or her preoccupations with mild, cheering influences and avoidance of the topics of the melancholic person's preoccupations.

these circumstances, receiving no longer from anything a lively impression, we cease to turn towards outer things, and the sense of inward loneliness grows upon us ... Where there is no strong intelligence to control this *blasé* condition, this psychic coldness and lack of interest, the issue of these states in which all seems so cold and hollow, the heart dried up, the world grown dead and empty, is often suicide or the deeper forms of insanity.[45]

James does not discuss melancholy any further in this chapter, but toward the end of the chapter he takes up the issue of the role that imagination plays in making unreal things seem real, as when one "realizes" the fact of a dead or distant friend's existence at the moment a portrait, letter or garment of one's friend is found.[46] This illustration suggests that melancholy has to do with absence and loss, and with the desire to recover the absent or lost object in some form or other.[47] We will see the relevance of this point when we consider James's own experience of melancholy later in this chapter.

Following his observation in his chapter in *The Varieties* on the sick soul that "if we are to touch the psychology of religion at all seriously, we must be willing to forget conventionalities, and dive below the smooth and lying official conversational surface,"[48] James goes on to discuss some of the "many kinds of pathological depression," beginning with the type that he describes as "mere passive joylessness and dreariness, discouragement, dejection, lack of taste and zest and spring."[49] He cites Theodule Ribot's proposal of the name *anhedonia* to designate this condition and quotes Ribot'sreference to a case of a young girl who was afflicted with a liver disease that altered her constitution to such a degree that she no longer experienced pleasure in things—like her doll—that had previously convulsed her with laughter.[50] James also cites the case of a Catholic philosopher, Fr. Auguste Gratry, who writes of his experience as a young man of a severe state of nervous exhaustion due to mental isolation and excessive study. He described his symptoms as "an incurable and intolerable desolation, verging on despair," of "having

45. Ibid. See Griesinger, *Mental Pathology and Therapeutics*, 50, 98.

46. Ibid., 303.

47. James mentions here the example of the imaginative child for whom a doll represents another object and does so even if there is little resemblance between it and what it is held to stand for (ibid., 303–4).

48. James, *The Varieties of Religious Experience*, 145.

49. Ibid.

50. Ibid., 145–46; Ribot, *The Psychology of the Emotions*, 54. This illustration may have been the basis for James's comment in the first chapter of *The Varieties of Religious Experience* that there are those who would claim that "William's melancholy about the universe is due to bad digestion—probably his liver his torpid" (10).

every idea of heaven taken away from me" and the sense that words like *happiness, joy, light, affection,* and *love* "were now devoid of sense."[51] No doubt he could still have talked about these things, "but I had become incapable of feeling anything in them, of understanding anything about them, of hoping anything from them, or of believing them to exist."[52]

From these cases of melancholy involving the sense of an incapacity for joyous feeling James moves to a second and much worse form of melancholy, that is, a "positive and active anguish, a sort of psychical neuralgia wholly unknown to normal life."[53] He notes that this form of melancholy can assume various expressions, including a sense of loathing, of irritation and exasperation, of self-mistrust and self-despair, and of suspicion, anxiety, trepidation and fear.[54] The afflicted person may engage in self-accusation or accuse outside powers and "may or may not be tormented by the theoretical mystery of why he should so have to suffer."[55]

James observes that only a relatively small proportion of these cases "connect themselves with the religious sphere of experience at all," but he quotes from a letter written by a patient in a French asylum who alludes to God and then asks himself why he does so, because all he has known so far has been the devil. This patient admits that the letter will prove that he is insane, but, if so, he is unable to keep himself from being either crazy or an idiot, for "I am defenseless against the invisible enemy who is tightening his coils around me."[56] James suggests that this letter shows two things. On the one hand, "the entire consciousness of the poor man is so choked with the feeling of evil that the sense of there being any good in the world is lost for him altogether."[57] On the other hand, "the querulous temper of his misery keeps his mind from taking a religious direction." Instead, it tends "towards irreligion; and it has played, so far as I know, no part whatever in the construction of religious systems."[58]

---

51. James, *The Varieties of Religious Experience*, 146–47; Gratry, *Souvenirs de ma Jeunesse*, 119–21.

52. James, *The Varieties of Religious Experience*, 147. This letter is from Roubinovitch and Toulouse, *Le Mélancolie*, 170.

53. James, *The Varieties of Religious Experience*, 147.

54. Ibid.

55. Ibid., 148.

56. Ibid.

57. Ibid., 149.

58. Ibid.

RELIGIOUS MELANCHOLY

A third type of melancholy, then, is *religious* melancholy, and it, James suggests, is typically "cast in a more melting mood" than the preceding type.[59] Leo Tolstoy and John Bunyan are prime examples of religious melancholy.

The Case of Leo Tolstoy

Noting that Tolstoy's book of confessions is "a wonderful account of the attack of melancholy which led him to his own religious conclusions," James indicates that Tolstoy's melancholy is "a well-marked case of *anhedonia*, of passive loss of appetite for all life's values."[60] It is also an example of "how the altered and estranged aspect which the world assumed in consequence of this stimulated Tolstoy's intellect to a gnawing, carking questioning and effort for philosophic relief."[61] To understand this passive loss of appetite for all life's values James proposes that his listeners think of themselves as "suddenly stripped of all the emotion with which your world now inspires you, and try to imagine it *as it exists*, purely by itself, without your favorable or unfavorable, hopeful or apprehensive comment."[62] James suggests that it will be "almost impossible for you to realize such a condition of negativity and deadness."[63] This, however, is what the person who suffers from religious melancholy experiences.

James also observes that in Tolstoy's case "the sense that life had any meaning whatever was for a time wholly withdrawn," and the result "was a transformation in the whole expression of reality."[64] Anticipating his lecture on conversion, which will emphasize religious regeneration, he suggests that "a not infrequent consequence of the change operated in the subject is a transfiguration of the face of nature in his eyes," and "a new heaven seems to shine upon a new earth."[65] But in the case of melancholy "there is usually a similar change, only it is in the reverse direction," for the "world now looks remote, strange sinister, uncanny" and its "color is gone, its breath is cold,

---

59. Ibid.

60. Ibid. *Anhedonia* is "a psychological condition marked by an inability to experience pleasure" (Agnes, *Webster's New World*, 55).

61. James, *The Varieties of Religious Experience*, 149.

62. Ibid., 150.

63. Ibid.

64. Ibid., 151.

65. Ibid.

there is no speculation in the eyes it glares with."[66] To illustrate this sense of the deadness of the world James draws on a text by Georges Dumas that contains the testimonies of asylum patients who suffer from pathological melancholy:

> "It is as if I lived in another century," says one asylum patient.—"I see everything through a cloud," says another, "things are not as they were, and I am changed."—"I see," says a third, "I touch, but the things do not come near me, a thick veil alters the hue and look of everything."—"Persons move like shadows, and sounds seem to come from a distant world." . . .—"I weep false tears, I have unreal hands; the things I see are not real things."[67]

James observes that these "are expressions that naturally rise to the lips of melancholy subjects describing their changed state."[68] He adds, however, that for some of these subjects the change produces in them a profound astonishment: "The strangeness is wrong. The unreality cannot be. A mystery is concealed, and a metaphysical solution must exist. If the natural world is so double-faced and unhomelike, what world, what thing is real? An urgent wondering and questioning is set up, a poring theoretic activity, and in the desperate effort to get into right relations with the matter, the sufferer is often led to what becomes for him a satisfying religious solution."[69]

Tolstoy, he suggests, is a case in point:

> At about the age of fifty, Tolstoy relates that he began to have moments of perplexity, of what he calls arrest, as if he knew not "how to live," or what to do. It is obvious that these were moments in which the excitement and interest which our functions naturally bring had ceased. Life had been enchanting, it was now flat sober, more than sober, dead. Things were meaningless whose meaning had always been self-evident. The questions "Why?" and "What next?" began to beset him more and more frequently. At first it seemed as if such questions must be answerable, and as if he could easily find the answers if he would take the time; but as they ever became more urgent, he perceived that it was like those first discomforts of a sick man, to which he pays but little attention till they run into one continuing suffering,

66. Ibid.

67. Ibid., 151–52; Dumas, *La Tristesse et la Joie*. These comments are similar to Wilhelm Greisinger's observation noted earlier that patients suffering from melancholia will say, "I see, I hear, but the objects do not reach me, it is as if there were a wall between me and the outer world!" (*Mental Pathology and Therapeutics*, 50).

68. James, *The Varieties of Religious Experience*, 152.

69. Ibid.

The Sick Soul

and then he realizes that what he took for a passing disorder means the most momentous thing in the world for him, means his death."[70]

James goes on to quote several pages from Tolstoy's book of confession.[71] The account begins with Tolstoy's feeling "that something had broken within me on which my life had always rested, that I had nothing left to hold on to, and that morally my life had stopped."[72] An "invincible force" impelled him to "get rid of my existence, in one way or another," and although he did not *wish* to kill himself, this force "which drew me away from life was fuller, more powerful, more general than any mere desire."[73] He notes the strangeness of the fact that although this was a time in his life when, as far as his outer circumstances were concerned, he ought to have been completely happy. After all, he "had a good wife who loved me and whom I loved, good children and a large property which was increasing with no pains taken on my part," he "was more respected by my kinsfolk and acquaintances than I had ever been," and "without exaggeration I could believe my name already famous."[74] Why then was he "hiding the rope in order not to hang myself to the rafters of the room where every night I went to sleep alone," and why was he "no longer going shooting, lest I should yield to the too easy temptation of putting an end to myself with my gun"?[75] He could give "no reasonable meaning" to what was happening to him.

Then, however, he realized that this was precisely the point, for life itself is essentially meaningless and without purpose, and this is "the literal uncontestable truth which every one may understand."[76] But then he began to ask himself whether this is really so. He wondered if there might be something he had failed to notice or comprehend? Consequently, he "sought for an explanation in all the branches of knowledge acquired by men," and he "questioned painfully and protractedly and with no idle curiosity."[77] For days and nights he searched for evidence that life is not without meaning, and he did so "like a man who is lost and seeks to save himself—and I found nothing."[78]

70. Ibid, 152–53.
71. Ibid., 153–56; see Tolstoy, *My Confession and the Spirit of Christ's Teaching*.
72. James, *The Varieties of Religious Experience*, 153.
73. Ibid.
74. Ibid., 153–54.
75. Ibid.
76. Ibid., 155.
77. Ibid.
78. Ibid.

And yet, while his intellect was engaged in this search, something else in him was working too, and it was this "something else" that inhibited him from ending his life. This was "a consciousness of life" that "was like a force that obliged my mind to fix itself in another direction and draw me out of my situation of despair."[79] Tolstoy says that he "can call this by no other name than that of a thirst for God" and observes that "this craving for God had nothing to do with the movement of my ideas,—in fact, it was the direct contrary of that movement,—but it came from my heart."[80] He says that it "was like a feeling of dread that made me seem like an orphan and isolated in the midst of all these things that were so foreign," and yet, "this feeling of dread was mitigated by the hope of finding the assistance of someone."[81]

James notes that he will discuss Tolstoy's recovery in a later lecture (on the divided self) but for the moment he suggests that what Tolstoy was experiencing was

> not the simple ignorance of ill, but something vastly more complex, including natural evil as one of its elements, but finding natural evil no such stumbling block and terror because it now sees it swallowed up in supernatural good. The process is one of redemption, not of mere reversion to natural health, and the sufferer, when saved, is saved by what seems to be a second birth, a deeper kind of conscious being than he could enjoy before.[82]

The Case of John Bunyan

James suggests that we find "a somewhat different type of religious melancholy" in John Bunyan's autobiography, for whereas "Tolstoy's preoccupations were largely objective, for the purpose and meaning of life in general was what so troubled him," Bunyan's troubles "were over the condition of his own personal self."[83] James explains:

> He was a typical case of the psychopathic temperament, sensitive of conscience to a diseased degree, beset by doubts, fears,

---

79. Ibid., 156.

80. Ibid.

81. Ibid. In the 1987 edition of his confession this passage is translated: "It was a feeling of fear, abandonment, loneliness, and all that was strange to me, and a sense of hope that someone would help me" (Tolstoy, *A Confession and Other Religious Writings*, 63).

82. James, *The Varieties of Religious Experience*, 156.

83. Ibid., 157. Bunyan, *Grace Abounding to the Chief of Sinners*, 1797 edition.

and insistent ideas, and a victim of verbal automatisms, both motor and sensory. These were usually texts of Scripture which, sometimes damnatory and sometimes favorable, would come in a half-hallucinatory form as if they were voices, and fasten on his mind and buffet it between them like a shuttlecock. Added to this were a fearful melancholy self-contempt and despair.[84]

James goes on to quote several paragraphs from *Grace Abounding*—paragraphs in which Bunyan recalls that as his condition grew worse and worse, a condition that lasted for several years, "I was more loathsome in my own eyes than was a toad; and I thought I was so in God's eyes too."[85] He was also "sorry that God had made me a man" for the beasts, birds, and fishes. "had not a sinful nature" nor were they "obnoxious to the wrath of God" and destined "to go to hell-fire after death."[86] He declares that "I could therefore have rejoiced, had my condition been as any of theirs," and "I blessed the condition of the dog or horse, for I knew that they had no soul to perish under the everlasting weight of Hell or Sin, as mine was like to do." [87]

James indicates, however, that, like Tolstoy, Bunyan "saw the light again,"[88] and James adds that he will also be relating that part of Bunyan's story in his lecture on the divided self. I will pick up on James's further discussion of the cases of Leo Tolstoy and John Bunyan in chapter 5.

The Case of Henry Alline

James concludes his discussion of religious melancholy with a brief allusion to Henry Alline, an evangelist who worked in Nova Scotia a century earlier. He cites a passage in Alline's autobiographical writings that "vividly describes the high-water mark of the religious melancholy which formed its beginning."[89] In describing that period in his life, Alline notes that he looked on animals with envy, "wishing with all my heart I was in their place, that I might have no soul to lose."[90] And when he saw birds flying overhead, he would think to himself, "Oh, that I could fly away from my danger and

---

84. James, *The Varieties of Religious Experience*, 157.

85. Ibid.

86. Ibid. 157–58. James is quoting from segments of paragraphs 78, 79, 82, 84, 87, 88, 104, and 105 of Bunyan's *Grace Abounding to the Chief of Sinners* (1797 edition); they are on pages 23–25 and 29 of the 1987 edition.

87. James, *The Varieties of Religious Experience*, 158.

88. Ibid., 159.

89. Ibid.; see Alline, *The Life and Journals of the Rev. Mr. Henry Alline*, 25–26.

90. James, *The Varieties of Religious Experience*, 159.

distress! Oh, how happy should I be if I were in their place!"[91] For him, happiness in his present form of a human being would be forever elusive. As James observes, "Envy of the placid beasts seems to be a very widespread affection in this type of sadness."[92] As with the cases of Tolstoy and Bunyan, James returns to the case of Henry Alline in his lecture on the divided self, and he also discusses Alline in his concluding lecture on conversion. I will pick up on these discussions of the case of Henry Alline in chapters 5 and 6.

THE CASE OF THE FRENCH SUFFERER

Finally, James considers one additional type of melancholy, stating: "The worst kind of melancholy is that which takes the form of panic fear."[93] He does not explain why this type of melancholy is worse than the other types already considered. Instead, he immediately provides an illustration, noting he has in hand "an excellent example" of it.[94] He expresses his thanks to the sufferer for giving him permission to print it and explains that "the original is in French, and though the subject was evidently in a bad nervous condition at the time of which he writes, his case has otherwise the merit of extremely simplicity."[95] He adds, "I translate freely."[96] Thus, he creates the impression that the sufferer is a Frenchman, and since several of his earlier examples of pathological melancholy have been Frenchmen, listeners or readers would have no reason to suspect that this particular sufferer was not French. But, in fact, the anonymous "French Sufferer" is James himself.[97]

91. Ibid.

92. Ibid.

93. Ibid., 159–60. In chapter 3 we saw that, for mind-cure, the saving grace of religion is not that it addresses the problem of willfulness but that it addresses the more fundamental problem of fear. Also, James discusses the instinct of fear in his chapter on instincts in *The Principles of Psychology* 2:415–22. He views fear as one of three types of instincts—the others are lust and anger—that are "the most exciting emotions of which our nature is susceptible" (415). He notes that the evolution of the human species has led to a "decrease of frequency of proper occasions for fear" and, in fact, it has become possible for large numbers of people "to pass from the cradle to the grave without ever having had a pang of genuine fear" (415–16). He notes that many of us "need an attack of mental disease to teach us the meaning of the word" (416).

94. James *The Varieties of Religious Experience*, 160.

95. Ibid.

96. Ibid.

97. For biographers and other scholars this case is unquestionably that of James himself. His son Henry testified that his father had informed him that the case was his own; see Beam, *Gracefully Insane*, 46–47. James also informed the French translator of *Varieties of Religious Experience*, who had asked James if he could provide him the

As R. W. B. Lewis relates in his study of the James family, the experience occurred in January 1870.[98] James had received his medical degree the previous June and had decided that he would simply "vegetate" for a year. This decision prompted his mother to complain to his younger brother Henry, who was in Europe at the time, that William was resting too much. He spent the summer and fall reading, and as Lewis points out, a surviving notebook lists a "staggering collection of philosophical and literary texts in several languages" that James read during these six months of vegetating.[99] However,

> Darkness began to close in at the start of the winter. On December 21, he confessed in his journal to being unfitted by "Nature and life . . . for any affectionate relations with other individuals," and that he recognized more than ever the limits of his personal faculties. Humanly estranged and incapable, he expressed again a tired acceptance of a spectator's role in life: "I may not study, make or enjoy—but . . . I can find some real life in the mere respect for other forms of life as they pass, even if I can never embrace them as a whole or incorporate them with myself."[100]

As Lewis notes, however, this "solution" to his sense of estrangement from others did not suffice, for "around January 10, 1870, William suffered a 'dorsal collapse,' in his phrase, evidently more severe than anything he had yet known. After three weeks of agony, compounded by other sources of depression, James wrote in his diary that he had arrived at the moment of crisis. 'Today, I about touched bottom, and perceive plainly that I must face the choice with open eyes: shall I *frankly* throw the moral business overboard, as one unsuited to my innate aptitudes, or shall I follow it, and it alone, making everything else merely stuff for it?'"[101] Lewis notes that James "went on, in the same February 1 entry, to say that he had not hitherto given any real trial to 'the moral interest,' but had deployed it chiefly to hold in

---

original document, that the document "is my own case—acute neurasthenic attack with phobia. I naturally disguised the *provenance!* [i.e., source]. So you may translate freely," see Menand, "William James and the Case of the Epileptic Patient," 6. As James had suggested in *The Varieties of Religious Experience* that he was translating the original French freely, there is a note of humor in the fact that he granted the French translator permission to translate the English version freely.

98. See also Allen, *William James: A Biography*, 162–67.
99. Lewis, *The Jameses: A Family Narrative*, 200–201.
100. Ibid., 201.
101. Ibid. (italics original). As *dorsal* applies to the back, James was suggesting that his back, which had been causing considerable pain, finally gave out, and that he became essentially immobile. See Agnes, *Webster's New World*, 427.

check certain bad habits, tendencies to 'moral degradation' (another allusion, probably, to auto-eroticism)."[102] Lewis suggests that there "was a slight stir of possibility in the final lines, but it did not endure."[103] Within days, James did in fact "touch bottom."[104]

Here, then, is the full account of James's experience of melancholy, which took "the form of panic fear," as presented in *The Varieties of Religious Experience*:

> Whilst in this state of philosophic pessimism and general depression of spirits about my prospects, I went one evening into a dressing-room in the twilight to procure some article that was there; when suddenly there fell upon me without any warning, just as if it came out of the darkness, a horrible fear of my own existence. Simultaneously there arose in my mind the image of an epileptic patient whom I had seen in the asylum, a black-haired youth with greenish skin, entirely idiotic, who used to sit all day on one of the benches, or rather shelves against the wall, with his knees drawn up against his chin, and the coarse gray undershirt, which was his only garment, drawn over them inclosing his entire figure. He sat there like a sort of sculptured Egyptian cat or Peruvian mummy, moving nothing but his black eyes and looking absolutely non-human. This image and my fear entered into a species of combination with each other. *That shape am I*, I felt, potentially. Nothing that I possess can defend me against that fate, if the hour for it should strike for me as it struck for him. There was such a horror of him, and such a perception of my own merely momentary discrepancy from him, that it was as if something hitherto solid within my breast gave way entirely, and I became a mass of quivering fear. After this the universe was changed for me altogether. I awoke morning after morning with a horrible dread at the pit of my stomach, and with a sense of the insecurity of life that I never knew before, and that I have never felt since. It was like a revelation; and although the immediate feelings passed away, the experience has made me sympathetic with the morbid feelings of others ever since. It gradually faded, but for months I was unable to go out into the dark alone.[105]

---

102. Ibid.
103. Ibid., 202.
104. Ibid.
105. Ibid., 160–61 (italics original).

The Sick Soul

The account continues: "In general I dreaded to be left alone. I remember wondering how other people could live, how I myself had ever lived, unconscious of that pit of insecurity beneath the surface of life. My mother in particular, a very cheerful person, seemed to me a perfect paradox in her unconsciousness of danger, which you may well believe I was very careful not to disturb by revelations of my own state of mind. I have always thought that this experience of melancholia of mine had a religious bearing."[106] James adds that when his "correspondent" (whic is, of course, himself) was asked to explain more fully what he meant by these last words—i.e., that he has always thought that this experience of his had a religious bearing, the answer he wrote was this: "I mean that the fear was so invasive and powerful that if I had not clung to scripture-texts like 'The eternal God is my refuge,' etc. 'Come unto me, all ye that labor and are heavy-laden,' etc. 'I am the resurrection and the life,' etc., I think I should have grown really insane."[107]

James adds two footnotes to this example of the worst kind of melancholy. One is in reference to the sufferer's statement that he "awoke morning after morning with a horrible dread at the pit of my stomach, and with a sense of the insecurity of life that I never knew before, and that I have never felt since."[108] The footnote relates this statement to John Bunyan's account of his tortured state after he succumbed to the devil's temptation to sell Christ. James quotes the following from Bunyan's *Grace Abounding to the Chief of Sinners*:

> Then was I struck into a very great trembling, insomuch that at some times I could, for days together, feel my very body, as well as my mind, to shake and totter under the sense of the dreadful judgment of God, that should fall on those that have sinned that most fearful and unpardonable sin. I felt also such clogging and heat at my stomach, by reason of this terror, that I was, especially at some times, as if my breast-bone would have split asunder . . . . Thus did I wind, and twine, and shrink, under the burden that was upon me; which burden also did so oppress me that I could neither stand, nor go, nor lie, either at rest or quiet.[109]

The other footnote occurs at the end of the correspondent's fuller explanation of what he meant by the statement that he has always thought that this experience of melancholia had a religious bearing. This footnote reads:

---

106. Ibid. 161.
107. Ibid.
108. Ibid., 160.
109. Ibid., 160–61; James is quoting from paragraphs 164–65 of Bunyan, *Grace Abounding to the Chief of Sinners*. These paragraphs are on page 42 of the 1987 edition.

"For another case of fear equally sudden, see HENRY JAMES: Society the Redeemed Form of Man, Boston, 1879, pp. 43ff."[110] James is referring here to his father's account of a devastating experience he suffered in May 1844 (he was thirty-three years old at the time) when he, his wife and two young sons were living in Windsor, England. William was two years old and Henry was one year old. His father described the event as follows:

> One day . . . towards the close of May [1844], having eaten a comfortable dinner, I remained at the table after the family had dispersed, idly gazing at the embers in the grate, thinking of nothing, and feeling only the exhilaration incident to a good digestion, when suddenly—in a lightning-flash as it were—"fear came upon me, and trembling, which made all my bones to shake." To all appearance it was a perfectly insane and abject terror, without ostensible cause, and only to be accounted for, to my perplexed imagination, by some damnèd shape squatting invisible to me within the precincts of the room, and raying out from his fetid personality influences fatal to life. The thing had not lasted ten seconds before I felt myself a total wreck; that is, reduced from a state of firm, vigorous, joyful manhood to one of almost helpless infancy. The only self control I was capable of exerting was to keep my seat. I felt the greatest desire to run incontinently to the foot of the stairs and shout for help to my wife,—to run to the roadside even, and appeal to the public to protect me; but by an immense effort I controlled these frenzied impulses, and determined not to budge from my chair till I had recovered my lost self-possession. This purpose I held to for a good long hour, as I reckoned time, beat upon meanwhile by an ever growing tempest of doubt, anxiety, and despair, and absolutely no relief from any truth I had ever encountered save a most pale and distant glimmer of the divine existence, when I resolved to abandon the vain struggle, and communicate without more ado what seemed my sudden burden of inmost, implacable unrest to my wife.[111]

After a few days had passed, Henry James Sr. consulted several physicians, all of whom said he had simply overworked his brain. He had been engaged in exegetical work on the book of Genesis, and perhaps the fact that he was working on Genesis and not some other biblical text contributed to his "tempest of doubt, anxiety, and despair." They recommended the water

---

110. Ibid., 161.

111. From William James, ed., *The Literary Remains of the Late Henry James*, 58–59. Also quoted in Feinstein, *Becoming William James*, 68.

cure at a nearby resort.[112] While there, he complained about having to listen to the "endless 'strife of tongues' about diet, regimen, disease, politics, etc., etc.," and he imagined "how sweet it would be to find oneself no longer man, but one of those innocent and ignorant sheep pasturing upon that placid hillside, and drinking in eternal dew and freshness from Nature's lavish bosom!"[113]

Some scholars have questioned the reliability of Henry James Sr.'s account of this experience of terror because it was written thirty-five years after the event itself. Howard Feinstein suggests that by then "the experience had been refracted by evangelical imagery and, like all of his mature works, the tale was intended to illustrate a well-developed theological position."[114] Feinstein adds that it also reflects the influence of John Bunyan. But the more critical question for our purposes here is the reliability of William James's account of his experience of panic fear. After all, it appeared in *The Varieties* some thirty-three years after the event occurred, and given the fact that the source of the account is fictional, we may wonder if there are other features of the case that were not in his mind at the time the experience occurred. For example, his own footnote reference to Bunyan's experience may suggest that he was engaging in a rather self-conscious attempt to give his experience a religious aura that it may not have had at the time it actually happened, and that this allusion to Bunyan was also a deliberate effort to link his experience to his father's experience. Furthermore, even as his father invoked Job 4:14—"Fear came upon me, and trembling, which made all my bones to shake"—so William James in his account of his experience of panic fear cites several biblical passages to which he clung in order to retain his sanity.

In her discussion of the experience, Linda Simon picks up on James's own association of his experience with that of his father. Noting that his panic attack begs for comparison with the "vastation" that his father

---

112. Lewis, *The Jameses*, 52.

113. Quoted in Mattheissen, *The James Family*, 162. Also quoted in Erikson, *Identity: Youth and Crisis*, 153–54. His longing to be one of "those innocent and ignorant sheep" recalls Henry Alline's envy of the beasts because they "have no soul to lose" and of the birds who are able simply "to fly away from danger and distress," quoted in James, *The Varieties of Religious Experience*, 159. It also recalls John Bunyan's observation: "Now again I blessed the condition of the dog and toad, and counted the estate of everything that God had made, far better than this dreadful state of mine, and such as my companions was: yea, gladly would I have been in the condition of dog and horse, for I knew they had no soul to perish under the everlasting weights of hell for sin, as mind was like to do" (*Grace Abounding to the Chief of Sinners*, 29).

114. Feinstein, *Becoming William James*, 68–69; see also Habegger, *The Father*, 211–12.

experienced in Windsor when William was a toddler, Simon points out the "inescapable parallels" between their testimonies: "Both attacks occurred suddenly at a moment of apparent calm. Central to both experiences was a crouching, motionless, yet threatening figure. Both attacks rendered the victims immobile, generated long depression, and seemed to have some religious connection."[115] However, in her view, William's version "has a stronger psychological veracity" as he "presented himself as depressed to begin with, not hopeful, cheerful, and vigorous as Henry Sr. claimed to have been—a claim that his son later recognized was false."[116] Furthermore: "In Henry's version, some powerful 'influences fatal to life' had 'ray[ed] out from [the figure's] fetid personality,' and threatened to annihilate him." In contrast, "William, reflecting changes in psychological theory since 1844, understood the figure to emanate from the workings of his own mind."[117] The figure, after all, was a young patient he had encountered, probably in his role as a medical student.[118]

On the other hand, Simon thinks that William's account has less veracity than that of his father when it comes to its religious associations. Whereas "Henry's fear and trembling led him to discover [Emmanuel] Swedenborg, a discovery that changed his perspective forever" William "attests to a religious epiphany that seems gratuitous." In fact: "The religious connection that William ascribed to the experience . . . seems only to justify including the anecdote in a volume about religious experiences. There is nothing in James's correspondence or journal entries for the period in which the attack occurred to reveal any religious conversion or epiphany; on the contrary, he insists on his inability to participate in religious ritual and doubts the existence of God."[119]

---

115. Simon, *Genuine Reality*, 126.

116. Ibid.

117. Ibid., 126–27. It is noteworthy that in the "intimate friend" account in chapter 2—"The Reality of the Unseen"—of *The Varieties of Religious Experience*, the friend felt the presence of "*something* that was indescribably *stronger* than the ordinary certainty of companionship when we are in the close presence of ordinary living people" (60; italics original). As I noted in footnote 90 to chapter 2, I have raised the question whether this "intimate friend" was James himself. See Capps, *Men, Religion, and Melancholia*, 37–42. If this is in fact the case, it may provide an association between this experience and that of Henry James Sr.

118. There has been a great deal of discussion as to whether James was himself a patient at McLean Hospital, also known as Somerville Asylum. I have reviewed this discussion and have concluded that this was probably a case of mistaken identity, for there is substantial evidence that James's brother Robertson (Bob) was a patient at McLean Hospital. See Capps, "Was William James a Patient at McLean Hospital for the Mentally Ill?"

119. Simon, *Genuine Reality*, 127.

The Sick Soul

Simon may well be right. James may have added the Scripture-texts in order to justify the inclusion of the experience in *The Varieties*. On the other hand, I think that the concluding sentence of the account itself is genuine: "I have always thought that this experience of melancholia of mine had a religious bearing."[120] This is a very modest, understated association of the experience with the religious. No conversion, no epiphany, but an association nonetheless. It is similar in tone to James's responses to Pratt's questionnaire (as discussed in chapter 2).[121]

Other connections between the two accounts are worth noting. There is the fact that both father and son write about revealing the experience to the same woman, but whereas his father reported his experience to his wife—William's mother—William makes an explicit note of the fact that he did not tell his mother about it because he did not want to disturb her "by revelations of my own state of mind."[122] The fact that the relationship was a mother-son relationship may well have been a factor in William James's reluctance to tell her.[123] But in any event Erik Erikson suggests that there was not a great deal of difference between father and son in this regard. In fact, "that the father, as he further reports, in his moment of distress reluctantly turned to his wife while the son assures us that he did not wish to disturb his unaccountably cheerful mother, makes one wonder how much anxiety it took for the self-made men of that day to turn to the refuge of woman."[124]

---

120. James, *The Varieties of Religious Experience*, 161.

121. It is also worth noting that James cites several examples in *The Varieties of Religious Experience* in which individuals mentioned the role that a particular biblical verse played in helping to resolve their psychological struggles or conflicts. The Matthew 11:28 citation—"Come unto me, all *ye* that labor and are heavy laden, and I will give you rest" (KJV)—seems especially relevant to what James was undergoing at the time. Moreover, it is not inconceivable that he would have thought of the immediately following verses—"Take my yoke upon you, and learn of me; for I am meek and lowly in heart; and ye shall find rest unto your souls. For my yoke *is* easy, and my burden is light" (Matthew 11:29–30, KJV). These verses, in other words, could have had a calming effect and reduced his feelings of panic fear. They would also have supported his suggestion in his lectures on the religion of healthy-mindedness, that mind-curers "have demonstrated that a form of regeneration by relaxing, by letting go . . . is within the reach of persons who have no conviction of sin" (ibid., 111). See also his essay "The Gospel of Relaxation" in *Talks to Teachers*, 99–112.

122. James, *The Varieties of Religious Experience*, 161.

123. I have written rather extensively about the association between melancholia and the mother-son relationship. See Capps, *Men, Religion, and Melancholia*; Capps, *Men and Their Religion*; Capps, *At Home in the World*; and Capps, *The Resourceful Self*. I derive this association from Freud's discussion of the lost object in "Mourning and Melancholia."

124. Erikson, *Identity: Youth and Crisis*, 153.

Another noteworthy connection is that even as his father's experience led to the discovery of the writings of Emmanuel Swedenborg, so William in the aftermath of his experience began reading a series of philosophical essays by French philosopher Charles Renouvier, and through these readings he discovered grounds for taking a new approach to life. He notes that Renouvier had defined free will as "the sustaining of a thought *because I choose to* when I might have other thoughts."[125] Instead of assuming that this is the definition of an illusion, James decided that he would believe Renouvier's definition of free will. In effect, "my first act of free will shall be to believe in free will," and "for the remainder of the year, I will abstain from the more speculative and contemplative *Grübelei* in which my nature takes most delight, and voluntarily cultivate the feeling of moral freedom, by reading books favorable to it, as well as by acting."[126] By *Grübelei* James means the "questioning mania" to which he refers in *The Principles of Psychology*, a state of interminable doubt and inquiry.[127] This, then, will be his new approach to life:

> Hitherto, when I have felt like taking a free initiative, like daring to act originally, without carefully waiting for contemplation of the external world to determine all for me, suicide seemed the most manly form to put my daring into; now, I will go a step further with my will, not only act with it, but believe as well; believe in my individual reality and creative power. My belief, to be sure, *can't* be optimistic—but I will posit life (the real, the good) in the self-governing *resistance* of the ego to the world. Life shall [be built in] doing and suffering and creating.[128]

As Erikson notes, William James commented sometime thereafter on the marked difference between himself then and himself a year earlier, and Erikson cites his father's observation that William had "given up the notion that all mental disorder requires to have a physical basis."[129] Erikson suggests that the first insight—that he could exercise choice over the thoughts that he would allow himself to think—was directly related to the second insight, "the abandonment of physiological factors as fatalistic arguments against a neurotic person's continued self-determination."[130] Erikson adds

125. Lewis, *The Jameses*, 204.
126. Ibid., 204–5.
127. See footnote 38.
128. Quoted in Lewis, *The Jameses*, 205. Incidentally, the material in square brackets represents an insertion by Lewis into the quotation from James.
129. Erikson, *Identity: Youth and Crisis*, 154.
130. Ibid., 155.

that these insights together "are the basis of psychotherapy, which, no matter how it is described and conceptualized, aims at the restoration of the patient's power of choice."[131] Perhaps James thereby severed the causal link between his habit of auto-eroticism and mental disorder—a link that would certainly have been in his mind as he considered the fate of the epileptic patient in the asylum. (It was commonly believed at the time that auto-erotic behaviors were the root cause of epilepsy.)

Significantly, James has nothing to say in *The Varieties* about the role played by the affirmation of "will" in resolving a melancholic crisis such as the one experienced by the "French Sufferer." Perhaps James assumed that to affirm the role of the will in resolving melancholia would reveal the true identity of this afflicted individual (himself), for James had written a great deal about the will in *The Principles of Psychology* and in his well-known essays in popular philosophy published in 1896, the lead essay of which was titled "The Will to Believe."[132] But another possible explanation is that at the time of writing *The Varieties* he no longer believed that he could lift himself from the depths by his own act of will. In the summer of 1900, writing despondently to his wife from Bad-Nauheim, he said that he had "*no strength at all*" and though he had tried to summon up a "will to believe . . . it is no go. The Will to Believe won't work."[133] As R. W. B. Lewis points out, "James was now inclined to locate the source of psychic renewal, not in a conscious act of will, but much rather in the activities of the subconscious . . . If *The Principles of Psychology* can be seen as William James's autobiography into the 1880s and the hard-won victory over the 'obstructed will,' *The Varieties* carries the personal story through the breakdown of energy at the turn of the century and the new alertness to the under-consciousness."[134]

If James was now less inclined to think of one's recovery from the worst form of melancholy in terms of an act of will and more inclined to think of it as a "new alertness to the under-consciousness," it may be the case that there were buried inner resources that he drew upon in his return from the depths of despair. An important clue in this regard is his suggestion to his daughter Margaret that painful as melancholy is, it is sent to us for "enlightenment."[135]

The enlightenment in this case occurred, I believe, when James was presented with a mental image of his "potential self." As he observed in his

---

131. Ibid.

132. James, *The Principles of Psychology*, 2:486–592; James, *The Will to Believe and Other Essays in Popular Philosophy*, 1–31.

133. Quoted in Lewis, *The Jameses*, 511 (italics original).

134. Ibid.

135. Rubin, *Religious Melancholy and Protestant Experience in America*, 20.

account of the experience he was already in a state of "philosophic pessimism and general depression of spirits about my prospects," and this was compounded by the "horrible fear of my own existence," which suddenly fell upon him. This fear in turn was accompanied by the mental image of an epileptic patient whom he had seen in the asylum. The combination of the horrible fear and the mental image of the patient produced the thought, "*That shape am I*, I felt, potentially." After all, nothing that James himself possessed could defend him against that fate if the hour should strike for him as it did for the other young man. This, I believe, was the moment of enlightenment: *That shape am I*, potentially, and against this fate I am utterly defenseless.

This account of James's recognition of himself—potentially—in the image of the young man he had seen in the asylum is, as he suggests, an account of the worst form of melancholy, which is that of panic fear. There is no sense of his superiority over the other young man. Nor is there an expression of pity, the kind of pity that those who are secure can express toward those who are insecure. There was simply an overwhelming sense that this young man could be himself. As he goes on to say about the cases—Tolstoy, Bunyan, and the French Sufferer—which he has presented in his lectures on the sick soul: "One of them gives us the vanity of mortal things; another the sense of sin; and the remaining one describes the fear of the universe;—and in one or other of these three ways it always is that man's original optimism and self-satisfaction get leveled with the dust."[136] James, of course, is the one whose melancholy describes the fear of the universe, thus making it all the more likely that his reference to "William's melancholy about the universe" in his opening lecture is an allusion to himself; though, of course, he would reject the idea that it was due to something as inconsequential as "bad digestion."[137]

Following the case of the French Sufferer, James notes that up to this point in his lectures on the sick soul in none of the cases he has presented "was there any intellectual insanity or delusions about matters of fact."[138] But if one were disposed to consider cases of "really insane melancholia, with its hallucinations and delusions, it would be a worse story still—desperation absolute and complete, the whole universe coagulating about the sufferer into a material of overwhelming horror, surrounding him without opening

---

136. James, *The Varieties of Religious Experience*, 161.

137. Ibid., 10. Rather, as we have seen, it was related to what he called his "dorsal collapse."

138. Ibid., 161–62.

The Sick Soul

or end."[139] In such cases there would not be "the conception or intellectual perception of evil, but the grisly blood-freezing heart-palsying sensation of it close upon one, and no other conception or sensation able to live for a moment in its presence."[140] Observing that our usual refined optimisms and intellectual and moral consolations are utterly irrelevant in the presence of a need like this, he concludes: "Here is the real core of the religious problem. Help! Help! No prophet can claim to bring a final message unless he says things that will have a sound of reality in the ears of victims such as these. But the deliverance must come in as strong a form as the complaint, if it is to take effect; and that seems a reason why the coarser religions, revivalistic, orgiastic, with blood and miracles and supernatural operations, may possibly never be displaced. Some constitutions need them too much."[141]

CONCLUSION

This brief reference to insane melancholy leads James to return to the distinction between the healthy-minded and the sick soul. He notes that we can now see "how great an antagonism may naturally arise between the healthy-minded way of viewing life and the way that takes all this experience of evil as something essential."[142] To what we might call "the morbid-minded" view, "healthy-mindedness pure and simple seems unspeakably blind and shallow," but to "the healthy-minded" view "the way of the sick soul seems unmanly and diseased."[143] In fact, "with their grubbing in rat-holes instead of living in the light; with their manufacture of fears, and preoccupation with every unwholesome kind of misery, there is something almost obscene about these children of wrath and cravers of a second birth. If religious intolerance and hanging and burning could again become the order of the day, there is little doubt that, however it may have been in the past, the healthy-minded would at present show themselves the less indulgent party of the two."[144]

However, James suggests that when we take an impartial view of this dispute between the healthy-minded and the morbid-minded ways of looking at life, "we are bound to say that morbid-mindedness ranges over the

---

139. Ibid., 162.
140. Ibid.
141. Ibid.
142. Ibid.
143. Ibid.
144. Ibid., 162–63.

wider scale of experience."[145] To be sure, "the method of averting one's attention from evil, and living simply in the light of good is splendid as long as it will work"; and "it will work with many persons; it will work far more generally than most of us are ready to suppose; and within the sphere of its successful operation there is nothing to be said against it as a religious solution."[146] And yet, "it breaks down impotently as soon as melancholy comes; and even though one be quite free from melancholy one's self, there is no doubt that healthy-mindedness is inadequate as a philosophical doctrine, because the evil facts which it refuses positively to account for are a genuine portion of reality; and they may after all be the best key to life's significance, and possibly the only openers of our eyes to the deepest levels of truth."[147]

This, then, is where morbid-mindedness affords a truer vision of the universe than healthy-mindedness, for the "normal process of life contains moments as bad as any of those which insane melancholy is filled with, moments in which radical evil gets its innings and takes its solid turn."[148] After all,

> The lunatic's visions of horror are all drawn from the material of daily fact. Our civilization is founded on the shambles, and every individual existence goes out in a lonely spasm of helpless agony. If you protest, my friend, wait till you arrive there yourself! To believe in the carnivorous reptiles of geologic times is hard for our imagination—they seem too much like mere museum specimens. Yet there is no tooth in any one of these museum-skulls that did not daily through long years of the foretime hold fast to the body struggling in despair of some fated living victim.[149]

And nothing has fundamentally changed in the meantime:

> Forms of horror, just as dreadful to their victims, if on a smaller spatial scale, fill our world about us to-day. Here on our very hearths and in our gardens the infernal cat plays with the panting mouse, or holds the hot bird fluttering in her jaws. Crocodiles and rattlesnakes and pythons are at this moment vessels of life as real as we are; their loathsome existence fills every minute of every day that drags its length along; and whenever they or

145. Ibid., 163.
146. Ibid.
147. Ibid.
148. Ibid.
149. Ibid., 163–64.

other wild beasts clutch their living prey, the deadly horror which an agitated melancholic feels is the literally right reaction on the situation.[150]

These are no placid beasts. James's father could long to be a sheep pasturing on the placid hillside, Henry Alline could think of himself as a bird flying away from danger and distress, and John Bunyan could envy the dog and the toad because they have no fear for the fate of their souls. But James uses the image of prehistoric reptiles and modern-day cats, crocodiles, rattlesnakes and pythons to make the sober point that there is no escape from the evil that the one who suffers from melancholia sees with such clear-sighted keenness. And perhaps most horrific of all is the randomness of evil, the way it selects one victim and lets the other, temporarily, escape. In a footnote to this passage James cites the case of a group of travelers who suddenly hear a cracking sound in the bushes and the next instant a tiger has pounced upon one of their party and carried him off.[151] Similarly, James realized that nothing he possessed could defend him against the fate of the black-haired youth with greenish skin if the hour for this terrifying fate "should strike for me as it struck for him."[152]

Thus, unlike his father, Alline, and Bunyan, who contrast their melancholic state with that of the animals, James suggests that the utterly heartless manner in which the animals clutch their living prey provides insight into the human experience of melancholy, their common link being the fact that the universe itself abounds with evil. William James continues: "It may indeed be that no religious reconciliation with the absolute totality of things is possible. Some evils, indeed, are ministerial to higher forms of good; but it may be that there are forms of evil so extreme as to enter into no good system whatsoever, and that, in respect of such evil, dumb submission or neglect to notice is the only practical resource."[153] But this, he notes, is an issue that he will need to take up later. For now the conclusion to be drawn is that the religious systems which incorporate these "pessimistic elements" into their worldview are the most complete, and here he cites Buddhism and Christianity in particular. They, he notes, "are essentially religions of deliverance" for they are based on the understanding that "the man must die to an unreal life before he can be born into the real life."[154] James adds

150. Ibid., 164.
151. Ibid.
152. Ibid., 160.
153. Ibid., 165.
154. Ibid.

that he will devote the next lecture on the divided self and the process of its unification to "some of the psychological conditions of this second birth."[155]

James would probably resist the suggestion that he began to experience a "second birth" that evening when, in a state of philosophic pessimism and general depression of spirits, he went into a dressing-room to procure some article that was there and suddenly there fell upon him, without any warning, just as if it came out of the darkness, a horrible fear of his own existence. But something changed in him as he saw in his mind the image of an epileptic patient he had seen in the asylum, and he realized that nothing that he possessed could defend him against the same fate if the hour for it should strike for him as it did for this other young man.

But if he would have resisted the suggestion that he himself experienced a "second birth," this is largely because the term has been employed in ways that have rendered it almost meaningless. *Enlightenment*, with its connotations of insight, understanding and illumination is less likely to be misinterpreted and misunderstood. And the fact that this is the word James used in his fatherly letter to his suffering daughter makes it all the more significant and meaningful.

155. Ibid.

5

THE DIVIDED SELF AND THE PROCESS OF ITS UNIFICATION

JAMES BEGINS HIS LECTURE on "The Divided Self and the Process of Its Unification" by referring to his preceding lecture on the sick soul. He recalled that the "lecture was a painful one, dealing as it did with evil as a pervasive element of the world we live in" and that "at the close of it we were brought into full view of the contrast between the two ways of looking at life which are characteristic respectively of what we called the healthy-minded, who need to be born only once, and of the sick souls, who must be twice-born in order to be happy. The result is two different conceptions of the universe of our experience."[1]

James suggests that in the religion of the once-born, "the world is a sort of rectilinear or one-storied affair"; he also employs a monetary analogy to describe it, noting that "its accounts are kept in one denomination, whose parts have just the values which naturally they appear to have, and of which a simple algebraic sum of pluses and minuses will give the total worth"; thus, for the once-born, "happiness and religious peace consist in living on the plus side of the amount."[2] In contrast, in the religion of the twice-born "the world is a double-storied mystery," and

> peace cannot be reached by the simple addition of pluses and elimination of minuses from life. Natural good is not simply insufficient in amount and transient, there lurks a falsity in its very being. Cancelled as it all is by death if not by earlier enemies, it

1. James, *The Varieties of Religious Experience*, 166–88.
2. Ibid.

gives no final balance, and can never be the thing intended for our lasting worship. It keeps us from our real good, rather; and renunciation and despair of it are our first step in the direction of the truth. There are two lives, the natural and the spiritual, and we must lose the one before we can participate in the other.[3]

James asserts that in their extreme forms of pure naturalism and pure salvationism the two types are "violently contrasted," but "the concrete human beings whom we oftenest meet are intermediate varieties and mixtures."[4] Practically speaking, however, we all recognize the difference and understand, for example, "the disdain of the Methodist convert for the mere sky-blue healthy-minded moralist," and the healthy-minded moralist's aversion to what "seems to him to be the diseased subjectivism of the Methodist, dying to live, as he calls it, and making of paradox and the inversion of natural appearances the essence of God's truth."[5]

THE HETEROGENEOUS PERSONALITY

The twice-born religion is, however, the subject of this lecture, and to get the discussion started James begins with "the psychological basis of the twice-born character," noting that there "seems to be a certain discordancy or heterogeneity in the native temperament of the subject, an incompletely unified moral and intellectual constitution."[6] To illustrate this temperamental discord, James cites the French novelist Alphonse Daudet's lament that he is made up of two different selves: "Homo duplex, homo duplex!" Daudet relates the following event from when he was fourteen years old: "The first time that I perceived that I was two was at the death of my brother Henri, when my father cried out so dramatically, 'He is dead, he is dead!' While my first self wept, my second self thought, 'How truly given was that cry, how fine it would be at the theatre.'"[7] He says that "this horrible duality has often given me matter for reflection. Oh, this terrible second me, always seated

---

3. Ibid., 166–67.

4. Ibid., 167.

5. Ibid. He cites Emerson's observation in his essay "Spiritual Laws" that "our young people are diseased with the theological problems of original sin, origin of evil, predestination, and the like. These never presented a practical difficulty to any man—never darkened across any man's road, who did not go out of his way to seek them. These are the soul's mumps, and measles, and whooping-coughs" (Emerson, *Essays and Lectures*, 305).

6. James, *The Varieties of Religious Experience*, 167.

7. Ibid. See Daudet, *Notes sur la Vie*, 1.

whilst the other is on foot, acting, living, suffering, bestirring itself. This second me that I have never been able to intoxicate, to make shed tears, or put to sleep. And how it sees into things, and how it mocks!"[8]

James indicates that recent works on the psychology of character have had much to say on this point, and he cites a book on the various types of character by Frédéric Paulhan.[9] These works suggest that "some persons are born with an inner constitution which is harmonious and well balanced from the outset. Their impulses are consistent with one another, their will follows without trouble the guidance of their intellect, their passions are not excessive, and their lives are little haunted by regrets."[10] Others, however, "are oppositely constituted; and are so in degrees which may vary from something so slight as to result in a merely odd or whimsical inconsistency, to a discordancy of which the consequences may be inconvenient in the extreme."[11]

To illustrate "the more innocent kinds of heterogeneity" James cites a paragraph from the autobiography of Annie Besant, the British theosophist who was a leader in India's movement for independence. Besant writes:

> I have ever been the queerest mixture of weakness and strength, and have paid heavily for the weakness. As a child I used to suffer tortures of shyness, and if my shoe-lace was untied would feel shamefacedly that every eye was fixed on the unlucky string; as a girl I would shrink away from strangers and think myself unwanted and unliked, so that I was full of eager gratitude to anyone who noticed me kindly . . . Combative on the platform in defense of any cause I cared for, I shrink from quarrel or disapproval in the house, and am a coward at heart in private while a good fighter in public.[12]

James observes that "this amount of inconsistency will only count as amiable weakness; but a stronger degree of heterogeneity may make havoc of the subject's life."[13] There are persons, he notes, "whose existence is little more than a series of zigzags, as now one tendency and now another gets the upper hand. Their spirit wars with their flesh, they wish for incompatibles, wayward impulses interrupt their most deliberate plans, and their lives are one long drama of repentance and of effort to repair misdemeanors and mistakes."[14]

8. James, *The Varieties of Religious Experience*, 168; Daudet, *Notes sur la Vie*, 1.
9. James, *The Varieties of Religious Experience*, 168; see Paulhan, *Les Caracteres*.
10. James, *The Varieties of Religious Experience*, 168.
11. Ibid.
12. Ibid., 168–69; see Besant, *Annie Besant: An Autobiography*, 82.
13. James, *The Varieties of Religious Experience*, 169.
14. Ibid.

The Inheritance Theory

What accounts for such heterogeneity? James notes that the heterogeneous personality "has been explained as the result of inheritance—the traits of character of incompatible and antagonistic ancestors are supposed to be preserved alongside each other."[15] He cites an article by Smith Baker in the September 1893 issue of the *Journal of Nervous and Mental Disease* that makes this point, but he is hesitant to accept it: "This explanation may pass for what it is worth—it certainly needs corroboration."[16]

In his chapter on reasoning in *The Principles of Psychology* James suggested that inheritance theories are contradicted by overwhelming evidence that the human brain is extremely malleable and elastic, that man is, "*par excellence, the educable* animal"; this being the case, "the theory that what was acquired habit in the ancestor may become [a] congenital tendency in the offspring" is questionable, especially because there is little empirical evidence in its support: "So vast a superstructure is raised upon this principle that the paucity of empirical evidence for it has alike been [a] matter of regret to its adherents, and of triumph to its opponents."[17]

James goes on in *The Varieties* to note that "whatever the cause of heterogeneous personality may be, we find the extreme examples of it in the psychopathic temperament," and "all writers about that temperament make the inner heterogeneity prominent in their descriptions."[18] Frequently it is only this trait of heterogeneity "that leads us to ascribe that temperament to a man at all," and this means that a person with a psychopathic temperament "is simply a man of sensibility in many directions, who finds more difficulty than is common in keeping his spiritual house in order and running his furrows straight, because his feelings and impulses are too keen and too discrepant mutually."[19]

The Psychopathic Temperament

In these introductory comments on the psychopathic temperament of the heterogeneous personality James mentions that he introduced the subject of the psychopathic temperament in his first lecture, specifically in the section of the lecture where he anticipated objections to his use of the insights of

---

15. Ibid.
16. Ibid. See Baker, "Etiological Significance of Heterogeneous Personality."
17. James, *The Principles of Psychology*, 2:367–68.
18. James, *The Varieties of Religious Experience*, 169.
19. Ibid., 169–70.

abnormal psychology to study religious experience. He emphasized there that he does not subscribe to a "medical materialism" that seeks to account for "the spiritual judgments of human beings" on psychophysical grounds alone, and to underscore this point James cites the "discordancy" to which so many persons of heightened religious sensibility are subject; James points out that "the impossibility of holding strictly to the medical tests" based on psychophysical evidence only "is seen in the theory of the pathological causation of genius promulgated by recent authors," one of whom has stated that genius "is a symptom of hereditary degeneration."[20]

On the other hand, James points out that these very authors contradict their own claims by choosing not to impugn the *works* of genius. Thus, he sees no reason to commend the psychopathic temperament per se. There is nothing inherently admirable about the traits and characteristics that are commonly attributed to it, including "borderland insanity, crankiness, insane temperament, loss of mental balance."[21] However, when these "peculiarities and liabilities" are combined "with a superior quality of intellect in an individual," there is greater probability that this individual "will make his mark and affect his age, than if his temperament were less neurotic."[22] And therefore, when a superior intellect and a psychopathic temperament coalesce in the same individual, "we have the best possible condition for the kind of effective genius that gets into the biographical dictionaries."[23] Such men, he adds, are not mere critics and interpreters of their age. Rather, "their ideas possess them [and] they inflict them, for better or worse, upon their companions or their age."[24]

THE UNIFYING OF THE INNER SELF

Continuing his discussion of the heterogeneous personality in his lecture on the divided self, James introduces the theme of unification:

> Now, in all of us, however constituted, but to a degree the greater in proportion as we are intense and sensitive and subject

---

20. Ibid., 16. These authors are discussed in Nisbet, *The Insanity of Genius and the General Inequality of Human Faculty Physiologically Considered*, xvi–xxiv.

21. James, *The Varieties of Religious Experience*, 22.

22. Ibid., 22–23.

23. Ibid., 23–24.

24. Ibid., 24. From this consideration of the psychopathic temperament James moves immediately to "religious phenomena" and specifically to melancholy, "an essential moment in every complete religious evolution" (ibid.) He follows the same procedure in his chapter on the divided self.

to diversified temptations, and to the greatest degree if we are decidedly psychopathic, does the normal evolution of character chiefly consist in the straightening out and unifying of the inner self. The higher and the lower feelings, the useful and the erring impulses, begin by being a comparative chaos within us—they must end by forming a stable system of functions in right subordination.[25]

Although this is a normal process, one is likely to be unhappy during "the period of order-making and struggle."[26] Also, "if the individual be of tender conscience and religiously quickened, the unhappiness will take the form of moral remorse and compunction, of feeling inwardly vile and wrong, and of standing in false relations to the author of one's being and appointer of one's spiritual fate."[27] James observes that "this is the religious melancholy and 'conviction of sin' that have played so large a part in the history of Protestant Christianity," wherein "the man's interior is a battleground for what he feels to be two deadly hostile selves, one actual, the other ideal."[28] He cites Saint Paul's lament—"What I would, that do I not; but what I hate, that I do"—and adds that one experiences "Self-loathing, self-despair; an unintelligible and intolerable burden to which one is mysteriously the heir."[29]

CASES OF THE DISCORDANT PERSONALITY

Following his citation of Saint Paul, James indicates that he now wishes to quote from "some typical cases of discordant personality, with melancholy in the form of self-condemnation and sense of sin."[30] His suggestion that these are cases of religious melancholy underscores the intimate connection between his preceding lectures on the sick soul and the present lecture on the divided self and the process of its unification. His first example is that of Saint Augustine.

---

25. Ibid., 170.
26. Ibid.
27. Ibid.
28. Ibid., 170–71.
29. Ibid., 171. The biblical citation is from Romans 7:15 (KJV).
30. James, *The Varieties of Religious Experience*, 171.

The Case of Saint Augustine

James's observation that religious melancholy and "conviction of sin" have played a large part in the history of Protestant Christianity may have led listeners—and readers—to assume that James's first illustration of the divided self would be that of a Protestant Christian. Instead, he says that "Saint Augustine's case is a classic example."[31] He continues: "You all remember his half-pagan, half-Christian bringing up at Carthage, his emigration to Rome and Milan, his adoption of Manicheism and subsequent skepticism, and his restless search for truth and purity of life."[32] And then, "distracted by the struggle between the two souls in his breast, and ashamed of his own weakness of will, when so many others whom he knew and knew of had thrown off the shackles of sensuality and dedicated themselves to chastity and the higher life, he heard a voice in the garden say, '*Sume, lege*' (take and read), and opening the Bible at random, saw the text, 'not in chambering and wantonness,' etc., which seemed directly sent to his address, and laid the inner storm to rest forever."[33]

James goes on to observe that "Augustine's psychological genius has given an account of the trouble of having a divided self which has never been surpassed," and he cites several passages from the *Confessions*. For example, he quotes the following from book 8, chapter 5:

> The new will which I began to have was not yet strong enough to overcome the other will, strengthened by long indulgence. So these two wills, one old, one new, one carnal, the other spiritual, contended with each other and disturbed my soul. I understood by my own experience what I had read, "flesh lusteth against

---

31. Ibid.

32. James, *The Varieties of Religious Experience*, 171. James says that Augustine was brought up in Carthage. In fact, he was born and reared in Thagaste, modern Souk Abras, in Algeria, some two hundred miles west of Carthage. However, he went to the University of Carthage where, according to his father's plans for him, he studied law. James bases his observation that Augustine's upbringing was "half pagan" and "half Christian" on the fact that Augustine's father, Patricius, was a civil servant of the Roman state and his mother, Monica, was a devout Christian from a Christian family. The classics scholar E. R Dodds notes the fact that Augustine carried these conflicting parental voices within himself, and that he vacillated between them until the conflict was finally settled with his conversion to Christianity when he was thirty-two years old. See Dodds, "Augustine's *Confessions*"; see also Capps, "Augustine's *Confessions*."

33. James, *The Varieties of Religious Experience*, 171–72. The biblical text is from Romans 13:13 (KJV). James does not cite the edition of the *Confessions* from which he is quoting, but the quotations differ from the most accessible translations of his time (by Edward B. Pussey and J. G. Pilkington), so it's possible that they are his own translations.

> spirit, and spirit against flesh." It was myself indeed in both the wills, yet more of myself in that which I approved in myself than in what I disapproved in myself. Yet it was through myself that habit had attained so fierce a mastery over me, because I had willingly come whither I willed not. Still bound to earth, I refused, O God, to fight on thy side, as much afraid to be freed from all bonds, as I ought to have feared being trammeled by them.[34]

Augustine suggests that his inability to fight on God's side against the old carnal will is like a drowsy person trying to wake up but falling asleep again: "There was naught in me to answer thy call, 'Awake, thou sleeper,' but only drawling, drowsy words, 'Presently; yes, presently; wait a little while.' But the 'presently' had no 'present,' and the 'little while' grew long."[35]

James also picks up on Augustine's observation in chapter 7 of book 8 of the *Confessions* that he was afraid that God would hear him too soon and heal him at once of his disease of lust, which he wanted to satiate rather than to see extinguished. Then, however, in chapter 11 of book 8 Augustine indicates that he said within himself, "Come, let it be done now," and as he said it, he "was on the point of the resolve."[36] But he did not succeed, so he made another effort "and almost succeeded, yet I did not reach it, and did not grasp it, hesitating to die to death, and live to life; and the evil to which I was so wonted held me more than the better life I had not tried."[37]

James's quotations from the *Confessions* conclude with Augustine's failure and he does not return to Augustine's *Confessions* in his lectures on conversion. It is noteworthy, however, that precisely at this point in his narrative (as James briefly mentions) Augustine relates that he heard a voice from a nearby house like that of a boy or girl chanting over and over again, "Take up and read. Take up and read." He began to reflect on whether children made use of any such chant in some kind of game, but he could not recall any such instances, so he doubted that he was hearing the actual voices of children. So he checked the flow of his tears and got up, because he interpreted this as a divine command given to him to open the book and to read the first chapter that he should come to. He hurried back to where his friend Alypius was sitting because this is where he had put the book when he had gotten up and, suddenly, in the midst of his torment the chaste

---

34. James, *The Varieties of Religious Experience*, 172. The biblical passage he cites is from Galatians 5:17 (KJV).
35. Ibid.
36. Ibid.
37. Ibid., 172–73.

dignity of continence appeared to him from across the garden, encouraging him to come to her. When he did so, she reached out to him and lifted him up and embraced him.[38]

As James indicates, Augustine opened the book and his eyes fell on Romans 13:13-14: "Not in rioting and drunkenness, not in chambering and impurities, not in strife and envying; but put ye on the Lord Jesus Christ, and make not provision for the flesh, to fulfil the lusts thereof" (KJV).[39] Augustine adds that he wished to read no further, "nor was there need to do so," for instantly, "at the end of this sentence, as if before a peaceful light streaming into my heart, all the dark shadows of doubt fled away."[40] He closed the book and with a calm countenance he related to Alypius all that had happened to him. Alypius responded by telling Augustine what had happened to him after Augustine had left him, and noted that after Augustine had shown him what *he* had read he had looked at what came next, and it said: "Him that is weak in the faith receive him" (Romans 14:1, KJV).[41] Alypius applied this weakness in the faith to himself so these words strengthened him. Thus, as Augustine suggests, "by a good resolution and purpose, which were entirely in keeping with his character, wherein both for a long time and for the better he had greatly differed from me, he joined me without any painful hesitation."[42]

Then the two of them went into the house and related the story of what had happened to Augustine's mother. She was "filled with exultation and triumph," and she blessed God, "who is able to do exceeding abundantly above all that we ask or think" (Ephesians 3:20, KJV).[43] Augustine notes that "she saw that through me you had given her far more than she had long begged for by her piteous tears and groans. For you had converted me to yourself, so that I would seek neither wife nor ambition in this world, for I would stand on that rule of faith where, so many years before, you had showed me to her. You turned her mourning into a joy far richer than that she had desired, far dearer and purer than that she had sought in grandchildren born of my flesh."[44]

---

38. Augustine, *The Confessions of St. Augustine*, 201.

39. The NRSV reads, "Instead, put on the Lord Jesus Christ, and make no provision for the flesh, to gratify its desires."

40. Augustine, *The Confessions of St. Augustine*, 202.

41. Ibid. The verse continues, "but not to doubtful disputations" (KJV). The NRSV reads: "Welcome those who are weak in the faith, but not for the purpose of quarreling over opinions."

42. Ibid.

43. Ibid.

44. Ibid., 203.

The rule of faith is a reference to a dream Augustine's mother had when he was a student in Carthage in which she saw the two of them standing on the same rule—a wooden measuring rod—and he was coming towards her. At the time, he had taken the dream to mean that she should not despair of becoming what he already was, to which she had replied, "No, it was not said to me, 'Where he is, there also are you,' but 'Where you are, there also is he.'"[45] Now, he notes that this dream was fulfilled nine years later. As for his reference to grandchildren, his mother had recently arranged his engagement to a young woman of high social standing. She had done so because when he was a student in Carthage he fathered a child, a son named Adeodatus (which means "gift of God") out of wedlock, and the woman and their son had lived with him ever since. Now that he was engaged to a more suitable woman his son's mother returned to Africa and was not heard from again, but Adeodatus remained with him. With Augustine's conversion to his mother's faith and to the monastic ideal, his engagement to marry was terminated.[46]

Following his quotations from Augustine's *Confessions* James observes: "There could be no more perfect description of the divided will, when the higher wishes lack just that last acuteness, that touch of explosive intensity, of dynamogenic quality (to use the slang of the psychologists), that enables them to burst their shell, and make irruption efficaciously into life and quell

---

45. Ibid., 90–91.

46. Augustine indicates that his son Adeodatus was baptized into the Christian faith with Augustine and Alypius the following Easter Sunday. He also describes a book that he and Adeodatus produced together titled *On the Teacher* in which they engaged in a dialogue. Adeodatus was sixteen years old at the time. Following the death of Augustine's mother the father and son returned from Milan, where Augustine was a professor of Rhetoric, to Augustine's hometown of Thagaste in northern Africa, and three years later Adeodatus died. Augustine also relates Adeodatus's emotional response at the funeral of his grandmother Monica in book 9, chapter 12 of the *Confessions*, noting that he and his friends hushed the boy when he burst out in lamentation because they "did not think it fitting to solemnize that funeral with tearful cries and groans" (ibid., 224). See also my reflections on this father-son relationship in Capps, *The Child's Song*, chapter 2.

The Divided Self and the Process of Its Unification

the lower tendencies forever."[47] James adds that he will have more to say about this higher excitability in a later lecture.[48]

The Case of Henry Alline

James's second example of the discordant personality is from the autobiography of Henry Alline, the Nova Scotian evangelist "of whose melancholy I read a brief account in my last lecture."[49] He introduces the following citation from Alline's autobiography with the observation that the young man's sins were of "the most harmless order, yet they interfered with what proved to be his truest vocation, so they gave him great distress."[50] Alline writes: "I was now very moral in my life, but found no rest of conscience. I now began to be esteemed in young company, who knew nothing of my mind all this while, and their esteem began to be a snare to my soul, for I soon began to be fond of carnal mirth, though I still flattered myself that if I did not get drunk, nor curse, nor swear, there would be no sin in frolicking and carnal mirth, and I thought God would indulge young people with some (what I called simple or civil) recreation."[51]

Alline continued to keep up a round of duties and did not allow himself any open vices, so he got along very well in periods of health and prosperity: "But when I was distressed or threatened by sickness, death, or heavy storms of thunder, my religion would not do, and I found there was

---

47. James, *The Varieties of Religious Experience*, 173. James explains the meaning of the term *dynamogenic* in *The Principles of Psychology* in his chapter on the production of movement. He notes not only that every sensorial stimulus sends a special discharge into certain particular muscles dependent on the special nature of the stimulus in question, but that this stimulus stimulates the muscles more generally. He notes that Dr. Ch. Féré has provided experimental proof of this. The strength of the contraction of a subject's hand was measured by a self-registering dynamometer. Normally, the maximum strength of a subject's hand remains the same from day to day. But if the subject receives a sensorial impression at the same time, the contraction is sometimes weakened but more often it is strengthened. This reinforcing effect has been named *dynamogeny*. An example is the dynamogenic effect of musical notes, especially their loudness and heights. When these notes are loud and merry, the dynamogenic effect increases but when they are quiet and sad the muscular strength diminishes. Colored lights have the same effect. Blue lights had negligible effect on a subject's muscular contraction but red lights almost doubled the effect. See James, *The Principles of Psychology*, 2:379–80. See also Féré, *Sensation et Mouvement*, chapter 14.
48. He is referring here to his second lecture on conversion.
49. James, *The Varieties of Religious Experience*, 173.
50. Ibid.
51. Ibid. See Alline, *The Life and Journal of the Rev. Mr. Henry Alline*. This and the following quotations are from 27–30.

something wanting, and would begin to repent my going so much to frolics, but when the distress was over, the devil and my own wicked heart, with the solicitations of my associates, and my fondness for young company, were such strong allurements, I would again give way, and thus I got to be very wild and rude, at the same time kept up my rounds of secret prayer and reading."[52] God, however, "not being willing that I would destroy myself, still followed me with his calls, and moved with such power on my conscience, that I could not satisfy myself with my diversions."[53] At times, when in the very midst of a mirthful diversion, "I would have such a sense of my lost and undone condition that I would wish myself from the company," and after it was over, "I would make many promises that I would attend no more on these frolics, and would beg forgiveness for hours and hours."[54] But, before long, the temptation would recur, and he would give way: "No sooner would I hear the music and drink a glass of wine," and "I would find my mind elevated and soon proceed to any sort of merriment or diversion that I thought was not debauched or openly vicious."[55] Then he would return home and feel "as guilty as ever," and sometimes he would be unable to close his eyes for some hours after he had gone to bed. He exclaims: "I was one of the most unhappy creatures on earth."[56]

Alline goes on to relate that he was often "the chief contriver and ringleader of the frolics," and that he made great efforts to disguise his agony lest the others would take note of it. He felt he would rather have been in a wilderness in exile than to be in the others' company, where he was acting the hypocrite and feigning a merry heart. Being in company with these "merry companions" was "a toil and torment, but the devil and my own wicked heart drove me about like a slave."[57] And all this time, "conscience would roar night and day."[58]

THE PROCESS OF UNIFICATION

As I noted, James returns to Henry Alline's story in his concluding lecture on conversion, but for now he simply observes that Alline, like Saint Augustine, "emerged into the smooth waters of inner unity and peace," and

52. James, *The Varieties of Religious Experience*, 173–74.
53. Ibid., 174.
54. Ibid.
55. Ibid.
56. Ibid.
57. Ibid., 175.
58. Ibid.

he asks his listeners "to consider more closely some of the peculiarities of the process of unification, when it occurs."[59] He notes that "it may come gradually, or it may occur abruptly; it may come through altered feelings or through altered powers of action; or it may come through new intellectual insights, or through experiences which we shall later have to designate as 'mystical.'"[60] But "however it comes, it brings a characteristic sort of relief; and never such extreme relief as when it is cast into the religious mould."[61]

Cases of Counterconversion

Yet "religion is only one out of many ways of reaching unity" and "the process of remedying inner incompleteness and reducing inner discord is a general psychological process, which may take place with any sort of mental material, and need not necessarily assume the religious form."[62] For example, "the new birth may be away from religion into incredulity; or it may be from moral scrupulosity into freedom and license; or it may be produced by the irruption into the individual's life of some new stimulus or passion, such as love, ambition, cupidity, revenge, or patriotic devotion."[63] In all these instances "we have precisely the same psychological form of event,—a firmness, stability, and equilibrium succeeding a period of storm and stress and inconsistency," and "in these non-religious cases the new man may also be born either gradually or suddenly."[64]

To illustrate the fact that there is the same psychological process in these instances as in the cases of Saint Augustine and Henry Alline, James cites the case of the French philosopher Théodore Jouffrey, who writes about his experience of "counter-conversion," a term that James attributes to Edwin Diller Starbuck.[65] James notes that Jouffrey's "doubts had long ha-

59. Ibid.
60. Ibid.
61. Ibid.
62. Ibid.
63. Ibid.
64. Ibid., 176.
65. Ibid. In a footnote James cites Starbuck's manuscript collection. Later, in his lectures on conversion James also cites Starbuck's book *The Psychology of Religion*, published in 1899. As David Wulff points out, for this book Starbuck analyzed autobiographical questionnaire responses from 192 subjects, the great majority of whom were Protestant Americans, and he also obtained 1,265 replies to a far briefer questionnaire that enabled him to demonstrate the coincidence of conversion with the onset of puberty. Although he showed that the true dawning of the spiritual life occurs most commonly during the years of physiological and particularly sexual maturation, he

rassed him," but that he dated "his final crisis from a certain night when his disbelief grew fixed and stable, and where the immediate result was sadness at the illusions he had lost."⁶⁶ As Jouffrey describes it,

> Vainly I clung to these last beliefs as a shipwrecked sailor clings to the fragments of his vessel; vainly, frightened at the unknown void in which I was about to float, I turned with them towards my childhood, my family, my country, all that was dear and sacred to me: the inflexible current of my thought was too strong,—parents, family, memory, beliefs, it forced me to let go of everything. The investigation went on more obstinate and more severe as it drew near its term, and did not stop until the end was reached. I knew then that in the depth of my mind nothing was left that stood erect . . . The days which followed this discovery were the saddest of my life.⁶⁷

The emotional tone of this account may appear to raise questions about James's earlier suggestion that when the inner unity occurs "it brings a characteristic sort of relief." But, as James points out, Jouffrey's disbelief "grew fixed and stable," which suggests that as time went on he was no longer involved in a hopeless struggle between belief and disbelief.

In a footnote to his citation from Jouffrey's account of his counter-conversion James cites a case from Starbuck's manuscript collection of a woman who rejected the idea that there is a God. She writes:

> A way down in the bottom of my heart, I believe I was always more or less skeptical about "God"; skepticism grew as an undercurrent, all through my early youth, but it was controlled and covered by the emotional elements in my religious growth. When I was sixteen I joined the church and was asked if I loved God. I replied "Yes," as was customary and expected. But instantly with a flash something spoke within me, "No, you do not." I was haunted for a long time with shame and remorse for my falsehood and for my wickedness in not loving God, mingled with fear that there might be an avenging God who would punish me in some terrible way.⁶⁸

---

emphasized that the latter is merely the occasion and not the cause of religious awakening. Moreover, he noted that religion becomes so differentiated from its sources, even opposed to them in some cases, that in time their connection is no longer evident. See Wulff, *Psychology of Religion*, 26.

66. James, *The Varieties of Religious Experience*; see Jouffrey, *Mèlanges Philosophiques*, 83.

67. James, *The Varieties of Religious Experience*, 176–77.

68. Ibid., 177.

At age nineteen she had an attack of tonsillitis and before she had completely recovered she heard a story "about a brute who had kicked his wife downstairs, and then continued the operation until she became insensible."[69] She says that she

> felt the horror of the thing keenly. Instantly this thought flashed through my mind: "I have no use for a God who permits such things." This experience was followed by months of stoical indifference to the God of my previous life, mingled with feelings of positive dislike and a somewhat proud defiance of him. I still thought there might be a God. If so he would probably damn me, but I should have to stand it. I felt very little fear and no desire to propitiate him. I have never had any personal relations with him since this painful experience.[70]

James notes that this case "exemplifies how small an additional stimulus will overthrow the mind into a new state of equilibrium when the process of preparation and incubation has proceeded far enough."[71] He compares it to the "proverbial last straw added to the camel's burden or that touch of a needle which makes the salt in a supersaturated fluid suddenly begin to crystallize out."[72] Of course, readers of this narrative could suggest that the young woman might have viewed the experience in another way, that it swept away her belief in a God who seems indifferent to the evils in the world so that a new understanding of God as continually working against such evils may take its place. Readers might even want to explore the relationship between her tonsillitis and the story of the brute who kicked his wife downstairs. But James does not take this approach. Rather, he is interested in the psychological process in which an internal division is overcome and a sense of inner unity takes its place, and he is especially interested in this regard in the seemingly insignificant factor that tips the scale to a new state of equilibrium.

In the same footnote he refers to another case of "counter-conversion" in which the proverbial last straw or touch of a needle also applies. This is a story told by Leo Tolstoy of a twenty-six-year-old man who was on a hunting expedition and, as he prepared for bed, he began to pray, which was his custom from childhood. His brother, who was lying on the hay nearby, looked at him and when he had finished praying said to him "Do you still keep up that thing?" Tolstoy comments:

69. Ibid.
70. Ibid.
71. Ibid.
72 Ibid., 177–78.

Nothing more was said. But since that day, now more than thirty years ago, S. has never prayed again; he never takes communion, and does not go to church. All this, not because he became acquainted with convictions of his brother which he then and there adopted; not because he made any new resolution in his soul, but merely because the words spoken by his brother were like the light push of a finger against a leaning wall already about to tumble by its own weight. These words but showed him that the place wherein he supposed religion dwelt in him had long been empty, and that the sentences he uttered, the crosses and bows he made during his prayer, were actions with no inner sense. Having once seized their absurdity, he could no longer keep them up.[73]

Here, Tolstoy adds to James's last straw and touch of a needle the push of a finger against a leaning wall. A seemingly inconsequential query by the young man's brother was all that was needed to end the matter. And as Tolstoy observes, this did not involve a new resolution but rather simply *not* doing what he had formerly done.

The Experience of a New Stimulus or Passion

Next, James cites two illustrations of the type of "new birth" that is produced "by the irruption into the individual's life of some new stimulus or passion, such as love, ambition, cupidity, revenge, or patriotic devotion."[74] The first, from John Foster's *Essays on Decision of Character*, is "a case of sudden conversion to avarice."[75] Foster relates the story of a young man who wasted a large patrimony in "revels with a number of worthless associates who called themselves his friends, and who, when his last means were exhausted, treated him of course with neglect or contempt."[76] Reduced to absolute want, "he one day went out of the house with an intention to put an end to his life; but wandering awhile almost unconsciously, he came to the brow of an eminence which overlooked what were lately his estates. Here he sat down, and remained fixed in thought a number of hours, at the end of which he sprang from the ground with a vehement, exulting emotion. He had formed

---

73. Ibid., 178. Tolstoy, *My Confession*, 8; see Tolstoy, *A Confession and Other Religious Writings*, 20–21.
74. James, *The Varieties of Religious Experience*, 176.
75. Ibid., 178. See Foster, *Essays on Decision of Character*, letter 3.
76. James, *The Varieties of Religious Experience*, 178.

The Divided Self and the Process of Its Unification

his resolution, which was, that all these estates should be his again; he had formed his plan, too, which he instantly began to execute."[77]

The plan was that he would "seize the first opportunity, of however humble a kind, to gain any money, though it were ever so despicable a trifle, and resolved absolutely not to spend, if he could help it, a farthing of whatever he might obtain."[78] For example, he saw a heap of coals that had been shot out of carts on the pavement in front of a house and offered to shovel or wheel them away: "He received a few pence for the labor and then, in pursuance of the saving part of the plan, requested some small gratuity of meat and drink, which was given him."[79] Foster ends his account with the observation that "he more than recovered his lost possessions, and died an inveterate miser, worth £60,000."[80]

James's use of the word "avarice" and Foster's suggestion that the man died an "inveterate miser" suggest that neither James nor Foster holds him in the highest esteem. But the point here is that he made a resolution and he remained faithful to it throughout his life, a life that might otherwise have ended in suicide.

In a footnote James cites another example of new birth that is "produced by the irruption into the individual's life of some new stimulus or passion."[81] He notes that it is from a document that has come into his possession and that it represents "in a vivid way what is probably a very frequent sort of conversion, if the opposite of 'falling in love,' falling out of love, may be so termed."[82] He adds that falling in love "also conforms frequently to this type, a latent process of unconscious preparation often preceding a sudden awakening to the fact that the mischief is irretrievably done," and James observes that the "free and easy tone in this narrative gives it a sincerity that speaks for itself."[83] It begins: "For two years of this time I went through a very bad experience, which almost drove me mad. I had fallen violently in love with a girl who, young as she was, had a spirit of coquetry like a cat. As I look back on her now, I hate her, and wonder how I could ever have fallen so low as to be worked upon to such an extent by her attentions. Nevertheless, I fell into a regular fever, could think of nothing else; whenever I was alone, I pictured her attractions, and spent most of the time when I should have

---

77. Ibid.
78. Ibid., 178–79.
79. Ibid., 179.
80. Ibid.
81. Ibid., 176.
82. Ibid., 179.
83. Ibid.

been working, in recalling our previous interviews, and imagining future conversations."[84]

He goes on to relate that she "was very pretty, good humored, and jolly to the last degree, and intensely pleased with my admiration" but "she would give me no decided answer, yes or no, and the queer thing about it was that whilst pursuing her for her hand, I secretly knew all along that she was unfit to be a wife for me, and that she would never say yes."[85] As they lived in the same boarding house, he saw her "continually and familiarly" for a year or so but "our closer relations had to be largely on the sly and this fact, together with my jealousy of another one of her male admirers, and my own conscience despising me for my uncontrollable weakness, made me so nervous and sleepless that I really thought I should become insane."[86]

Another "queer thing was the sudden and unexpected way in which it all stopped."[87] This is how it happened: "I was going to my work after breakfast one morning, thinking as usual of her and my misery, when, just as if some outside power laid hold of me, I found myself turning round and almost running to my room, where I immediately got out all the relics of her which I possessed, including some hair, all her notes and letters, and ambrotypes on glass."[88] He burned the former and crushed the latter beneath his heel and "in a sort of fierce joy of revenge and punishment. I now loathed and despised her altogether, and as for myself I felt as if a load of disease had suddenly been removed from me. That was the end."[89] He never spoke or wrote to her again and has never had a loving thought towards her: "In fact, I have always rather hated her memory, though now I can see that I had gone unnecessarily far in that direction."[90] Nonetheless, "from that happy morning onward I regained possession of my own proper soul, and have never since fallen into any similar trap."[91]

James says that this case of falling out of love "seems to me an unusually clear example of two different levels of personality, inconsistent in their dictates, yet so well balanced against each other as for a long time to fill

---

84. Ibid.

85. Ibid., 180.

86. Ibid.

87. Ibid.

88. Ibid. An *ambrotype* is an early kind of photograph consisting of a glass negative backed by a dark surface so that it actually appears positive. See Agnes, *Webster's New World*, 44.

89. James, *The Varieties of Religious Experience*, 180.

90. Ibid.

91. Ibid.

The Divided Self and the Process of Its Unification

the life with discord and dissatisfaction."[92] But then "not gradually, but in a sudden crisis, the unstable equilibrium is resolved, and this happens so unexpectedly that it is as if, to use the writer's words, 'some outside power laid hold.'"[93] Noting that Professor Starbuck has an analogous case in which hatred suddenly turned into love, he suggests that Starbuck "seems right in conceiving all such sudden changes as results of special cerebral functions unconsciously developing until they are ready to play a controlling part, when they make irruptions into the conscious life."[94] James adds that when he discusses sudden conversions in his second of two lectures on conversion, he "will make as much use as I can of this hypothesis of subconscious incubation."[95]

CONVERSIONS OF THE RELIGIOUS TYPE

At this point in the lecture James returns to religious conversions, the topic he introduced earlier with his cases of Saint Augustine and Henry Alline.

The Case of Horace Fletcher

His first case is that of Horace Fletcher, who wrote about his experience in his book titled *Menticulture*.[96] James suggests that this is a case of "the simplest possible type, an account of the conversion to the systematic religion of healthy-mindedness of a man who must already have been naturally of the healthy-minded type."[97] This case, he adds, "shows how, when the fruit is ripe, a touch will make it fall."[98]

---

92. Ibid.
93. Ibid.
94. Ibid.
95. Ibid. As these two cases involve conflicting emotions of love and hate, it is noteworthy that James and Starbuck were expressing views similar to those that Josef Breuer and Sigmund Freud had only recently formulated. See Breuer and Freud, *Studies on Hysteria*.
96. James, *The Varieties of Religious Experience*, 181. James quotes from Fletcher's chapter titled "A Personal Experience," in *Menticulture*, 25–43. The title of Fletcher's *Menticulture* is a play on the word *horticulture* and expresses his conviction that negative mental processes can be gotten rid of in the same way that weeds can be eradicated from a field or garden. As I noted in chapter 3 on healthy-mindedness, Fletcher was also the author of *Happiness as Found in Forethought minus Fearthought*.
97. James, *The Varieties of Religious Experience*, 181.
98. Ibid., 181.

James picks up on Fletcher's account of his conversation with a friend who had realized self-control through the practice of Buddhist discipline.[99] The friend told Fletcher that he could realize the same self-control, but that in order to do so he needed to "get rid of anger and worry." Following this conversation, Fletcher could think of nothing other than the words "get rid, get rid," and he notes that "the idea must have continued to possess me during my sleeping hours, for the first consciousness in the morning brought back the same thought, with the revelation of a discovery, which framed itself into the reasoning, 'If it is possible to get rid of anger and worry, why is it necessary to have them at all?'"[100] He "felt the strength of the argument, and at once accepted the reasoning. The baby had discovered that it could walk. It would scorn to creep any longer."[101]

From the moment that he realized that these cancer spots of worry and anger were removable, they began to disappear. Also, although he was initially on guard only against anger and worry, in time he began to notice "the absence of the other depressing and dwarfing passions." He wondered if the elimination of anger and worry would "yield to indifference and sloth," but in fact the opposite has happened: "I feel such an increased desire to do something useful that it seems as if I was a boy again and the energy for play has returned."[102] This feeling that he had regained the energy he experienced when he was a boy was especially significant because he had had an experience when he was a boy that he believes was responsible for his tendency to worry: "I was standing under a tree which was struck by lightning, and received a shock from the effects of which I never knew exemption until I had dissolved partnership with worry."[103] Since then "lightning and thunder have been encountered under conditions which would formerly have caused great depression and discomfort, without experiencing a trace of either."[104]

Fletcher says he recognizes that "pure Christianity and pure Buddhism, and the Mental Sciences and all Religions, fundamentally teach what has been a discovery to me," but that "none of them have presented it in the light of a simple and easy process of elimination."[105] Fletcher also notes

---

99. The friend was Professor Ernest Francisco Fenollosa, whom he had previously met in Japan. The conversation took place in Fenollosa's apartment in Boston. Fletcher, *Menticulture*, 25–26, notes that the odor of incense in the room added to the calming effect of the experience.

100. Ibid.

101. Ibid.

102. Ibid., 183.

103. Ibid.

104. Ibid.

105. Ibid., 182.

that he has not been concerned "as to what the results of this emancipated condition may be."[106] He has no doubt that "the perfect health aimed at by Christian Science may be one of the possibilities," but he hasn't made any moves in that direction. Nor is he "wasting any of this precious time formulating an idea of a future existence or a future Heaven," for "the Heaven that I have within myself is as attractive as any that has been promised or that I can imagine; and I am willing to let the growth lead where it will, as long as the anger and their brood have no part in misguiding it."[107]

James does not comment on Fletcher's account. Instead, he notes that the older medicine spoke of two ways in which one might recover from a bodily disease—one gradual (*lysis*) the other abrupt (*crisis*)—and he suggests that in the spiritual realm "there are also two ways, one gradual, the other sudden, in which inner unification may occur."[108] He suggests that Leo Tolstoy and John Bunyan, both of whom he discussed in his lectures on the sick-soul, may serve again as examples. They are examples "of the gradual way, though it must be confessed at the outset that it is hard to follow these windings of the hearts of others, and one feels that their words do not reveal their total secret."[109]

The Case of Leo Tolstoy

James begins his reflections on Tolstoy's rebirth by noting that with Tolstoy it was a matter of pursuing "unending questioning," which led to "one insight after another."[110] He explains: "First he perceived that his conviction that life was meaningless took only this finite life into account. He was looking for the value of one finite term in that of another, and the whole result could only be one of those indeterminate equations in mathematics which end with $0=0$. Yet this is as far as the reasoning intellect by itself can go, unless irrational sentiment or faith brings in the infinite. Believe in the infinite as common people do, and life grows possible again."[111]

Thus, Tolstoy began to look at the situation as common people do, and eventually he "came to the settled conviction—he says it took him two years to arrive there—that his trouble had not been with life in general, not with the common life of common men, but with the life of the upper, intellectual,

106. Ibid., 183.
107. Ibid.
108. Ibid.
109. Ibid., 183–84.
110. Ibid., 184.
111. Ibid.

artistic classes, the life which he had personally always led, the cerebral life, the life of conventionality, artificiality, and personal ambition."[112] Tolstoy realized that "he had been living wrongly and must change," and that happiness lay in working for basic physical needs, renouncing lies and vanities, relieving common wants, living simply, and believing in God.[113] As he writes in his confessions, "I remember one day in early spring, I was alone in the forest, lending my ear to its mysterious noises. I listened, and my thought went back to what for these three years it always was busy with—the quest of God. But the idea of him, I said, how did I ever come by the idea? And again there arose in me, with this thought, glad aspirations towards life. Everything in me awoke and received a meaning."[114]

Then why look further? "He is there: he, without whom one cannot live. To acknowledge God and to live are one and the same thing. God is what life is. Well, then! Live, seek God, and there will be no life without him."[115] He describes the change in him that followed this resolution to seek God: "After this things cleared up within me and about me better than ever, and the light has never wholly died away. I was saved from suicide. Just how or when the change took place I cannot tell. But as insensibly and gradually as the force of life had been annulled within me, and I had reached my moral death-bed, just as gradually and imperceptibly did the energy of life come back."[116] What was strange about this was that the energy that came back was nothing new: "It was my ancient juvenile force of faith, the belief that the sole purpose of my life was to be *better*.[117] He "gave up the life of the conventional world, recognizing it to be no life, but a parody on life," and as James indicates he "embraced the life of the peasants, and has felt right and happy, or at least relatively so, ever since."[118]

In James's view, Tolstoy's melancholy was not merely due to "an accidental vitiation of his humors, though it was doubtless also that,"[119] for his mel-

---

112. Ibid., 184–85.

113. Ibid., 185.

114. Ibid. James is quoting here from Tolstoy's *My Confession*. See Tolstoy, *A Confession and Other Religious Writings*, 64–65.

115. James, *The Varieties of Religious Experience*, 185.

116. Ibid.

117. Ibid.

118. Ibid.

119. Ibid., 185–86. It is obvious that James does not believe that the traditional view that melancholy is caused by bodily fluids provides a full explanation for the fact that Tolstoy became melancholic. On the other hand, he may be suggesting here that Tolstoy had been experiencing some changes in his physical health or vitality, and that these changes contributed to his susceptibility to melancholy. This would be consistent with

ancholy "was logically called for by the clash between his inner character and his outer activities and aims."[120] In this regard, Tolstoy, despite the fact that he was a literary artist, "was one of those primitive oaks of men to whom the superfluities and insincerities, the cupidities, complications, and cruelties of our polite civilization are profoundly unsatisfying, and for whom the eternal veracities lie with more natural and animal things. His crisis was the getting of his soul in order, the discovery of its genuine habitat and vocation, the escape from falsehoods into what for him were ways of truth. It was a case of heterogeneous personality tardily and slowly finding its unity and level."[121] James concludes his account of Tolstoy's conversion with this somewhat ironic comment: "And though not many of us can imitate Tolstoy, not having enough, perhaps, of the aboriginal human marrow in our bones, most of us may at least feel as if it might be better for us if we could."[122]

The Case of John Bunyan

James makes the transition from Tolstoy to Bunyan by noting that Bunyan's recovery "seems to have been even slower," that for years Bunyan "was alternately haunted with texts of Scriptures, now up and now down, but at last with an ever growing relief in his salvation through the blood of Christ."[123] He cites Bunyan's account of how, over a period of time, the positive texts began to overcome the negative ones, and eventually "those dreadful Scriptures of God" ceased to trouble him anymore. Bunyan exclaims: "Now could I see myself in Heaven and Earth at once: in Heaven by my Christ, by my Head, by my Righteousness and Life, though on Earth by my body or person."[124] James notes that Bunyan went on to become "a minister of the gospel, and in spite of his neurotic constitution, and of the twelve years he lay in prison for his non-conformity, his life was turned to active use."[125] He "was a peacemaker and doer of good, and the immortal Allegory which he wrote has brought the very spirit of religious patience

---

James's view that physiological problems generally contribute to psychological difficulties. As we saw earlier, James's dorsal (back) problems played a significant role in his own susceptibility to melancholy.

120. James, *The Varieties of Religious Experience*, 185–86.

121. Ibid., 186.

122. Ibid.

123. Ibid.

124. Ibid., 187. James is quoting from paragraph 233 of Bunyan's *Grace Abounding to the Chief of Sinners* (1797 ed.). This paragraph is on p. 60 of the 1987 edition.

125. James, *The Varieties of Religious Experience*, 187.

home to English hearts."¹²⁶ The immortal allegory is, of course, Bunyan's *The Pilgrim's Progress*.¹²⁷

CONCLUSION

James concludes that neither Bunyan nor Tolstoy could become what he has called "healthy-minded," for both "had drunk too deeply of the cup of bitterness ever to forget its taste, and their redemption is into a universe two stories deep."¹²⁸ Both "realized a good which broke the effective edge of his sadness; yet the sadness was preserved as a minor ingredient in the heart of the faith by which it was overcome," but "the fact of interest for us is that as a matter of fact they could and did find *something* welling up in the inner reaches of their consciousness, by which such extreme sadness could be overcome."¹²⁹ James notes that Tolstoy refers to this *something* as "*that by which men live*."¹³⁰ This, in James's view, "is exactly what it is, a stimulus, an excitement, a faith, a force that re-infuses the positive willingness to live, even in full presence of the evil perceptions that erewhile made life seem unbearable."¹³¹ James adds that Tolstoy's "later works show him implacable to the whole system of official values: the ignobility of fashionable life; the infamies of empire; the spuriousness of the church; the vain conceit of the professions; the meannesses and cruelties that go with great success; and every other pompous crime and lying institution of this world. To all patience with such things his experience has been for him a permanent ministry of death."¹³²

Similarly, Bunyan "leaves the world to the enemy," declaring that "I must pass a sentence of death upon everything that can properly be called a thing of this life, even to reckon myself, my wife, my children, my health, my enjoyment, and all, as dead to me, and myself as dead to them; to trust in God through Christ, as touching the world to come; and as touching this world, to count the grave my house, to make my bed in darkness, and to say to corruption, Thou art my father, and to the worm, Thou art my mother and sister."¹³³ The original auditors of James's lectures would probably have known that this

---

126. Ibid.
127. Bunyan, *The Pilgrim's Progress*.
128. James, *The Varieties of Religious Experience*, 187.
129. Ibid. (italics original).
130. Ibid. (italics original). See Tolstoy, *A Confession and Other Religious Writings*, 65.
131. James, *The Varieties of Religious Experience*, 187.
132. Ibid., 188.
133. Ibid. Bunyan, *Grace Abounding to the Chief of Sinners* (1987 ed.), 79.

passage from *Grace Abounding to the Chief of Sinners* follows his account of how he has been sentenced to twelve years in prison as "an upholder and maintainer of unlawful assemblies and conventicles, and for not conforming to the national worship of the Church of England."[134] Thus, when he goes on to write about having to part with his family (which James also quotes), this is not a declaration of his desire to transcend the things of this world, but of how difficult it has been to live without them. He writes:

> The parting with my wife and poor children hath oft been to me in this place, as the pulling the flesh from my bones; and that not only because I am somewhat too fond of these great mercies; but also because I should have often brought to my mind the many hardships, miseries and wants that my poor family was like to meet with, when I should be taken from them, especially my poor blind child, who lay nearer my heart than all I had besides; O the thought of the hardship I thought my blind one might go under, would break my heart to pieces.[135]

He goes on to relate how he was "in a very sad and low condition for many weeks," that he continually thought of his death by execution, and that, given the state he was in, he would undoubtedly "make a scrabbling shift to clamber up the ladder" and "either with quaking or other symptoms of fainting, give occasion to the enemy to reproach the way of God and his people, for their timorousness."[136] But then he began to consider that he might "have an opportunity to speak my last words to a multitude which I thought would come to see me die; and thought I, if it must be so, if God will but convert one soul by my very last words, I shall not count my life thrown away, nor lost."[137] James concludes that although the "hue of resolution" is evident in Bunyan's text, "the full flood of ecstatic liberation seems never to have poured over poor John Bunyan's soul."[138]

Then, noting that the examples he has provided in this lecture "may suffice to acquaint us in a general way with the phenomenon technically called 'Conversion,'" James concludes his lecture on the divided self and its process of unification by indicating that in the next lecture he will invite his auditors to study the "peculiarities and concomitants" of conversion in greater detail.[139]

---

134. Ibid., 78.
135. Ibid., 80.
136. Ibid., 81.
137. Ibid., 81–82.
138. James, *The Varieties of Religious Experience*, 188.
139. Ibid.

6

The Psychology of Religious Conversion

James's lectures on conversion concluded the first set of the Gifford Lectures. Although, as we have seen, much of the preceding lecture on the divided self focused on conversion, James clearly felt that he needed to say more about the more minute features of the conversion process. He also wanted to consider the recent empirical studies of conversion undertaken by Edwin Diller Starbuck, George Albert Coe, James Leuba, and others. Although he does not specifically say that the focus of these lectures is the *psychology* of religious conversion, this is essentially what the two lectures are about.

He begins the first lecture on conversion with a paragraph that connects the focus of the previous lecture on the divided self and the subject of this lecture. He writes:

> To be converted, to be regenerated, to receive grace, to experience religion, to gain an assurance, are so many phrases which denote the process, gradual or sudden, by which a self hitherto divided, and consciously wrong, inferior and unhappy, becomes unified and conscious right, superior and happy, in consequence of its firmer hold upon religious realities. This at least is what conversion signifies in general terms, whether or not we believe that a direct divine operation is needed to bring such a moral change about.[1]

---

1. James, *The Varieties of Religious Experience*, 189.

Acknowledging the general nature of this description, he indicates that he intends to enter into a more minute study of the process of conversion but that before he does so he proposes to "enliven our understanding of the definition" of conversion that he has just offered by focusing on a concrete example.

THE CASE OF STEPHEN BRADLEY

The example is the case of "an unlettered man, Stephen H. Bradley, whose experience is related in a scarce American pamphlet."[2] James indicates that he has selected this case "because it shows how in these inner alterations one may find one unsuspected depth below another, as if the possibilities of character lay disposed in a series of layers or shells, of whose existence we have no premonitory knowledge."[3]

James notes that Bradley thought he had already been fully converted at the age of fourteen. This belief was based on a momentary vision in which he saw the Savior in human form. The Savior's arms were extended, and he said to young Stephen, "Come." The next day he "rejoiced with trembling" and soon thereafter his happiness was so great that he wanted to die, as this world no longer had a place in his affections, and "every day appeared as solemn to me as the Sabbath."[4] At the same time he underwent a thoroughgoing moral change: "Previous to this time I was very selfish and self-righteous; but now I desired the welfare of all mankind, and could with a feeling heart forgive my worst enemies, and I felt as if I should be willing to bear the scoffs and sneers of any person, and suffer anything for His sake, if I could be the means in the hands of God, of the conversion of one soul."[5]

Nine years later, in 1829, Bradley heard of a religious revival that was taking place in his own neighborhood. Many of the young converts would approach him and ask him if he had religion and he would generally reply that he hoped that he did. This did not satisfy them because they said that they *knew* that they had it. So he asked them to pray for him. Then one Sabbath day he went to hear a Methodist preacher at the Academy and the preacher spoke of the ushering in of Judgment Day. As he listened he trembled involuntarily on the bench where he was sitting "though I felt nothing

---

2. The pamphlet is titled "A sketch of the life of Stephen H. Bradley, from the age of five to twenty-four years, including his remarkable experience of the power of the Holy Spirit on the second evening of November, 1829."
3. James, *The Varieties of Religious Experience*, 189.
4. Ibid., 190.
5. Ibid.

at heart." The next evening he returned, and the preacher again "represented the terrors of that day in such a manner that it appeared as if it would melt the heart of stone."[6] When the preacher finished an old gentleman turned to Bradley and said, "This is what I call preaching." Bradley agreed, but his feelings "were still unmoved by what he said, and I did not enjoy religion." He believed, though, that the old gentleman did.[7]

Later that evening he had an "experience of the power of the Holy Spirit." He had returned home immediately after the meeting, "and when I got home I wondered what made me feel so stupid."[8] He went to bed and "felt indifferent to the things of religion until I began to be exercised by the Holy Spirit." This began about five minutes after he went to bed. At first he felt his heart beating very quickly, which caused him to think that perhaps something was physically wrong with him, but he was not alarmed because he felt no pain. As his heart increased in its beating, he became convinced that it was the work of the Holy Spirit, and he "began to feel exceedingly happy and humble and such a sense of unworthiness as I never felt before."[9] He spoke out saying, "Lord, I do not deserve this happiness, or words to that effect," and a stream resembling air in feeling came into his mouth and heart and continued for five minutes or more, taking complete possession of his soul. His heart felt as if it would burst, "but it did not stop until I felt as if I were unutterably full of the love and grace of God."[10]

While this was occurring, a thought arose in his mind: "What can it mean?" All at once his memory became exceedingly clear, "and it appeared to me just as if the New Testament was placed open before me, eighth chapter of Romans, and as light as if some candle lighted was held for me to read the 26th and 27th verses of that chapter, and I read these words: 'The Spirit helpeth our infirmities with groaning which cannot be uttered.'"[11]

Because his heart was beating, he groaned like a person in distress even though he was not in any pain, and his brother, hearing the sound, came into his room and asked him if he had a toothache. He said no and advised his brother to go back to sleep. But he did not want to sleep because he was so happy. As his heart stopped its rapid beating, he felt as though there were angels hovering around his bed and he said to them, "O ye affectionate

---

6. Ibid., 190.
7. Ibid.
8. Ibid., 191.
9. Ibid.
10. Ibid.
11. Ibid.

angels! How is it that ye can take so much interest in our welfare, and we take so little interest in our own?"[12]

With some difficulty he fell asleep, and his first thoughts in the morning were, "What has become of my happiness? And feeling a degree of it in my heart, I asked for more, which was given to me as quick as thought."[13] When he got up to dress himself he "found to my surprise that I could but stand" and this felt to him "as if it was a little heaven upon earth."[14] His soul felt as completely raised above the fear of death "and like a bird in a cage, I had a desire, if it was the will of God, to get released from my body and to dwell with Christ, though willing to live to do good to others, and to warn sinners to repent."[15] He went downstairs feeling as solemn as if he had lost all of his friends. He initially thought that he would not tell his parents about it, but when he looked at the eighth chapter of Romans, it seemed as though every verse almost spoke and confirmed the experience to be truly the Word of God, and it was "as if my feelings corresponded with the meaning of the word."[16] So he told his parents, and as he did so he felt that they could see that it was not his own voice that spoke as his speech seemed entirely under the control of the Spirit within him. He felt that what was happening to him was similar to the Apostles on the day of Pentecost, "with the exception of having power to give it to others, and doing what they did."[17] After breakfast he went to his neighbors to converse with them on religion, "which was something "I could not have been hired to have done before this," and at their request he "prayed with them, though I had never prayed in public before."[18]

In conclusion, Bradley expresses the feeling that "I have discharged my duty by telling the truth, and hope by the blessing of God, it may do some good to all who shall read it," and adds, "He has fulfilled his promise in sending the Holy Spirit down into our hearts, or mine at least, and I now defy all the Deists and Atheists in the world to shake my faith in Christ."[19]

James does not comment on Bradley's account of his conversion. He simply says: "So much for Mr. Bradley and his conversion, of the effect of

---

12. Ibid., 192.
13. Ibid.
14. Ibid.
15. Ibid.
16. Ibid.
17. Ibid., 192–93.
18. Ibid., 193.
19. Ibid.

which upon his later life we gain no information."[20] This observation suggests that James would be interested in knowing whether or not Bradley's conversion had permanent effects and, if so, what they may have been. He indicates, however, that he is now prepared to focus on "the constituent elements of the conversion process."[21]

ASSOCIATION THEORY AND RELIGIOUS CONVERSION

James begins his consideration of the constituent elements of the conversion process with a reference to the concept or theory of Association: "if you open the chapter on Association, of any treatise on Psychology, you will read that a man's ideas, aims, and objects form diverse internal groups and systems, relatively independent of one another."[22] Thus, each "aim" that a person follows "awakens a certain specific kind of interested excitement, and gathers a certain group of ideas together in subordination to it as its associates; and if the aims and excitements are distinct in kind, their groups of ideas may have little in common."[23] If, however, "one group is present and engrosses the interest, all the ideas connected with other groups may be excluded from the mental field."[24]

To illustrate the fact that these groups of ideas may have little in common James cites the example of the president of the United States who goes camping in the wilderness for a vacation, and in doing so he "changes his system of ideas from top to bottom."[25] The anxieties associated with his office have lapsed into the background and have been replaced by "the habits of a son of nature."[26] Persons who have known him only as the President would not know him as the same person if they witnessed him in the role of the camper. Moreover, if he never went back to his presidential role, he would, for all practical intents and purposes, be "a permanently transformed

20. Ibid.

21. Ibid.

22. James has a chapter on association in his own *The Principles of Psychology*, 2:550–604; see also James, *Psychology: The Briefer Course*, 120–46. This chapter includes a history of the concept of association, which can be traced to Aristotle, but, in James's view, was first formulated by Thomas Hobbes in *Leviathan*, and is also represented in the writings of David Hume and the French psychologist M. Ribot. He critiques recent attempts by Herbert Spencer and others to replace the concept of association with the concept of similarity.

23. James, *The Varieties of Religious Experience*, 193.

24. Ibid.

25. Ibid.

26. Ibid.

being."[27] Our ordinary alterations of character as we pass from one aim to another are not transformations because each of them is so rapidly succeeded by another, but "whenever one aim grows so stable as to expel definitively its potential rivals from the individual's life, we tend to speak of the phenomenon, and perhaps to wonder at it, as a "transformation."[28]

James notes that the most thoroughgoing of such alternations are evidenced in the divided self, as discussed in the preceding lecture, where two aims conflict with one another. A less complete example is the simultaneous existence of two or more different groups of aims with one group in command and instigating all activity while the others "are only pious wishes, and never practically come to anything."[29] James observes that Saint Augustine's aspirations to a purer life were, temporarily, an example of the subordinate aim. Another example would be if the president were to wonder if his presidential engagements were not all vanity and whether the life of a woodchopper would be a more wholesome destiny. James contends that such fleeting aspirations are not mere whimsies. Rather they exist on the remoter outskirts of the mind, and the real self of the man, the center of his energies, is occupied with an entirely different system. As life goes on, there is a constant change of our interests, and a consequent change of place of our systems of ideas, from more central to more peripheral, and from more peripheral to more central parts of consciousness."[30]

Noting that these changes in our system of ideas from central to peripheral and peripheral to central involve our emotions, James uses the language of "hot" and "cold" to describe the process, with the "hot" parts of personal desire and volition as the centers of our dynamic energy, and the "cold" parts leaving us indifferent and passive.[31] If there is great oscillation

27. Ibid., 194.

28. Ibid.

29. Ibid. James presents several cases of alternating personality in his chapter on "The Consciousness of Self" in *The Principles of Psychology*, 1:379–93.

30. James, *The Varieties of Religious Experience*, 194. James notes that when he was a youth his father read aloud from a Boston newspaper the part of Lord Gifford's will that established the very lectureship that he was now engaged in. At that time he "did not think of being a teacher of philosophy, and what I listened to was as remote from my own life as if it related to the planet Mars. Yet here I am, with the Gifford system part and parcel of my very self, and all my energies, for the time being, devoted to successfully identifying myself with it" (ibid., 194–95). This, then, is an example of how something can move from the periphery to the center of one's consciousness.

31. James's article "What Is an Emotion?" published in the journal *Mind* in 1884 is especially relevant here. So, too, are his chapter on "The Emotions" in *The Principles of Psychology*, 2:442–85, and his abbreviated chapter on "Emotion" in *Psychology: The Briefer Course*, 240–57.

in the emotional interest, with the hot places rapidly shifting from one system to another, then we have "the wavering and divided self we heard so much of in the previous lecture."[32] On the other hand, if the focus of excitement and heat comes to lie permanently within a certain system, and if the change is a religious one, "we call it a *conversion,* especially if it be by crisis, or sudden."[33]

James suggests calling this hot place in a person's consciousness, this group of ideas to which one devotes oneself and out of which one works, "the habitual center of [one's] personal energy," and he points out that "it makes a great difference to a man whether one set of his ideas, or another, be the center of his energy; and it makes a great difference, as regards any set of ideas which he may possess, whether they become central or remain peripheral in him. To say that a man is 'converted' means, in these terms, that religious ideas previously peripheral in his consciousness, now take a central place, and that religious aims form the habitual center of his energy."[34] The question that this raises is just "*how* the excitement changes in a person's mental system and *why* aims that were peripheral become at a certain moment central."[35] Although psychology can give a general description of what happens, it is unable "in a given case to account accurately for all the single forces at work."[36] In fact,

> Neither an outside observer nor the Subject who undergoes the process can explain fully how particular experiences are able to change one's center of energy so decisively, or why they so often have to bide their hour to do so. We have a thought, or we perform an act, repeatedly, but on a certain day the real meaning of the thought peals through us for the first time, or the act has suddenly turned into a moral impossibility. All we know is that there are dead feelings, dead ideas, and cold beliefs, and there are hot and live ones; and when one grows hot and alive within us, everything has to re-crystallize.[37]

Lacking the capacity to account for all the single forces at work in this process, we fall back, as James puts it, "on the hackneyed symbolism of a mechanical equilibrium."[38] If we view the mind as "a system of ideas, each

---

32. James, *The Varieties of Religious Experience*, 196.
33. Ibid.
34. Ibid.
35. Ibid.
36. Ibid.
37. Ibid., 197.
38. Ibid. An example would be a perfectly balanced weighing scale or even the

with the excitement it arouses, and with tendencies impulsive and inhibitive, which mutually check or reinforce one another," we know that this collection of ideas "alters by subtraction or by addition in the course of experience, and the tendencies alter as the organism gets more aged."[39] On the one hand, "a mental system may be undermined or weakened by this interstitial alteration just as a building is, and yet for a time keep upright by dead habit."[40] On the other hand, "a new perception, a sudden emotional shock, or an occasion which lays bare the organic alteration, will make the whole fabric fall together; and then the center of gravity sinks into an attitude more stable, for the new ideas that reach the center in the rearrangement seem now to be locked there, and the new structure remains permanent."[41]

James notes that formed associations of ideas and habits usually have a retarding effect on such changes in equilibrium while new information, however acquired, "plays an accelerating part in the changes." Also, "the slow mutation of our instincts and propensities" has an enormous influence, and "all these influences may work subconsciously or half unconsciously."[42] In a footnote James refers to the case of Théodore Jouffrey, whose counter-conversion was presented in the preceding lecture on the divided self. Jouffrey writes: "Down this slope it was that my intelligence had glided, and little by little it had got far from its first faith. But this melancholy revolution had not taken place in the broad daylight of my consciousness. It had gone on in silence, by an involuntary elaboration of which I was not the accomplice; and although I had in reality long since ceased to be a Christian, yet, in the innocence of my intention, I should have shuddered to suspect it, and thought it calumny had I been accused of such a falling away."[43] James adds that in cases where the individual's subconscious life is fully developed and thus "in whom motives habitually ripen in silence, you get a case of which you can never give a full account, and in which, both to the Subject and the

---

wooden rule that Saint Augustine's mother dreamed about (see chapter 5).

39. Ibid.
40. Ibid.
41. Ibid. James's allusion to the "center of gravity" is noteworthy here because, in his chapter on association, he mentions that David Hume compared the law of association with the law of gravity; and he cites in this connection M. Ribot's observation that the "discovery of the ultimate law of our psychologic acts [i.e., the law of association] has this, then, in common with many other discoveries: it came late and seems so simple that it may justly astonish us" (James, *The Principles of Psychology*, 1:597).
42. James, *The Varieties of Religious Experience*, 197–98.
43. Ibid., 198; see Jouffrey, *Mélanges Philosophiques*.

onlookers, there may be an element of marvel," largely because it seemed to happen without any forewarning.[44]

Also, since emotions, especially those that are intensely felt, are potent factors in the precipitation of mental rearrangements, they typically play a powerful role in religious conversions, and James suggests that emotions especially characteristic of religious conversions are hope, happiness, security, and resolve.[45] For example, happiness played a very prominent role in Stephen Bradley's conversion, and resolve was especially powerful in Saint Augustine's conversion.

THE ROLE OF MENTAL PROCESSES IN RELIGIOUS CONVERSION

At this point in the lecture, James introduces the contributions of Edwin Diller Starbuck and James Leuba to the psychology of religious conversion.[46] He expresses appreciation for Starbuck's empirical approach to the psychology of conversion, noting, for example, that his statistical studies show that the conversions that occur in young people brought up in evangelical circles are quite similar to the growth into a larger spiritual life which is a normal phase of adolescence in every class of human beings. The age is the same, usually falling between fourteen and seventeen; the symptoms are the same (the sense of incompleteness and imperfection, brooding, depression, morbid introspection, sense of sin, anxiety about the hereafter, distress over doubts); and the result is the same—"a happy relief and objectivity as confidence in self gets greater through the adjustment of one's faculties to the wider outlook" that the experience affords, and this means, in effect, that conversion "is in its essence a normal adolescent phenomenon, incidental to the passage from the child's small universe to the wider intellectual and spiritual life of maturity."[47]

Leuba's work, which is more theoretical, focuses on the religious aspects or features of conversion. James notes in this regard that Leuba, in his valuable article on the psychology of conversion, "subordinates the theological aspect of the religious life almost entirely to its moral aspect," for he defines the religious sense as "the feeling of unwholeness, of moral

44. James, *The Varieties of Religious Experience*, 198.
45. Ibid.
46. Ibid. James cites Starbuck's *The Psychology of Religion* and Leuba's "A Study in the Psychology of Religious Phenomena." Both were students of G. Stanley Hall at Clark University.
47. James, *The Varieties of Religious Experience*, 198–99.

imperfection, of sin, to use the technical word, accompanied by the yearning after the peace of unity," and he also says that the word *religion* "is getting more and more to signify the conglomerate of desires and emotions springing from the sense of sin and its release."[48]

Noting that the conception of conversion as fundamentally moral covers an immense number of cases, James considers the case of S. H. Hadley, who became an active rescuer of alcoholics in New York following his conversion.[49] Hadley tells about the night that he "sat in a saloon in Harlem, a homeless, friendless, dying drunkard." He had pawned or sold everything that would buy a drink, had not eaten for days and had been suffering from delirium tremors which he called "the horrors" for four nights. He recalled having often said that he would never be a tramp, "for when that time comes, if ever it comes, I will find a home in the bottom of the river." He realized that this time had come but "the Lord so ordered it that when that time did come I was not able to walk one quarter of the way to the river." As Hadley sat there thinking, he "seemed to feel some great and mighty presence" and later he learned that "it was Jesus, the sinner's friend." He went up to the bar, pounded it with his fist, said that he would never take another drink and felt that he would die on the street before morning. But then something said to him, "If you want to keep this promise, go and have yourself locked up." He went to the nearest station house and asked to be put into a cell.[50]

The cell he was placed in was narrow, and "it seemed as though all the demons that could find room came in that place with me."[51] But this was not the only company he had: "No, praise the Lord; that dear Spirit that came to me in the saloon was present, and said, Pray. I did pray, and though I did not feel any great help, I kept on praying. As soon as I was able to leave my cell I was taken to the police court and remanded back to my cell. I was finally released, and found my way to my brother's house, where every care was given me."[52] While lying in bed that night, he thought of Jerry M'Auley's rescue mission on Water Street, and went there the following evening. The house was packed, and after listening to the testimonies of twenty-five or thirty persons, all of whom had been saved from rum, he made up his mind that he would either be saved or die there. When the invitation was given, he knelt down with a crowd of drunkards and as he listened to Mrs. M'Auley

---

48. Ibid., 201.

49. Ibid. Leuba presents the case of S. H. Hadley in "A Study in the Psychology of Religious Phenomena," 331–32, 384–85.

50. James, *The Varieties of Religious Experience*, 201–2.

51. Ibid., 202.

52. Ibid.

praying fervently for them "a conflict was going on for my poor soul!" A blessed whisper said, "Come," but the devil said, "Be careful." He halted, for a moment and then with a breaking heart said, "Dear Jesus, can you help me?" What happened next was indescribable: he felt "the glorious brightness of the noonday sun shine into my heart" and felt that he "was a free man." From that moment he has never wanted a drink of whiskey and has never had enough money to make him take one. He promised God that night that if he would take away his appetite for strong drink, he would work for him all his life. The excerpt from his account concludes that "he has done his part, and I have been trying to do mine."[53]

James notes that Leuba "rightly remarks that there is little doctrinal theology in such an experience, which starts with the absolute need of a higher helper, and ends with the sense that he has helped us"; and he adds that Leuba provides "other cases of drunkards' conversions which are purely ethical, containing, as recorded, no theological beliefs whatever."[54] He suggests, however, that "in spite of the importance of this type of regeneration, with little or no intellectual readjustment," Leuba "surely makes it too exclusive."[55] He notes that this type of regeneration "corresponds to the subjectively centered form of morbid melancholy, of which Bunyan and Alline were examples." But as James's earlier lecture on the sick soul demonstrated, "there are objective forms of melancholy also, in which the lack of rational meaning of the universe, and of life anyhow, is the burden that weighs upon one—you remember Tolstoy's case. So there are distinct elements in conversion, and their relations to individual lives deserve to be discriminated."[56] In a footnote James cites the case of John Stuart Mill, who emerged from a crisis of apathetic melancholy by reading Marmontel's *Memoirs* and William Wordsworth's poetry. James suggests that this is an example of a conversion that was intellectually inspired.[57]

---

53. Ibid, 202–3. Hadley's account of his conversion is from Leuba's article. James indicates that Hadley has also written a pamphlet titled "Rescue Mission Work," which includes accounts of other conversions from drunkenness. He adds that there is also a collection of cases in the appendix to Leuba's article. It is noteworthy that the conversion occurred when Hadley and the others were being prayed for by Mrs. M'Auley. There are parallels here between his conversion and that of Saint Augustine, who heard the voice of chastity from across the garden. Their voices may be reminiscent of the voice of the mother following birth and thus invite or support the view that one is experiencing a second birth.

54. Ibid., 203.

55. Ibid.

56. Ibid., 203–4.

57. Ibid., 204; see Mill, *Autobiography* 141, 148; see also Marmontel, *Memoirs of Jean Francois Marmontel*; and Wordsworth, *The Poetical Works of William Wordsworth*.

Thus, here, as with his earlier discussion of association theory and religious conversion, James emphasizes the importance of systems of ideas—ideas that are subject to emotional influence and moral aims but that are not reducible to them. However, it is important to note that James does not think of systems of ideas in a purely rational sense, for as he emphasizes in his chapter on association in *The Principles of Psychology*, ideas typically come to us in the form of images or visualized objects. For example, "rooms, landscapes, buildings, pictures, or persons with whose look we are very familiar, surge up before the mind's eye with all the details of their appearance complete, as soon as we think of any one of their component parts."[58] Thus, "some persons, in reciting printed matter by heart, will seem to see each successive word, before they utter it, appear in its order on an imaginary page," and "a certain chess player, one of those heroes who train themselves to play several games at once blindfold, is reported to say that in bed at night after a match the games are played all over again before his mental eye, each board being pictured as passing in turn through each of its successive stages."[59]

There are examples of such visualized objects in the religious conversions that James has already presented, such as those that involve Scripture texts that come to impress themselves on the mind and seem to leap off the page on which they are printed. There are also visual appearances of Christ and other spiritual personages. Thus, what James seems not to want to relinquish are the elements of the conversion experience that reflect the workings of the mind, including the play of the imagination.[60]

Following his observation that Leuba's examples tend to minimize the role played by mental processes in religious conversions, James goes on to note that some persons are simply unlikely to experience a religious conversion, and the reason for this is that "religious ideas cannot become the centre of their spiritual energy."[61] They may be excellent persons, servants of God in practical ways, but "they are either incapable of imagining the invisible; or else, in the language of devotion, they are life-long subjects of 'barrenness' and 'dryness.'"[62] In some cases this ineptitude for religious faith may be intellectual in its origin. Their religious faculties may be checked in their natural tendency to expand. They may, for example, have beliefs

---

58. James, *The Principles of Psychology*, 1:555.

59. Ibid.

60. See Pruyser's chapter "Illusion Processing in Religion" in *The Play of the Imagination*, 152–78.

61. James, *The Varieties of Religious Experience*, 204.

62. Ibid.

about the world that are inhibitive, such as the pessimistic and materialistic beliefs "within which so many good souls, who, in former times would have freely indulged their religious propensities, find themselves nowadays, as it were, frozen."[63] Or they may be inhibited by "the agnostic vetoes upon faith as something weak and shameful, under which so many of us today lie cowering, afraid to use our instincts."[64] James notes that "in many persons such inhibitions are never overcome. To the end of their days they refuse to believe, their personal energy never gets to its religious center, and the latter remains inactive in perpetuity."[65]

James also notes that there are persons for whom conversion is problematic because they are temperamentally ill-suited for it. As he puts it, they are simply "anesthetic on the religious side, deficient in that category of sensibility."[66] Suggesting that they are "spiritually barren," he notes that they "may admire and envy faith in others, but can never compass the enthusiasm and peace which those who are temperamentally qualified for faith enjoy."[67] On the other hand, there is the possibility that this temperamental deficiency may "turn out eventually to have been a matter of temporary inhibition" so that even late in one's life some release may take place, and the hardened heart "may soften and break into religious feeling."[68] Such cases, James concludes, "suggest the idea that sudden conversion is by miracle," and as long as such cases present themselves, "we must not imagine ourselves to deal with irretrievably fixed classes."[69]

Returning to Edwin Starbuck's work, James indicates that "there are two forms of mental occurrence in human beings, which lead to a striking difference in the conversion process, a difference to which Professor Starbuck has called attention."[70] Drawing once again on his own earlier work on association in *The Principles of Psychology*, he observes:

> You know how it is when you try to recollect a forgotten name. Usually you help the recall by working for it, by mentally running over the places, persons, and things with which the word was connected. But sometimes this effort fails: you feel then as if the harder you tried the less hope there would be, as though

---

63. Ibid.
64. Ibid.
65. Ibid.
66. Ibid., 204–205.
67. Ibid., 205.
68. Ibid.
69. Ibid.
70. Ibid.

the name were *jammed,* and pressure in its direction only kept it all the more from rising. And then the opposite expedient often succeeds. Give up the effort entirely; think of something altogether different and in half an hour the lost name comes sauntering into your mind, as Emerson says, as carelessly as if it had never been invited. Some hidden process was started in you by the effort, which went on after the effort ceased, and made the result come as if it came spontaneously.[71]

James concludes that there is thus "a conscious and voluntary way and an involuntary and unconscious way in which mental results may get accomplished; and we find both ways exemplified in the history of conversion, giving us two types, which Starbuck calls the *volitional type* and the *type by self-surrender* respectively."[72] In the *volitional* type, the regenerative change is usually gradual. Although it generally "consists in the building up, piece by piece, of a new set of moral and spiritual habits," there "are always critical points at which the movement forward seems much more rapid."[73] Starbuck compares this to the athlete who suddenly awakens to an understanding of the fine points of the game and to a real enjoyment of it; and to the musician who suddenly reaches a point where pleasure in the technique of the art falls away "and in some moment of inspiration he becomes the instrument through which music flows."[74] Thus, as James notes, "Even in the most voluntarily built-up sort of regeneration, there are passages of partial self-surrender interposed; and in the great majority of all cases, when the will has done its uttermost towards bringing one close to the complete unification aspired after, it seems that the very last step must be left to other forces and performed without the help of its activity. In other words, self-surrender becomes then indispensable."[75]

Noting that in many cases of the *voluntary* type of religious conversion "relief persistently refuses to come until the person ceases to resist, or to make an effort in the direction he desires to go," Starbuck cites the following statements by his correspondents: "I simply said, 'Lord, I have done all I can; I leave the whole matter with Thee;' and immediately there came to me a great peace"; or, "all at once it occurred to me that I might be saved, too,

---

71. Ibid.; see James, *The Principles of Psychology,* 1:587–88. He draws here on the work of Shadworth H. Hodgson, who notes that volition has no power of calling up images but only of rejecting and selecting from those that are offered through spontaneous associations. See Hodgson, *Theory of Practice,* 1:394–400.

72. James, *The Varieties of Religious Experience,* 206.

73. Ibid.

74. Ibid.

75. Ibid., 208.

if I would stop trying to do it all myself, and follow Jesus: somehow I lost my load."[76] Starbuck suggests—and James agrees—that there are two things occurring here in the mind of the candidate for conversion: the present incompleteness or wrongness ("sin") that one is eager to escape from and the positive ideal that one longs to embrace. Because for most of us the sense of present wrongness is a far more distinct piece of our consciousness than is the imagination of any positive ideal we can aim at, the sense of "sin" commands our attention. Yet, at the same time our conscious straining is letting loose subconscious allies behind the scenes, and these in their way "work toward rearrangement."[77] Moreover, the rearrangement toward which these deeper forces tend is different from what we consciously conceive, so this rearrangement may be interfered with by our conscious efforts.[78]

Thus, in Starbuck's view, to exercise one's personal will is to remain in the region where the imperfect self is emphasized, whereas when the subconscious forces take the lead, the better potential self is directing the operation. In effect, this self is no longer on the periphery but has become the organizing center. Thus, Starbuck advises one to relax and allow the larger Power which has been welling up in one's own being "to finish in its own way the work it has begun."[79] By yielding, one gives "one's self over to the new life, making it the center of a new personality, and living, from within, the truth of it which had before been viewed objectively."[80]

James observes that the theological way of this yielding or *self-surrender* is expressed in phrases like "Man's extremity is God's opportunity" while the physiological way of describing it would be, "Let one do all in one's own power, and one's nervous system will do the rest."[81] Or, to state it in the terms that James has been employing throughout the lecture, "When the new center of personal energy has been subconsciously incubated so long as to be just ready to open into flower, 'hands off' is the only word for us, it must burst forth unaided!'"[82]

James acknowledges that he has been using "the vague and abstract language of psychology" to describe the crisis that occurs in the conversion experience, but he believes that this language helps to explain "why

---

76. Ibid.; see Starbuck, *The Psychology of Religion*, 91.
77. James, *The Varieties of Religious Experience*, 209.
78. Ibid.
79. Ibid., 210; see Starbuck, *The Psychology of Religion*, 115.
80. James, *The Varieties of Religious Experience*, 210; see Starbuck, *The Psychology of Religion*, 115.
81. James, *The Varieties of Religious Experience*, 210.
82. Ibid.

self-surrender has been and always must be regarded as the vital turning-point of the religious life, so far as the religious life is spiritual and no affair of outer works and ritual and sacraments."[83] In fact, "the whole development of Christianity in inwardness has consisted in little more than the greater and greater emphasis attached to this crisis of self-surrender."[84] This means that "psychology and religion are in perfect harmony to this point, for both acknowledge that there are forces seemingly outside of the conscious individual which bring redemption to his life."[85] On the other hand, in defining these forces as "subconscious" and speaking of their effects as due to "incubation," psychology implies "that they do not transcend the individual's personality; and herein she diverges from Christian theology, which insists that they are direct supernatural operations of the Deity."[86] James suggests, however, that we need not consider this divergence final but leave the question in abeyance for a while, for "continued inquiry may enable us to get rid of some of the apparent discord."[87]

THE PSYCHOLOGY OF SELF-SURRENDER

At this point in the lecture James focuses on "the psychology of self-surrender" and its relevance to religious conversion. He begins by noting that "when you find a man living on the ragged edge of his consciousness, pent in to his sin and want and incompleteness, and consequently inconsolable, and then simply tell him that it is well with him, that he must stop his worry, break with his discontent, and give up his anxiety, you seem to him to come with pure absurdities."[88] This is because "the only positive consciousness he has tells him that all is *not* well, and the better way you offer sounds as if you proposed to him to assert cold-blooded falsehoods."[89] No, "'the will to believe' cannot be stretched as far as that. We can make ourselves more faithful to a belief of which we have the rudiments, but we cannot create a belief out of whole cloth when our perception actively assures us of its opposite. The better mind proposed to us comes in that case in the form of a pure negation of the only mind we have, and we cannot actively will a pure negation."[90]

83. Ibid.
84. Ibid., 210–11.
85. Ibid., 211.
86. Ibid.
87. Ibid.
88. Ibid.
89. Ibid., 212.
90. Ibid. "The Will to Believe" is the title of James's address to the philosophical

James suggests, therefore, that there are only two ways to get rid of anger, worry, fear, despair or other undesirable affections: "One is that an opposite affection should overpoweringly break over us, and the other is by getting so exhausted with the struggle that we have to stop,—so we drop down, give up, and *don't care* any longer. Our emotional brain-centers strike work, and we lapse into a temporary apathy."[91] He adds that there is documentary proof that this state of temporary exhaustion frequently forms part of the conversion crisis. James cites the case of the American clergyman David Brainerd, who relates that during a solitary walk on July 10, 1739, he suddenly became aware of the fact that all of his "contrivances and projects to effect or procure deliverance and salvation for myself were utterly in vain," and he felt "totally lost."[92] He continues:

> I saw that it was forever impossible for me to do anything towards helping or delivering myself, that I had made all the pleas I ever could have made to all eternity; and that all my pleas were vain, for I saw that self-interest had led me to pray, and that I had never once prayed from any respect to the glory of God . . . I saw that I had been heaping up my devotions before God, fasting, praying, etc., pretending, and indeed really thinking sometimes that I was aiming at the glory of God; whereas I never once truly intended it, but only my own happiness.[93]

---

clubs at Yale and Brown Universities and was published in the *New World* in June 1896. It was republished the following year as the first essay in his *The Will to Believe and Other Essays in Popular Philosophy*, 1–31. In the essay he discusses the fact that religion says essentially two things: First, that the best things are the more eternal things; and second, that we are better off now if we believe the first affirmation to be true. James goes on to suggest that in order to discuss the religious hypothesis, we need to treat it as a living option, and as such, it is a *momentous* option, for we have much to gain, even now, by our belief, and much to lose, even now, by our unbelief. It is also a *forced* option, because we cannot escape the issue by remaining skeptical and waiting for more light, for although we avoid error if religion is untrue, we lose the good if it is true as certainly as if we positively choose to disbelieve. James suggests that to preach skepticism on the grounds that there is insufficient evidence for religion is tantamount to telling us that yielding to our fear of being in error is better than yielding to our hope that it may be true (James, *The Will to Believe and Other Essays in Popular Philosophy*, 26). James concludes that the decision to believe or not believe is a personal one and that we ought "to respect one another's mental freedom" in this regard, for only then only will "we bring about the intellectual republic," and only then will "we have that spirit of inner tolerance without which all our outer tolerance is soulless" (ibid., 30).

91. James, *The Varieties of Religious Experience*, 212.

92. Ibid., 212–13. This and the following quotations from Brainerd's account are from Edwards and Dwight, *Memoirs of the Rev. David Brainerd*, 45–47.

93. James, *The Varieties of Religious Experience*, 213.

Brainerd remained in this state of mind from Friday to Sunday evening. That evening he was walking in the same solitary place and in a mournful melancholy state. He was attempting to pray "*but found no heart to engage in that or any other duty; my former concern, exercise, and religious affections were now gone. I thought that the Spirit of God had quite left me; but still was not distressed; yet disconsolate, as if there was nothing in heaven or earth could make me happy.*"[94] Brainerd continued his effort to pray, feeling "*very stupid and senseless,*" for nearly half an hour and then, "as I was walking in a thick grove, unspeakable glory seemed to open to the apprehension of my soul. I do not mean any external brightness, nor any imagination of a body of light, but it was a new inward apprehension or view that I had of God, such as I never had before, nor anything which had the least resemblance to it."[95]

James indicates that he has italicized "the passage which records the exhaustion of the anxious emotion."[96] He adds that in a large percentage, perhaps the majority of such accounts, the writers "speak as if the exhaustion of the lower and the entrance of the higher emotion were simultaneous" although they often speak as if "the higher activity drove the lower out."[97] In any event, what seems indisputable is the fact "that both conditions—subconscious ripening of the one affection and exhaustion of the other—must simultaneously have conspired, in order to produce the result."[98] In a footnote, James suggests that if we view the whole phenomenon as a change in equilibrium we could say that "the movement of new psychic energies towards the personal center and the recession of old ones toward the margin (or the rising of some objects above, and the sinking of others below the conscious threshold) were only two ways of describing an indivisible event."[99] James observes that Starbuck is right when he says that "self-surrender" and "new determination," though seeming to be such different experiences, are "really the same thing," for, as Starbuck notes, "Self-surrender sees the change in terms of the old self; determination sees it in terms of the new."[100]

James concludes his first lecture on conversion with the observation that there are persons who do not experience such exhaustion of their

---

94. Ibid. (italics original).
95. Ibid. (italics original).
96. Ibid., 214.
97. Ibid., 214–15.
98. Ibid., 215.
99. Ibid., 214.
100. Ibid., 214–15; see Starbuck, *Psychology of Religion*, 160.

capacity for feeling or even the absence of any acute previous feeling before the higher condition bursts forth. He suggests that these "are the most striking and memorable cases, the cases of instantaneous conversion to which the conception of divine grace has been most peculiarly attached."[101] James points to the case of Stephen Bradley is an example and indicates that other cases will be presented in the second lecture on conversion.

INSTANTANEOUS CONVERSIONS

James begins his second lecture on conversion with the observation that he will finish the subject of conversion by first considering "those striking instantaneous instances" in which "a complete division is established in the twinkling of an eye between the old life and the new."[102] These instantaneous conversions "of which Saint Paul's is the most eminent" often occur "amid tremendous emotional excitement and perturbation of the senses."[103] He suggests that conversion of this type is "an important phase of religious experience, owing to the part which it has played in Protestant theology, and it behooves us to study it conscientiously on that account."[104]

To provide the basis for a more generalized account James begins with a few concrete instances of this type of conversion experience. The first is Henry Alline whom he previously discussed in his lectures on the sick soul and on the divided self.[105] Here he focuses on Alline's report of March 26, 1775, the day "on which his poor divided mind became unified for good."[106] This report is far too lengthy to present here, but especially significant as far as the phenomenon of instantaneous conversion is concerned is his account of how he picked up an old Bible that was lying on a chair and "opening it without any premeditation, cast my eyes on the 38th Psalm, which was the first time I ever saw the word of God: it took hold of me with such power that it seemed to go through my whole soul, so that it seemed as if God was praying in, with, and for me."[107]

Just then his father called the family together for prayers, but he paid no attention to his father's prayer. Instead he continued praying in the words

---

101. James, *The Varieties of Religious Experience*, 215–16.
102. Ibid., 217.
103. Ibid.
104. Ibid.
105. Ibid., 159, 173–75.
106. Ibid., 217; see Alline, *The Life and Journal of the Rev. Henry Alline*. The full quotation includes excerpts from pages 31–40 of the journal.
107. James, *The Varieties of Religious Experience*, 218.

of the psalm. As he did so, he saw a light that he had seen on previous occasions, but it appeared different this time, for "as soon as I saw it, the design was opened to me, according to his promise, and I was obliged to cry out: Enough, enough, O Blessed God!"[108] The change in him was instantaneous. In less than half an hour after his soul was set at liberty, "the Lord discovered to me my labor in the ministry and call to preach the gospel."[109] Alline related to his parents the next morning what "God had done for my soul and declared to them the miracle of God's unbounded grace."[110]

James cites another case of instantaneous conversion, a young man mentioned by James Leuba in a then-recent article in the *American Journal of Psychology*. An Oxford graduate, he was the son of a clergyman. However: "between the period of leaving Oxford and my conversion I never darkened the door of my father's church, although I lived with him for eight years, making what money I wanted by journalism, and spending it in high carousal with anyone who would sit with me and drink it away. So I lived, sometimes drunk for a week together, and then a terrible repentance, and would not touch a drop for a whole month."[111] All this time, up to thirty-three years of age,

> I never had a desire to reform on religious grounds. But all my pangs were due to some terrible remorse I used to feel after a heavy carousal, the remorse taking the shape of regret after my folly in wasting my life in such a way—a man of superior talents and education. This terrible remorse turned me gray in one night, and whenever it came upon me I was perceptibly grayer the next morning. What I suffered in this way is beyond the expression of words. It was hell-fire in all its most dreadful tortures. Often did I vow that if I got over "this time" I would reform. Alas, in about three days I fully recovered, and was as happy as ever. So it went on for years, but, with a physique like a rhinoceros, I always recovered, and as long as I let drink alone, no man was as capable of enjoying life as I was.[112]

---

108. Ibid., 219. It is likely that verse 10 of Psalm 38 played a significant role in his new outlook because it refers to the fact that one had lost the light of one's eyes, i.e., become blind to the purposes of God. Also noteworthy is Psalm 38's emphasis on one's "foolishness" (v. 5) and one's unhealthy relationships (vv. 11–12, 16). As I noted in our discussion of his case in chapter 3, much of his spiritual struggle focused on his role as a ringleader among friends who were into "frolicking and carnal mirth" (ibid., 173–74).

109. Ibid., 219.

110. Ibid.

111. Ibid., 220; see Leuba, "A Study in the Psychology of Religious Phenomena."

112. James, *The Varieties of Religious Experience*, 221.

But then, without any preparation or anticipation, he had a conversion experience. He says that he "was converted in my own bedroom, in my father's rectory house at precisely three o'clock in the afternoon of a hot July day (July 13, 1886). I was in perfect health, having been off from the drink for nearly a month. I was in no way troubled about my soul. In fact, God was not in my thoughts that day. A young lady friend sent me a copy of Professor [Henry] Drummond's *Natural Law in the Spiritual World*, asking me my opinion of it as a literary work only. Being proud of my critical talents and wishing to enhance myself in my new friend's esteem, I took the book to my bedroom for quiet, intending to give it a thorough study, and then write her what I thought of it."[113] He read the words "He that hath the Son has life eternal, he that hath not the Son hath not life," and it was in the reading of these words "that God met me face to face."[114] He had previously read these words scores of times, but "I was now in God's presence and my attention was absolutely 'soldered' on to this verse, and I was not allowed to proceed with the book till I had fairly considered what these words really involved. Only then was I allowed to proceed, feeling all the while that there was another being in my bedroom, though not seen by me. The stillness was very marvelous, and I felt extremely happy."[115]

He goes on to relate that he suffered a temporary relapse. He succumbed to alcohol one more time but has subsequently never touched a drop of alcohol or smoked his pipe. He concludes: "Since I gave up to God all ownership in my own life, he has guided me in a thousand ways, and has opened my path in a way almost incredible to those who do not enjoy the blessing of a truly surrendered life."[116]

James cites a third case of instantaneous conversion, that of M. Alphonse Ratisbonne, a freethinking French Jew, to Catholicism.[117] Ratisbonne's older brother had been converted to Catholicism and had entered the priesthood, but he himself was irreligious and felt a certain antipathy toward his apostate brother. But when, at the age of twenty-nine, he was in Rome, he began to have conversations with a French gentleman who tried to convert him to the Catholic faith. The most this man was able to accomplish after two or three conversations was to get him to agree, half-jokingly,

---

113. Ibid. See Drummond, *Natural Law in the Spiritual World*.

114. James, *The Varieties of Religious Experience*, 221. He is referring here to John 3:36.

115. Ibid., 221. See Drummond, *Natural Law in the Spiritual World*.

116. James, *The Varieties of Religious Experience*, 223.

117. James indicates that the following account is from a letter that Ratisbonne wrote to a clerical friend. See Bussierre, *The Conversion of Marie Alphonse Ratisbonne Followed by a Letter from M. A. Ratisbonne to M. Dufriche-Desgenettes*.

to wear a religious medal around his neck and read a copy of a short prayer to the Virgin. However, the next day when he was coming out of a café, his friend was driving by in a carriage. The friend invited him to ride with him but asked him to wait for a few minutes while he performed some duty at a church. Instead of waiting outside, he entered the church. It was poor, small, and empty. No work of art attracted his attention, and he looked mechanically over its interior without having any particular thoughts. He later recalled that a black dog trotted by as he mused. Then, in an instant, "the dog had disappeared, the whole church had vanished [and] I no longer saw anything" or "more truly I saw, O my God, one thing alone."[118] He was lying prostrate on the ground, bathed in tears, when his friend called him back to life. He could not reply to his friend's questions, but finally he took the medal that he had put around his neck and kissed the image of the Virgin, radiant with grace, which was on the medal, and he exclaimed, "Oh, indeed, it was She! It was indeed She!" He had experienced a vision of the Virgin.[119]

Ratisbonne goes on to relate that he did not know where he was or even who he was, that he "only felt myself changed and believed myself another me; I looked for myself in myself and did not find myself."[120] But he felt in the bottom of his soul a "most ardent joy." He could not speak and had no desire to reveal what had happened but he felt something solemn and sacred within him which prompted him to ask for a priest. With his heart still trembling, he knelt before the priest, and although he was unable to give an account of the faith which he had acquired he felt that "in an instant the bandage had fallen from my eyes; and not one bandage only, but the whole manifold of bandages in which I had been brought up."[121] One after another the bandages disappeared "even as the mud and ice disappear under the rays of the burning sun."[122]

If he were asked how he came to this new insight—after all, "I had never opened a book of religion or even read a single page of the Bible," nor had he given any thought to the "dogma of original sin"—he could say only that "on entering that church I was in darkness altogether, and on coming out of it I saw the fullness of the light."[123] The closest analogy to what he experienced is that of a person born blind who suddenly gains his sight: "He sees but cannot define the light which bathes him and by means of which

118. James, *The Varieties of Religious Experience*, 225.
119. Ibid.
120. Ibid.
121. Ibid.
122. Ibid.
123. Ibid., 226.

he sees the objects which excite his wonder."[124] If, then, "we cannot explain physical light, how can we explain the light which is the truth itself?" All that he could say is that without having any knowledge of the letter of religious doctrine, he now intuitively perceived its sense and spirit:

> Better than if I saw them, I *felt* those hidden things; I felt them by the inexplicable effects they produced in me. It all happened in my interior mind; and those impressions, more rapid than thought, shook my soul, revolved and turned it, as it were, in another direction, towards other aims, by other paths.[125]

James says that he could cite many more cases, but that these three will suffice to show "how real, definite, and memorable an event a sudden conversion may be to him who has this experience."[126] At its height one seems to be a passive spectator or to be undergoing an astounding process performed upon oneself from above. Also, as "there is too much evidence of this for any doubt of it to be possible," theology, "combining this fact with doctrines of election and grace, has concluded that the spirit of God is with us at these dramatic moments in a peculiarly miraculous way, unlike what happens at any other juncture of our lives."[127]

James cites examples of Christian groups (such as the Moravian Protestants) that endorse instantaneous conversion as the norm, and he notes that in the Revivalism of Great Britain and America "we have, so to speak, the codified and stereotyped procedure to which this way of thinking has led."[128] But as far as the individuals who have had this experience are concerned, it has the feeling of being a miracle rather than a natural process: "Voices are often heard, lights seen, or visions witnessed; automatic motor phenomena occur; and it always seems, after the surrender of the personal will, as if an extraneous higher power has flooded in and taken possession. Moreover the sense of renovation, safety, cleanness, rightness, can be so marvelous and jubilant as well to warrant one's belief in a radically new substantial nature."[129]

James also cites passages from the writings of the New England Puritan Joseph Alleine and from Jonathan Edwards that offer doctrinal interpretations of these experiences, but he adds that whatever role "suggestion and

---

124. Ibid.
125. Ibid.
126. Ibid.
127. Ibid., 226–27.
128. Ibid., 228.
129. Ibid.

imitation may have played in producing them in men and women in excited assemblies," instantaneous conversions "have at any rate been in countless individual instances an original and un-borrowed experience."[130] If, then, we were "writing the story of the mind from the purely natural-history point of view, with no religious interest whatever, we should still have to write down man's liability to sudden and complete conversion as one of his most curious peculiarities."[131]

THE SUBCONSCIOUS REGION OF THE MIND

This very fact, however, raises the question whether these conversions are a miracle in which God is present in a way that is truly unique, or might this whole phenomenon "be a strictly natural process," one that is "divine in its fruits" but is "neither more nor less divine in its mere causation and mechanism than any other process, high or low, of man's interior life?"[132] By way of addressing this question, James asks his auditors "to listen to some more psychological remarks," and he returns to the discussion in his first lecture, on conversion as "the shifting of men's center of personal energy and the lighting up of new crises of emotion."[133] James points out that he explained this phenomenon "as partly due to explicitly conscious processes of thought and will, but as due largely also to the subconscious incubation and maturing of motives deposited by the experiences of life."[134] Noting that when ripe, these motives burst into flower, he proposes at this point to speak, in a somewhat less vague way than previously, about "the subconscious region, in which such processes of flowering may occur."[135]

James begins by observing that up until recently the unit of mental life that figured most prominently in psychology was the single "idea." Now, however, the expression "field of consciousness" has "come into vogue in the psychology books."[136] This expression reflects the tendency of psychologists to focus on the total mental state, or the entire wave of consciousness or field of objects present to the thought at any given time. These psychologists acknowledge that it is impossible to outline this wave or field with any

---

130. Ibid., 229–30. See Alleine, *The Solemn Warnings of the Dead*; see also Edwards, *Edwards on Revivals*.

131. James, *The Varieties of Religious Experience*, 229–30.

132. Ibid.

133. Ibid.

134. Ibid., 231.

135. Ibid.

136. Ibid.

definiteness, but several things can be said about this field of consciousness. One is that as our mental fields succeed one another, each has its center of interest around which the objects of which we are less and less attentively conscious fade to a margin so faint that its limits are impossible to determine. Another is that some fields are wide and others are narrower. A third is that we tend to value a wide field over a narrow field because with the wider field we see masses of truth together and often get glimpses of relations that we intuit rather than see. This is because these relations venture beyond the field into remote regions of objectivity. At other times— for example, of drowsiness, illness or fatigue—"our fields may narrow almost to a point, and we find ourselves correspondingly oppressed and contracted."[137]

Most important, individuals have constitutional differences with regard to the width or narrowness of their field of consciousness. There are those who are organizing geniuses with vast fields of mental vision. They are able to visualize a whole program of future operations. In contrast, ordinary persons lack this magnificent inclusive view: "They stumble along, feeling their way, as it were, from point to point, and often stop entirely."[138] Narrowest of all are "certain diseased conditions" in which "consciousness is a mere spark, without memory of the past or thought of the future, and with the present narrowed down to some one simple emotion or sensation of the body."[139] And yet, despite these differences in the width of the field of consciousness the important fact that this field-of-consciousness formula brings to our attention is "the indetermination of the margin."[140] Although the matter that exists on the margins is outside or beyond our conscious awareness, it nonetheless "helps both to guide our behavior and to determine the next movement of our attention."[141]

James likens this mental state to a magnetic field to which our center of energy is drawn like a compass needle. As for what exists beyond the margin, there is "our whole past store of memories" as well as "the entire mass of residual powers, impulses, and knowledges that constitute our empirical

---

137. Ibid.

138. Ibid.

139. Ibid., 231–32. It is noteworthy in this regard that the basis for a diagnosis of dementia is that there is evidence of memory impairment. See American Psychiatric Association, *Diagnostic and Statistical Manual of Mental Disorders*, 4th ed., 148; see also the diagnostic criteria of mild and major neurocognitive disorder in American Psychiatric Association, *Diagnostic and Statistical Manual of Mental Disorders*, 5th edition, 605–14. James also appears to have in mind persons whose consciousness is controlled by a single insistent or fixed idea. See James, *The Principles of Psychology*, 2:545.

140. James, *The Varieties of Religious Experience*, 232.

141. Ibid.

The Psychology of Religious Conversion 141

self."¹⁴² Elements of both are ready at hand to cross over the margin and enter the field. Moreover, the outlines between what is actual and what is only potential at any moment of our conscious life are so vaguely drawn "that it is always hard to say of certain mental elements whether we are conscious of them or not."¹⁴³

James notes in this connection that the most important step forward in psychology since he has been a student of the science was the discovery first made in 1886 that at least in certain subjects not only is there "the consciousness of the ordinary field, with its usual center and margin," but there is also "an addition thereto in the shape of a set of memories, thoughts, and feelings which are extra-marginal and outside of the primary consciousness altogether."¹⁴⁴ Also, these memories, thoughts, and feelings "must be classed as conscious facts of some sort" because they "are able to reveal their presence by unmistakable signs."¹⁴⁵ James calls this the most important step forward in psychology because, unlike other advances in psychology, "this discovery has revealed to us an entirely unsuspected peculiarity in the constitution of human nature."¹⁴⁶ Furthermore, "this discovery of a consciousness existing beyond the field, or subliminally as Mr. [Frederick] Myers terms it, casts light on many phenomena of religious biography."¹⁴⁷

James acknowledges that the demonstration of this phenomenon has largely been based on studies of unusually suggestible hypnotic subjects and hysteric patients, but "the elementary mechanisms of our life are presumably so uniform that what is shown to be true in marked degree of some persons is probably true in some degree of all, and may in a few be true in an extraordinarily high degree."¹⁴⁸ James suggests that the "most important consequence of having a strongly developed ultra-marginal life of this sort

142. Ibid.
143. Ibid.
144. Ibid.
145. Ibid.
146. Ibid.

147. Ibid., 233. James notes that he cannot provide in these lectures the evidence on which this discovery is based, but he indicates that it is presented in many recent books and cites in particular Alfred Binet's *Alterations in Personality*. Frederick Myers wrote several articles on "the subliminal consciousness" that were published in *Proceedings of the English Society for Psychical Research* in the early 1890s. Eugene Taylor notes in *William James on Exceptional Mental States* that "James's great attraction to Myers's work lay not in psychic phenomena themselves but rather in Myers's emphasis on growth-oriented aspects of the subconscious" (179). James's eulogy on "Frederick Myers's Service to Psychology" was published in 1901. See also Murphy and Ballou, *William James on Psychical Research*, 55–57, 211–39.

148. James, *The Varieties of Religious Experience*, 233.

is that one's ordinary fields of consciousness are liable to incursions from it of which the subject does not guess the source, and which, therefore, take for him the form of unaccountable impulses to act, or inhibitions of action, of obsessive ideas, or even of hallucinations of sight or hearing."[149] The impulses may, for example, take the form of automatic speech or writing, the meaning of which one may not understand even when uttering it. James notes that Myers has given the name of *automatism*, sensory or motor, emotional or intellectual, to this whole sphere of effects—a term that indicates that they "are due to 'uprushes' into the ordinary consciousness of energies originating in the subliminal parts of the mind."[150]

He states that the simplest example of an automatism is a posthypnotic suggestion: "You give a hypnotized subject, adequately susceptible, an order to perform a certain act—usual or eccentric, it makes no difference—after he wakes from his hypnotic sleep," and "when the signal comes or the time upon which you have told him that the act must ensue, he performs it."[151] However, in doing so he has no recollection of the suggestion, and he invariably comes up with an improvised pretext for why he is doing it, especially if it involves an eccentric behavior. It is even possible to suggest to a subject "to have a vision or hear a voice at a certain interval after waking, and when the time comes the vision is seen or the voice heard, with no inkling on the subject's part of its source."[152]

James also cites the use of suggestion with hysterical patients, noting that in "the wonderful explorations by Binet, Janet, Breuer, Freud, Mason, Prince and others of the subliminal consciousness of patients with hysteria we have revealed to us whole systems of underground life, in the shape of memories of a painful sort which lead a parasitic existence, buried outside of the primary fields of consciousness, and making irruptions there into with hallucinations, pains, convulsions, paralyses of feeling and of motion, and the whole procession of symptoms of hysteric disease of body and of mind. Alter or abolish by suggestion these subconscious memories and the patient immediately gets well. His symptoms were automatisms, in Mr. Myers's use of the word."[153]

149. Ibid., 234.
150. Ibid.
151. Ibid.
152. Ibid.
153. Ibid., 234–35. In his Lowell Lectures, delivered at the Lowell Institute in Boston in 1896, James devoted a whole lecture to the topic of automatisms. At the close of the lecture he noted that one can verify the reality of the subliminal for oneself and he suggested that his auditors might experiment with the technique of automatic writing between now and the next lecture. See Taylor, *William James on Exceptional Mental*

James acknowledges that these "clinical records sound like fairy-tales when one first reads them, yet it is impossible to doubt their accuracy."[154] Moreover, they not only throw a wholly new light on our natural constitution but also make a further step inevitable. He explains: "Interpreting the unknown after the analogy of the known, it seems to me that hereafter, wherever we meet with a phenomenon of automatism, be it motor impulses, or obsessive idea, or unaccountable caprice, or delusion, or hallucination, we are bound first of all to make search whether it be not an explosion, into the fields of ordinary consciousness, of ideas elaborated outside of these fields in subliminal regions of the mind. We should look, therefore, for its source in the Subject's subconscious life."[155] In the case of hypnotic suggestion, we ourselves create the source so we know it directly. In the case of hysteria, the lost memories need to be extracted from the patient's subliminal regions by one or another of the methods employed by the authors he has mentioned.[156] In other pathological cases, such as insane delusions or psychopathic obsessions, the source may be more difficult to discover, but it too may be found in the subliminal regions of the mind. James concludes that much work still needs to be done in developing methods of discovering

---

States, 52. In his lecture in *The Varieties of Religious Experience* on the reality of the unseen (lecture 3) James cites a case of automatic writing (62). Later, in his lecture on other characteristics of religious experience (lecture 19) he notes that motor automatisms, although rarer than the sense of a divine or spiritual presence, tend to be even more convincing, for here "the evidence is dynamic; the God or spirit moves the very organs of their body" (Taylor, *William James on Exceptional Mental States*, 478). In a footnote, he cites the case of a friend of his, "a first-rate psychologist," who has told him that "the appearance of independent actuation in the movements of his arm, when he writes automatically, is so distinct that it obliges him to abandon a psychophysical theory which he had previously believed in, the theory, that we have no feeling of the discharge downwards of our voluntary motor-centers. We must normally have such a feeling, he thinks, or the *sense of an absence* would not be so striking as it is in these experiences" (ibid.). He concludes the footnote by citing two recent books that the author claims are not his words but those of Jehovah in the one case, and of a prophet in the other (ibid.).

154. James, *The Varieties of Religious Experience*, 235.

155. Ibid.

156. James does not cite the writings by Janet, Breuer, Freud, Mason, or Prince here. But he discusses the work of Pierre Janet and Alfred Binet on hysteria in a section of his chapter on the relations of minds to other things, a chapter titled "'Unconsciousness' in Hysterics" in *The Principles of Psychology*, 1:202–14. He is also referring here to Josef Breuer and Sigmund Freud's *Studies on Hysteria*, published in 1895. Morton Prince's "Contributions to the Study of Hysteria and Hypnosis," presented at the 1891 meeting of the American Neurological Association, was published in 1899. R. Osgood Mason was a New York physician who had written on cases of multiple personality disorder. See Taylor, *William James on Exceptional Mental States*, 81–82.

and verifying these sources, but he suggests that religious experiences can play an important role in this regard.[157]

THE FRUITS FOR LIFE

Following this discussion of the subconscious region of the mind, James recalls the cases of Henry Alline, Stephen Bradley, David Brainerd and the Oxford graduate. He notes that if we view their experiences from the psychological side only—thus leaving aside the question of their value for the future spiritual life of the individual—we will be inclined to class their experiences with other automatisms and to conclude that the real difference between instantaneous conversions and more gradual conversions is due to a rather simple psychological peculiarity, namely, that those who experience the instantaneous form have "a large region in which mental work can go on subliminally, and from which invasive experiences, abruptly upsetting the equilibrium of the primary consciousness, may come."[158] James says that he sees no reason why those who emphasize the instantaneous conversion (here he specifically mentions Methodists) should object to this psychological point of view, for as he argued in his very first lecture the worth of a thing cannot be decided by its origin.[159] Rather, our opinion of the significance and value of a human event or condition must be decided on empirical grounds exclusively, and this means that if "the *fruits for life* of the state of conversion are good, we ought to idealize and venerate it, even though it a piece of natural psychology; if not, we ought to make short work with it, no matter what supernatural being may have infused it."[160] This undoubtedly explains why he made note of the fact that in the case of the conversion of Stephen Bradley we have no information regarding the conversion's effect on his later life.

On the other hand, if the *fruits for life* are the basic criterion for the worth of a conversion, how do we apply this criterion? In his view, this

---

157. In a footnote James acknowledges that there are cases in which a religious experience may not involve an irruption from the subliminal region, for example, an experience that is more accurately ascribed to a merely physiological nerve storm, or "discharging lesion" like that of epilepsy. It is also possible that a religious experience may be adequately explained by a mystical or theological hypothesis. But he wishes for the moment to limit himself to the more "scientific" view and later discuss "the question of its absolute sufficiency as an explanation of all the facts" (James, *The Varieties of Religious Experience*, 236).

158. Ibid., 237.

159. Ibid., 18–19.

160. Ibid., 237 (italics original).

needs to be determined on a case-by-case basis, for there is no distinctive mark that separates persons who have experienced a religious conversion from those who have not. After all, the human qualities that are said to be the signs or expressions of the second birth are to be found among persons who have not experienced a religious conversion. However, if we consider an individual convert we cannot ignore "the extraordinary momentousness of the fact of his conversion to the individual himself who gets converted."[161] There are higher and lower limits of possibility set to each person's life, so "when we touch our own upper limit and live in our own highest center of energy, we may call ourselves saved, no matter how much higher someone else's center may be."[162] Thus, "what is attained is often an altogether new level of spiritual vitality, a relatively heroic level, in which impossible things have become possible, and new energies and endurances are shown."[163] Furthermore, the "personality is changed, the man *is* born anew, whether or not his psychological idiosyncrasies are what give the particular shape to his metamorphosis."[164] Thus, although James endorses George Albert Coe's view that "the ultimate test of religious values is nothing psychological, nothing definable in terms of *how it* happens, but something ethical, definable only in terms of *what is attained*,"[165] the word "ethical" does not really capture what he himself has in mind, as he is thinking of the fruits for life in a more self-generative sense. One is, after all, a new person.[166]

James concludes his discussion of the *fruits for life* criterion with a brief clarification of his position with regard to the spiritual aspects of the instantaneous conversion. He seeks to make clear that in arguing that a well developed subliminal self is a necessary *condition* for being converted in the instantaneous way he is not excluding the idea that higher spiritual agencies are involved in the conversion experience. In fact, he suggests that the possession of a fully developed subconscious region may be the very avenue through which these spiritual agencies make themselves known to an individual. Thus, the "perception of external control which is so essential a feature in conversion might, in some cases at any rate, be interpreted as the orthodox interpret it: forces transcending the finite individual might impress him on condition of his being what we may call a subliminal

161. Ibid., 239.
162. Ibid.
163. Ibid., 241.
164. Ibid.
165. Ibid.; Coe, *The Spiritual Life,* 144 (italics original to James).
166. See my discussion of the new person in Capps, *The Resourceful Self,* 135–37, 156. This sense of being a new person may involve a process of self-recognition due to the fact that one's subliminal self has entered one's field of conscious awareness.

human specimen."[167] But in any case, "the *value* of these forces would have to be determined by their effects, and the mere fact of their transcendency would of itself establish no presumption that they were more divine than diabolical."[168] In short, "the notion of a subconscious self certainly ought not at this point of our inquiry to be held to *exclude* all notion of a higher penetration." The point, rather, is that "if there be higher powers able to impress us, they may get access to us only through the subliminal door."[169]

ASSURANCE AND HAPPINESS

In the concluding segment of the lecture James focuses on the feelings that immediately fill the hour of the conversion experience. The first one to be considered is the sense of higher control, which is not always but very often present. Noting examples of it in Henry Alline, Stephen Bradley and David Brainerd he suggests "the need of such a higher controlling agency" by a brief reference that the French Protestant Adolphe Monod makes to the crisis of his own conversion. It occurred in Naples when he was in his early adulthood.

Monod says that his sadness at the time "was without limit," and that it had gotten such possession of him that "it filled my life from the most indifferent external acts to the most secret thoughts, and corrupted at their source my feelings, my judgment, and my happiness."[170] Monod realized that "to expect to put a stop to this disorder by my reason and my will, which were themselves diseased, would be to act like a blind man who should pretend to correct one of his eyes by the aid of the other equally blind one."[171] It was evident that he had "no resource save in *some influence from without*," and at that very moment he remembered the promise of the Holy Ghost and he learned, from necessity, "what the positive declarations of the Gospel had never succeeded in bringing home to me."[172] And so, he believed "for the first time in my life, in this promise, in the only sense in which it answered the needs of my soul, in that, namely, of a real external supernatural action, capable of giving me thoughts, and taking them away from me, and exerted on me by a God as truly master of my heart as he is of the rest of nature."[173]

167. James, *The Varieties of Religious Experience*, 242–43.
168. Ibid., 243.
169. Ibid. Italics original.
170. Ibid.; see Monod, *Souvenirs de sa vie*.
171. James, *The Varieties of Religious Experience*, 243–44.
172. Ibid., 244.
173. Ibid.

In effect, Monod abandoned all his "personal resources" and from this day onwards "a new interior life began for me."[174] His melancholy had not disappeared "but it had lost its sting," and hope "had entered my heart."[175]

James notes the "admirable congruity of Protestant theology with the structure of the mind as shown in such experiences," for this theology emphasizes that "in the extreme of melancholy the self that consciously *is* can do absolutely nothing."[176] He quotes rather extensively from Martin Luther's commentary on Paul's Epistle to the Galatians and notes that Luther's main point in this selection is that "the more literally lost you are, the more literally you are the very being whom Christ's sacrifice has already saved."[177] James adds that "faith that Christ has genuinely done his work was part of what Luther meant by faith, which so far is faith in a fact intellectually conceived of," but he notes that this is only one part of Luther's faith, the other part being far more vital: "This other part is something not intellectual but immediate and intuitive, the assurance, namely, that I, the individual I, just as I stand, without one plea, etc., am saved now and forever."[178]

Noting that he prefers to call this "the state of assurance" rather than "the faith-state," James suggests that its characteristics can be easily enumerated, although "it is probably difficult to realize their intensity, unless one has been through the experience one's self."[179] The central characteristic is "the loss of all of worry, the sense that all is ultimately well with one, the peace, the harmony, the *willingness to be,* even though the outer conditions should remain the same."[180] He notes that "a passion of willingness, of acquiescence, of admiration, is the glowing center of this state of mind."[181]

The second characteristic of the state of assurance is "the sense of perceiving truths not known before."[182] Here James cites Leuba's observation

---

174. Ibid.

175. Ibid.

176. Ibid.

177. Ibid., 245; see Luther, *A Commentary upon the Epistle of Paul to the Galatians.*

178. James, *The Varieties of Religious Experience,* 246. The term "faith-state" occurs in a quotation from Leuba's "A Study in the Psychology of Religious Phenomena," 345–47. Leuba observes that the faith-state is "that state of confidence, trust, union with all things, following upon the achievement of moral unity," and that its value "lies in the fact that it is the psychic correlate of a biological growth reducing contending desires to one direction; a growth which expresses itself in new affective states and new reactions; in larger, nobler, more Christ-like activities."

179. James, *The Varieties of Religious Experience,* 247–48.

180. Ibid., 248 (italics original).

181. Ibid.

182. Ibid.

that the mysteries of life become clear but are difficult if not impossible to express in words. In fact, one finds oneself at a loss for words.[183] James indicates that he will take up this feature of the experience later in his lectures on mysticism.

Finally, a third feature of this state of assurance is "the objective change which the world often appears to undergo."[184] Here James reminds readers of his comment in his lecture on the sick soul that "when we come to study the phenomenon of conversion or religious regeneration, we shall see that a not infrequent consequence of the change operated in the subject is a transfiguration of the face of nature in his eyes."[185] In his discussion of religious melancholy and, more specifically, the case of Leo Tolstoy he had noted that when one is in the depths of melancholy there is usually a similar change but in the reverse direction, for to the melancholy person the world "looks remote, strange, sinister and uncanny, its very color is gone, and its breath is cold."[186] Now, in his discussion of the state of assurance that the religious conversion effects he notes that the "appearance of newness beautifies every object," and that this is "the precise opposite of that other sort of newness, that dreadful unreality and strangeness in the appearance of the world, which is experienced by melancholy patients."[187]

Suggesting that "this sense of clean and beautiful newness within and without is one of the commonest entries in conversion records," James cites Jonathan Edwards's account of this sense of inner and external newness: "After this my sense of divine things gradually increased and became more and more lively, and had more of that inward sweetness. The appearance of everything was altered; there seemed to be, as it were, a calm, sweet cast, or appearance of divine glory, in almost everything. God's excellency, his wisdom, his purity and love, seemed to appear in everything; in the sun, moon, and stars; in the clouds and blue sky; in the grass, flowers, and trees; in the water and all nature."[188] Edwards adds that among all the works of nature, scarcely anything "was as sweet to me as thunder and lightning; formerly nothing had been so terrible to me. Before, I used to be uncommonly terrified with thunder and to be struck with terror when I saw a thunderstorm rising; but now, on the contrary, it rejoices me."[189] James also cites a woman

---

183. Ibid. See Leuba, "A Study in the Psychology of Religious Phenomena," 352.
184. James, *The Varieties of Religious Experience*, 248.
185. Ibid., 151.
186. Ibid.
187. Ibid., 248.
188. Ibid., 248–49; see Dwight, *The Life of Jonathan Edwards*, 61.
189. James, *The Varieties of Religious Experience*, 248–49.

in Starbuck's manuscript collection who noted that the immediate effect of her conversion "was like entering another world, a new state of existence. Natural objects were glorified, my spiritual vision was so clarified that I saw beauty in every material object in the universe, the woods were vocal with heavenly music."[190]

James suggests that these and other reports of the objective change which the world appears to undergo invite us to take special note of one form of sensory automatism, that of hallucinatory or pseudohallucinatory luminous phenomena, which psychologists term *photisms*. Noting that "Saint Paul's blinding heavenly vision seems to have been a phenomenon of this sort," James cites several other examples of experiences of luminosity, including that of Charles Finney, who writes: "All at once the glory of God shone upon and round about me in a manner almost marvelous. A light perfectly ineffable shone in my soul that almost prostrated me on the ground. This light seemed like the brightness of the sun in every direction. It was too intense for the eyes ... I think I knew something, then, by actual experience, of that light that prostrated Paul on the way to Damascus. It was surely a light such as I could not have endured long."[191]

James also cites Leuba's case of a Mr. Peck, who went in the morning into the fields to work, and all of a sudden "the glory of God appeared in all his visible creation. I well remember we reaped oats, and how every straw and head of the oats seemed, as it were, arrayed in a kind of rainbow glory, or to glow, if I may so express it, in the glory of God."[192] In a footnote James suggests that these reports of sensorial photism "shade off into what are evidently only metaphorical accounts of the sense of new spiritual illumination."[193] He cites his earlier quotation from David Brainerd's account of his conversion experience in which Brainerd reports, "As I was walking in a thick grove, unspeakable glory seemed to open to the apprehension of my soul. I do not mean any external brightness, for I saw no such thing, nor any imagination of a body of light in the third heavens, or anything of that nature, but it was a new inward apprehension or view that I had of God."[194]

James also cites other examples from Starbuck's manuscript collection, in which the one who experiences conversion appears to be speaking metaphorically. One is a case that is similar to that of Stephen Bradley, who, as we

---

190. Ibid., 250.

191. Ibid., 252; see Finney, *Memoir Written by Himself*, 34.

192. James, *The Varieties of Religious Experience*, 253; see Leuba, "A Study in the Psychology of Religious Phenomena," 334–35, 353.

193. James, *The Varieties of Religious Experience*, 253.

194. Ibid.; see Edwards and Dwight, *Memoirs of the Rev. David Brainerd*, 46.

saw earlier, had a conversion experience after attending a revival meeting. This convert writes:

> A prayer meeting had been called for at close of evening service. The minister supposed me impressed by his discourse (a mistake—he was dull). He came and, placing his hand upon my shoulder, said: "Do you not want to give your heart to God?" I replied in the affirmative. Then said he, "Come to the front seat." They sang and prayed and talked with me. I experienced nothing but unaccountable wretchedness. They declared that the reason I did not "obtain peace" was because I was not willing to give up all to God. After about two hours the minister said we would go home. As usual, on retiring, I prayed. In great distress, I at this time simply said, "Lord, I have done all I can, I leave the whole matter with thee." Immediately, like a flash of light, there came to me a great peace, and I arose and went into my parents' bedroom and said, "I do feel so wonderfully happy." This I regard as the hour of conversion. It was the hour in which I became assured of divine acceptance and favor. So far as my life was concerned, it made little immediate change.[195]

James notes that, in this case, "the flash of light is metaphorical."[196] As a metaphor, it captures and conveys the young man's overwhelming sense of peace, happiness, and assurance of divine acceptance and favor. His observation that there was little immediate change in his life recalls James's earlier observation that this divine assurance reflects "the sense that all is ultimately well with one" and *the willingness to be* what God would have him be even though, at least for the time being, "the outer conditions should remain the same."[197]

Finally, James suggests that of all the elements of the conversion crisis the most characteristic is the ecstasy of happiness produced. He cites several examples of persons who experienced such intense happiness that they found it almost unbearable. Some wept for joy while others sang, shouted, or even bellowed. One of Starbuck's correspondents said that he "was as light as if walking on air. I felt as if I had gained greater peace and happiness than I had ever expected to experience."[198]

---

195. James, *The Varieties of Religious Experience*, 254.
196. Ibid.
197. Ibid., 248 (italics original).
198. Ibid., 256.

CONVERSION: TRANSIENT OR PERMANENT?

The fact that this state of happiness does not last indefinitely—one person said that it lasted about three days—provides a nice segue for James to conclude the lecture with a few reflections on "the question of the transiency or permanence of these abrupt conversions."[199] He suggests that some of his listeners and readers, aware that numerous backslidings and relapses take place, make these the basis for their interpretation of the conversion experience and therefore dismiss it as so much "hysterics." But this, he notes, is a rather shallow view, both psychologically and religiously, because it misses the point of serious interest "which is not so much the duration as the nature and quality of these shiftings of character to higher levels."[200] Being in love with another person is a useful analogy. Whether it lasts or not, "it reveals new flights and reaches of ideality while it lasts."[201] So too with the conversion experience: "That it should for even a short time show a human being what the high-water mark of his spiritual capacity is, this is what constitutes its importance,—an importance which backsliding cannot diminish, although persistence might increase it."[202] Thus, even if one "backslides"—and this is in no way a guaranteed outcome despite what critics of conversion experiences allege—one has, in fact, had an experience that informs one of one's spiritual capacities, and this makes the experience itself inherently valuable. On the other hand, if one continues to live in accordance with the implications of the conversion experience, one may, in fact, experience an increase in one's spiritual capacity.

James also notes that as a matter of fact all of the more striking instances of conversion that he has cited here have been permanent. The case on which there might be the most doubt is that of Alphonse Ratisbonne, due to the fact that "it suggests so strongly an epileptoid seizure."[203] And yet, as James points out, Ratisbonne's whole future was formed by the few minutes he spent in the small church in Rome, for he gave up his plans of marriage, became a priest, founded a mission of nuns in Jerusalem for the conversion of Jews and remained faithful to his religious vocation until his death in his eighties.[204] James also cites some statistics that Starbuck presents indicating that although a high percentage of the subjects he studied acknowledged

199. Ibid.
200. Ibid., 257.
201. Ibid.
202. Ibid.
203. Ibid.
204. Ibid.

some sort of backsliding (93 percent of the women and 77 percent of the men), only 6 percent experienced relapses from the religious faith which the conversion had confirmed. James ends the lecture with Starbuck's conclusion that the effect of a conversion is to bring with it "a changed attitude towards life, which is fairly constant and permanent, although the feelings fluctuate ... In other words, the persons who have passed through conversion, having once taken a stand for the religious life, tend to feel themselves identified with it, no matter how much their religious enthusiasm declines."[205]

CONCLUSION

James begins the first lecture following the lectures on conversion—the first of three lectures titled "Saintliness"—with the observation that the preceding lecture "left us in a state of expectancy" in that it left us with the question, "What may the practical fruits for life have been, of such seemingly happy conversions as those we heard of?"[206] He suggests that with this question "the really important part of our task opens, for you remember that we began all this empirical inquiry not merely to open a curious chapter in the natural history of human consciousness, but rather to attain a spiritual judgment as to the total value and positive meaning of all the religious trouble and happiness which we have seen."[207]

Yet, as we consider what James accomplishes in his lectures on conversion, it may well be the case that this empirical inquiry into the natural history of human consciousness is no less important than the task that looms ahead, for this inquiry has demonstrated that religious experiences are no less amenable to psychological study than other human experiences. In these lectures James has made a persuasive case for his emphasis on the mental states and processes involved in a religious conversion, a case for his use of association theory to illumine the fact that conversions typically involve a struggle between two conflicting selves, and a case for the concept of fields of consciousness to account for the sudden irruption of new insights and resolutions. These concepts deepen our understanding of what occurs in a religious conversion experience. Moreover, they enhance rather than diminish the significance and momentousness of these experiences. In fact, one could argue that James does more in behalf of these experiences than do the theologians who simply view them as instances of divine agency. James's view that they manifest the workings of the subconscious mind and

---

205. Ibid., 258; see Starbuck, *Psychology of Religion*, 360, 357.
206. James, *The Varieties of Religious Experience*, 259.
207. Ibid.

the evidence he provides in support of this view enable us to see that they reflect the resourcefulness of the human mind when a person is confronted with what seems to be a hopelessly insoluble situation or condition.[208]

Some readers of James's second lecture on conversion may feel that his use of research findings with hypnotized subjects and patients with hysteria to shed light on the various features of religious conversions demeans the religious conversion itself. Yet these very research findings enable him to take note of the fact that the religious conversion involves greater mental complexities than we normally attribute to it. Also, by invoking patients with hysteria he is able to make the point that the religious conversion may and often does contribute to the mental health of the individual, as it, too, contributes to the alteration and abolishment of demoralizing subconscious memories.[209] Thus, as he suggests, the most important fruit for life of the religious conversion experience is that it unleashes "the *willingness to be*" and it does so even though the outer conditions of one's life remain the same, for it is the case not only that all the other fruits for life depend upon *the willingness to be* but also that this very willingness is the first critical step toward *becoming* what one had never thought was even remotely possible.[210]

---

208. This is not, of course, to question or challenge Adolphe Monod's observation that prior to his conversion he "had then no resources save in *some influence from without*" (ibid., 244; italics original). The point, rather, is that he has come to the point where his mind is receptive to the resources available via its subconscious region.

209. Ibid., 235.

210. Ibid., 248.

7

The Saintly Character

James's second lecture on conversion completed the first set of the Gifford Lectures. The second set of lectures, which were presented a year later, begin with the topic of saintliness, and five of the ten lectures are on saintliness. The chapter in *The Varieties* titled "Saintliness" comprises the first three lectures, and the chapter titled "The Value of Saintliness" comprises the fourth and fifth lectures. I will focus here on the first chapter and on James's explication of what he calls "the saintly character."[1]

THE EXPERIENCE OF RELIGIOUS REGENERATION

As I noted in the conclusion to the preceding chapter, James begins his lectures on saintliness with the observation that the concluding lecture on conversion "left us in a state of expectancy" because it prompted us to ask, "What may the practical fruits for life have been, of such movingly happy conversions as those we heard of?"[2] He says that in order to answer this question, we must "first describe the fruits of the religious life, and then we must judge them," and he suggests that the descriptive task ought to be "the pleasantest portion of our business in these lectures."[3] He acknowledges that some features of this description "may be painful, or show human nature

---

1. James, *The Varieties of Religious Experience*, 259–325. The dictionary defines *character* as "the pattern of behavior or personality found in an individual or group" and indicates that a person is *characterized* by his or her "particular qualities, features, or traits." See Agnes, *Webster's New World*, 246.

2. James, *The Varieties of Religious Experience*, 259.

3. Ibid.

in a pathetic light, but it will be mainly pleasant, because the best fruits of religious experience are the best things that history has to show."[4] In fact, "the highest flights of charity, devotion, trust, patience, bravery to which the wings of human nature have spread themselves have been flown for religious ideals."[5]

To illustrate this fact he cites Charles Augustin Sainte-Beuve's history of the abbey of Port-Royal-des-Champs, near Paris.[6] Sainte-Beuve notes that if we penetrate beneath the diversity of circumstances, we find in Christians of different epochs certain qualities that result from the realization of a state of grace, whether this is by means of a jubilee, a general confession, or solitary prayer.[7] These qualities are a fundamental spirit of piety and charity, an inner state of love and humility, an infinite confidence in God, and a severity toward oneself accompanied by tenderness for others.[8] Sainte-Beuve cites Saint Teresa of Avila and the Moravian brothers of Herrnhut as exemplars of these qualities.[9] However, James points out that these "more eminent instances of regeneration" point to the fact that, generally speaking, persons who have experienced such regeneration differ from one another in how they manifest or express these fruits, and he suggests that the primary reason for these differences is that individuals have differing susceptibilities to emotional excitement, which in turn produce different impulses and inhibitions.[10] Thus, at any given moment our moral and practical attitude "is always a resultant of two sets of forces within us, impulses pushing us one way and inhibitions holding us back. 'Yes! yes!' say the impulses; 'No! no!' say the inhibitions."[11]

James goes on to note that we fail to realize how much our inhibitions hold us back because their influence is largely subconscious. But if some great emotional excitement intervenes, such inhibitions will snap like cobwebs.

---

4. Ibid.

5. Ibid., 259–60.

6. Sainte-Beuve, *Port-Royal*. Sainte-Beuve was a French literary critic. He was born in 1804 and died in 1869.

7. In the Roman Catholic Church a jubilee is a year proclaimed as a solemn time for gaining a plenary indulgence and for obtaining absolution, on certain conditions. See Agnes, *Webster's New World*, 773.

8. James, *The Varieties of Religious Experience*, 260. See Sainte-Beuve, *Port-Royal*, 1:106.

9. Ibid. Sainte-Beuve has reference here to the missionary movement founded in Herrnhut, a refugee village in Germany, by Christian David (Count) Zinzendorf in 1722.

10. James, *The Varieties of Religious Experience*, 260.

11. Ibid., 261.

He says he has seen a dandy appear in the street with his face covered with shaving-lather because a nearby house was on fire, and a woman will run among strangers in her nightgown if it is a question of saving her baby's life or her own. There are also situations in which neither emotional state is sovereign—the yes and no are mixed together—and in such situations an act of will is required to solve the conflict. Soldiers in combat situations are well acquainted with this experience. The dread of cowardice impels them to advance, but their fears impel them to run, and their wavering between the one and the other action is only resolved when they collectively, in a pitch of high emotion, either advance or retreat together.[12]

Thus, in cases of religious regeneration, the ignoble inhibitions aided by unworthy impulses vanish. This enables the noble and worthy intentions to become the center of one's personality or character, and it is at this point that the fruits of the religious life emerge: "Magnanimities once impossible are now easy; paltry conventionalities and mean incentives once tyrannical hold no sway. The stone wall inside of him has fallen [and] the hardness in his heart has broken down."[13] James suggests that the rest of us can imagine this experience "by re-calling our state of feeling in those temporary 'melting-moods' into which either the trials of real life, the theater, or a novel sometimes throw us. Especially if we weep! For it is then as if our tears broke through an inveterate inner dam, allowing our moral stagnancies to drain away, leaving us now washed and soft of heart and open to every nobler leading."[14] However, the difference between us and saintly persons is that our "customary hardness quickly returns" whereas in the cases of persons like Saint Teresa, "the melting mood seems to have held almost uninterrupted control," and however these exalted affections have come about, whether "by gradual growth or by a crisis," they have "come to stay."[15]

Before embarking on "the general history of the regenerate character," James cites several examples. He notes that the most numerous examples are those of reformed alcoholics, and he recalls the cases of S. H. Hadley and of the unnamed Oxford graduate mentioned in his lectures on conversion.[16] He also introduces the "classic case" of Colonel James Gardiner, who was cured of sexual temptation in a single hour.[17] As Gardiner was reported

---

12. Ibid., 261–63.
13. Ibid., 267.
14. Ibid.
15. Ibid., 267–68.
16. Ibid., 201–2, 220–23.
17. Ibid., 269; see Doddridge, *Some Remarkable Passages in the Life of the Honourable Colonel James Gardiner*, 23–32.

to have said: "I was effectively cured of all inclination to that sin I was so strongly addicted to that I thought nothing but shooting me through the head would have cured me of it; and all desire and inclination for it was removed, as entirely as if I had been a sucking child; nor did the temptation return to this day."[18] Gardiner also said that he "was much addicted to impurity before his acquaintance with religion; but that, as soon as he was enlightened from above, he felt the power of the Holy Ghost changing his nature so wonderfully that his sanctification in this respect seemed more remarkable than in any other."[19] James notes that these and similar cases are so reminiscent of the results of hypnotic suggestion "that it is difficult not to believe that subliminal influences play the decisive part in these abrupt changes of heart, just as they do in hypnotism."[20] He adds, "Suggestive therapeutics abound in records of cure, after a few sittings, of inveterate bad habits with which the patient, left to ordinary moral and physical influences, had struggled in vain. Both drunkenness and sexual vice have been cured in this way, action through the subliminal seeming thus in many individuals to have the prerogative of inducing relatively stable change. If the grace of God miraculously operates, it probably operates through the subliminal door."[21]

But if so, the problem is that it leaves unexplained the manner in which anything in this subliminal region operates, and this means, at least for the purposes of the lecture, that "we shall do well now to say good-by to the *process* of transformation altogether,—leaving it, if you like, a good deal of a psychological or theological mystery,—and to turn our attention to the fruits of the religious condition, no matter in what way they may have been produced."[22]

Although James said goodbye to the process of transformation in the lecture itself, he adds a footnote at this point in *The Varieties* in which he has more to say about the question of how anything operates in the subliminal region. He cites Starbuck's suggestion that there appears to be a cutting off

---

18. James, *The Varieties of Religious Experience*, 269; see Doddridge, *Some Remarkable Passages in the Life of the Honourable Colonel James Gardiner*, 23–32.

19. James, *The Varieties of Religious Experience*, 269.

20. Ibid., 269–70. In a footnote James cites Starbuck's case of a woman who, having been a smoker for fifteen years, tried to stop smoking when she was forty years old but to no avail. Then when she was fifty-three years old she was sitting by the fire smoking and a voice came to her. It was not a voice that she could hear but rather "as a dream or sort of double think." It said to her, "Louisa, lay down smoking." She replied, "Will you take the desire away?" Instead of answering it kept saying, "Louisa, lay down smoking." Finally, she got up, lay her pipe on the mantel shelf, and never smoked again or had the desire to do so. See Starbuck, *The Psychology of Religion*, 142.

21. James, *The Varieties of Religious Experience*, 270.

22. Ibid.

of the connection between higher and lower cerebral centers, and that this disconnection is often reflected in the way that his correspondents describe their experiences. For example, one correspondent noted that "temptations from without still assail me, but there is nothing *within* to respond to them."[23] Another correspondent said that "although Satan tempts me, there is as it were a wall of brass around me, so that his darts cannot touch me."[24]

James agrees that "functional exclusions of this sort must occur in the cerebral organ," and that "on the side accessible to introspection, their causal condition is nothing but the degrees of spiritual excitement, getting at last so high and strong as to be sovereign."[25] The problem is that "we do not know just why or how such sovereignty comes about in one person and not in another."[26] James suggests that perhaps the best we can do is "to give our imagination a certain delusive help" by means of "mechanical analogies."[27]

He provides a rather complicated analogy based on the idea that the human mind is a many-sided solid with different surfaces, and that it undergoes mental revolutions comparable to the spatial revolutions of this solid object. He imagines a lever raising one of these surfaces so that it is no longer subject to the pull of gravity. The lever would correspond to the emotional influences making for a new life, and the pull of gravity is the drawbacks and inhibitions to which the mind has become accustomed over a long period of time. If the lever fails to reach a certain level of efficacy, the changes it produces are unstable, and the mind relapses to its original state. But if the lever continues to raise the surface higher, it may reach a level where a critical point is passed, and the change becomes irreversible.[28] What especially interests James, therefore, is the role that emotions play in this process of transformation.

---

23. Ibid.
24. Ibid., 271.
25. Ibid.
26. Ibid.

27. Ibid. This is not the first time James mentions mechanical analogies to the functioning of the human mind. As I noted in chapter 6 he suggested the use of "the hackneyed symbolism of a mechanical equilibrium" to explain the shifts that occur in a person's mental system (ibid., 197).

28. Ibid.

THE SPECIFIC FRUITS OF SAINTLINESS

James begins his discussion of "the ripe fruits of religion in a character" by noting that the collective name for these fruits is "saintliness."[29] He says in a footnote that he uses this word, despite the fact that it sometimes has a "sanctimonious" connotation, because there is no other word that suggests "the exact combination of affections" that he will be describing in the course of his discussion.[30] In the text itself he notes that "the saintly character is the character for which spiritual emotions are the habitual center of the personal energy; and there is a certain composite photograph of universal saintliness, the same in all religions, of which the features can easily be traced."[31]

James suggests that this "composite photograph" has four primary features. First, there is "a feeling of being in a wider life than that of this world's selfish little interests; and a conviction, not merely intellectual, but as it were, sensible, of the existence of an Ideal Power."[32] James observes that in Christian saintliness "this power is always personified as God, but it may also take the form of abstract moral ideals, civic or patriotic utopias, or inner visions of holiness or right."[33] Second, there is "a sense of the friendly continuity of the ideal power with one's life, and a willing self-surrender to its control."[34] Third, there is "an immense elation and freedom as the outlines of the confining selfhood melt down."[35] Fourth, there is "a shifting of the emotional center towards loving and harmonious affections, towards 'yes, yes' and away from 'no,' where the claims of the non-ego are concerned."[36] These four "fruits" are typically mentioned in converts' descriptions of the changes that occur in them in the weeks, months, and years following their conversion experiences.

Having identified these four "ripe fruits of religion" James suggests that these "fundamental inner conditions have characteristic practical consequences."[37] He identifies four of these practical consequences. The first

---

29. Ibid.

30. Ibid.

31. Ibid. This reference to the "habitual center of the personal energy" recalls his proposal in his lectures on conversion that "to say that a man is 'converted' means that religious ideas, previously peripheral in his consciousness, now take a central place, and that religious aims form the habitual center of his energy" (ibid., 196).

32. Ibid., 272.

33. Ibid.

34. Ibid., 273.

35. Ibid.

36. Ibid.

37. Ibid.

is *Asceticism*. Here "the self-surrender may become so passionate as to turn into self-immolation," and "it may then so overrule the ordinary inhibitions of the flesh that the saint finds positive pleasure in sacrifice and asceticism, measuring and expressing as they do the degree of his loyalty to the higher power."[38]

The second is *Strength of Soul*. Here "the sense of enlargement of life may be so uplifting that personal motives and inhibitions, commonly omnipotent, become too insignificant for notice, and new reaches of patience and fortitude open up. Fears and anxieties go, and blissful equanimity takes their place."[39]

The third is *Purity*. James points out that "The shifting of the emotional center brings with it, first, an increase of purity."[40] Here "the sensitivity to spiritual discords is enhanced, and the cleansing of existence from aggressive and sensual elements becomes imperative."[41] This means that "occasions of contact with such elements are avoided" because "the saintly life must deepen its spiritual consistency and keep unspotted from the world," and "in some temperaments, this need for purity of spirit takes an ascetic turn, and weaknesses of the flesh are treated with relentless severity."[42]

The fourth is *Charity*. Here the shifting of the emotional center brings "an increase of charity, of tenderness for others" and the ordinary motives of antipathy toward others, especially those with whom one does not share a common bond, are inhibited. As James puts it, "The saint loves his enemies, and treats loathsome beggars as his brothers."[43]

In identifying these practical consequences of the ripe fruits of religion as reflected in saintliness, James does not identify the practical consequences of the third feature of universal saintliness—i.e., the immense elation and freedom that occurs when the outlines of the confining selfhood melt down. I would suggest, however, that the very elation and freedom that characterize this inner condition are, in fact, its practical consequences. Moreover, since the elation and freedom in this case are a function of the melting down of one's confining selfhood, one could argue that this inner condition is essentially the consequence of the first inner condition, which is that one experiences a feeling of being in a wider life than that of this

---

38. Ibid.
39. Ibid.
40. Ibid., 274.
41. Ibid.
42. Ibid.
43. Ibid., 273–74.

world's "selfish little interests."[44] Thus, there is a sense of *self-expansion* that is made possible by one's willing *self-surrender* to the ideal power.

THE SENSE OF A FRIENDLY PRESENCE

James indicates that he now needs "to give some concrete illustrations of these fruits of the spiritual tree."[45] He notes that "the sense of Presence of a higher and friendly power seems to be the fundamental feature in the spiritual life," so he introduces his consideration of the fruits of saintliness with illustrations of this sense of Presence.[46] He begins by noting that "quite apart from anything acutely religious, we all have had moments when the universal life seems to wrap us round with friendliness."[47] His first illustration, from Henry David Thoreau's *Walden*, centers on Thoreau's observation that his experiment of living in the woods was initially somewhat unpleasant because he felt all alone, without human company. But then in the midst of a gentle rain "I was suddenly sensible of such sweet and beneficent society in Nature, in the very pattering of the drops, and in every sight and sound around my house, an infinite and unaccountable friendliness all at once, like an atmosphere, sustaining me, as made the fancied advantages of human neighborhood insignificant, and I have never thought of them since. Every little pine-needle expanded and swelled with sympathy and befriended me. I was so distinctly made aware of the presence of something kindred to me, that I thought no place would ever be strange to me again."[48]

James notes that in the Christian consciousness "this sense of the enveloping friendliness becomes most personal and definite" and here he cites a passage from a sermon by Charles Voysey:

> It is the experience of myriads of trustful souls, that this sense of God's unfailing presence with them in their going out and their coming in, and by night and day, is a source of absolute repose and confident calmness. It drives away all fear of what may befall them. That nearness of God is a constant security against terror and anxiety. It is not that they are at all assured of physical safety, or deem themselves protected by a love which is denied to others, but that they are in a state of mind equally ready to be safe or to meet with injury. If injury [should] befall

---

44. Ibid., 272.
45. Ibid.,
46. Ibid.
47. Ibid.
48. Ibid., 275. See Thoreau, *Walden*, 206.

them, they will be content to bear it because the Lord is their keeper, and nothing can befall them without his will. If it be his will, then injury is for them a blessing and no calamity at all. Thus and thus only is the trustful man protected and shielded from harm.[49]

Voysey adds: "I for one—by no means a thick-skinned or hard-nerved man—am absolutely satisfied with this arrangement, and do not wish for any other kind of immunity from danger and catastrophe. Quite as sensitive to pain as the most highly strung organism, I yet feel that the worst of it is conquered, and the sting taken out of it altogether, by the thought that God is our loving and sleepless keeper, and that nothing can hurt us without his will."[50]

Noting that "more excited expressions of this condition are abundant in religious literature," and that he "could easily weary you with their monotony," James provides an extended account by Sarah Edwards, wife of Jonathan Edwards, of her experience as she lay in bed one night of "a constant, clear, and lively sense of the heavenly sweetness of Christ's excellent love, of his nearness to me, and of my dearness to him; with an inexpressibly sweet calmness of soul in an entire rest in him."[51] She sensed "a glow of divine love come down from the heart of Christ in heaven into my heart in a constant stream, like a stream or pencil of sweet light," and at the same time her "heart and soul all flowed out in love to Christ, so that there seemed to be a constant flowing and reflowing of heavenly love, and I appeared to myself to float or swim, in these bright, sweet beams, like the motes swimming in the beams of the sun, or the streams of his light which come in at the window."[52]

James concludes his discussion of the sense of a friendly presence with the observation that the annals of Catholic saintliness abound in records as ecstatic or even more ecstatic than that of Sarah Edwards, and he mentions the case of a Sister who experienced assaults of divine love that were so powerful that she begged God to "bear gently with my weakness or I shall expire under the violence of your love."[53]

---

49. Ibid., 275–76. See Voysey, *The Mystery of Pain and Death*, 258. Voysey (1828–1912) was subsequently tried as a heretic for denying the doctrine of everlasting hell and deprived of his living as vicar of Healaugh. It appears that his sense of an enveloping friendliness made it difficult if not impossible to believe in the doctrine of everlasting hell.

50. James, *The Varieties of Religious Experience*, 276.

51. Ibid. The account is from Jonathan Edwards's narrative of the revival in New England. See Edwards, *Edwards on Revivals*.

52. James, *The Varieties of Religious Experience*, 276.

53. Ibid., 278.

CHARITY AND TENDERNESS FOR OTHERS

This discussion of the sense of a friendly presence brings James to the fruits of saintliness, which he identified as *asceticism, strength of soul, purity,* and *charity*.[54] He begins with the fourth of these fruits—charity and tenderness for others—especially as reflected in brotherly love. He notes that these feelings are "a usual fruit of saintliness," and that they "have always been reckoned essential theological virtues, however limited may have been the kinds of service which the particular theology enjoined."[55] James suggests that brotherly love follows "logically from the assurance of God's friendly presence" because the idea of our brotherhood is "an immediate inference from that of God's fatherhood of us all."[56] Thus, when Christ bids us to love our enemies and do good to those who hate us, the reason he gives for this is that our heavenly Father "maketh his sun to rise on the evil and on the good, and sendeth rain on the just and on the unjust" (Matthew 5:44-45, KJV).

On the other hand, we should not attempt to explain this self-humility and charity toward others as the result of "the all-leveling character of theistic belief," for although these affections harmonize "with paternal theism beautifully," they are not "mere derivatives of theism."[57] After all, we find them in "the highest degree" in Stoicism, Hinduism and Buddhism. Thus, we should view them

> as coordinate parts of that great complex excitement in the study of which we are engaged. Religious rapture, moral enthusiasm, ontological wonder, cosmic emotion, are all unifying states of mind, in which the sand and grit of the selfhood incline to disappear, and tenderness to rule. The best thing is to describe the condition integrally as a characteristic affection to which our nature is liable, a region in which we find ourselves at home, a sea in which we swim; but not to pretend to explain its parts by deriving them too cleverly from one another. Like love or fear, the faith-state is a natural psychic complex, and carries charity with it by organic consequence.[58]

---

54. Ibid., 273–74.
55. Ibid., 278.
56. Ibid.
57. Ibid., 279.
58. Ibid. It is worth noting that in this instance he uses the term "faith state" whereas in his concluding chapter on conversion he preferred "state of assurance" (247).

Thus, the affections of charity and brotherly love can be explained in natural terms, but the experience of God's friendly presence is one of the ways in which they are activated.

James goes on to cite a case of mental pathology that illustrates the fact that these affections are inherent in the human organism. The case is presented in M. Georges Dumas's book on sadness and joy, in which Dumas "compares the melancholy and the joyous phases of circular insanity, and shows that, while selfishness characterizes the one, the other is marked by altruistic impulses."[59] Dumas observes that in her melancholy period Marie is stingy and useless, "but the moment the happy period begins, sympathy and kindness become her characteristic sentiments. She displays a universal goodwill, not only of intention, but in act . . . She becomes solicitous of the health of other patients, interested in getting them out, desirous to procure work to knit socks for some of them. Never since she has been under my observation have I heard her in her joyous period utter any but charitable opinions."[60] Commenting on the joyous periods that he has witnessed in others, Dumas observes that "unselfish sentiments and tender emotions are the only affective states to be found in them," and the individual's mind "is closed against envy, hatred, and vindictiveness, and wholly transformed into benevolence, indulgence, and mercy."[61]

James concludes that there is "an organic affinity between joyousness and tenderness, and their companionship in the saintly life need in no way occasion surprise."[62] He cites the narratives of conversion collected by Starbuck, noting that the happiness that they report is often accompanied by such statements as "I had more tender feelings for my family and friends"; or, "I spoke at once to a person with whom I had been angry"; or, "I felt everyone to be my friend."[63] James also returns to Sarah Edwards's account of her experience of the sense of Christ's presence. She notes that when she arose the following morning, "I felt a love to all mankind, wholly peculiar in its strength and sweetness, far beyond all that I had ever felt before. The power of that love seemed inexpressible. I thought, if I were surrounded by enemies, who were venting their malice and cruelty upon me, in tormenting me, it would be impossible that I should cherish any feelings towards them but those of love, and pity, and ardent desires for their happiness. I never

---

59. Ibid.; see Dumas, *La Tristesse et la Joie*.
60. James, *The Varieties of Religious Experience*, 279–80.
61. Ibid., 280.
62. Ibid.
63. Ibid.

before felt so far from a disposition to judge and censure others, as I did that morning."[64]

James also cites the case of Richard Weaver, a coal miner and a semi-professional pugilist in his younger days, who became a much-beloved evangelist. Weaver had a tendency to want to fight after he had been drinking, and once he pounded a man who had insulted a young woman. But he turned his life around and not only resisted the temptation to provoke a fight but refused to be drawn into a fight initiated by others.[65]

These cases prompt James to ask whether it is in fact possible to love your enemies, "not simply those who happen not to be your friends, but your *enemies*, your positive and active enemies."[66] Is Jesus's injunction to love your enemies "a bit of verbal extravagance, meaning that we should, as far as we can, abate our animosities," or should we take it literally? Apart from certain cases of intimate personal relationships, it has seldom been taken literally, but it prompts us to ask whether there can in general be a level of emotion so unifying, so capable of obliterating human differences "that even enmity may become an irrelevant circumstance," unable "to inhibit the friendlier interests aroused?"[67] If positive well-wishing could attain such a supreme degree of excitement, those who achieve it may well be considered superhuman: "Their life would be morally discrete from the life of other men," and there is no way of knowing "what the effects might be; they might conceivably transform the world."[68]

James points out, however, that, psychologically speaking, the precept to love your enemies is not self-contradictory. On the contrary: "It is merely the extreme limit of a kind of magnanimity with which, in the shape of pitying tolerance of our oppressors, we are fairly familiar. Yet if radically followed, it would involve such a breach with our instinctive springs of action as a whole, and with the present world's arrangements, that a critical point

---

64. Ibid. Sarah Edwards was criticized by the members of her husband's church in Northampton, Massachusetts, for her love of jewelry and nice clothes. The fact that the Edwards family lived better than most of the other townspeople became a matter of contention. The church elders would often express their criticism by forcing Edwards to make his family budget public and among the itemized budget items was an expenditure of eleven pounds for his wife's new locket and chain. The humiliation of being forced to reveal his family's budget led in turn to his request for a fixed salary instead of an amount to be determined annually. This request led to a salary dispute that dragged on for six years until the town finally agreed to his request. See Capps, *Young Clergy*, 84, 89.

65. Ibid., 281–83.
66. Ibid., 283.
67. Ibid.
68. Ibid.

would practically be passed, and we should be born into another kingdom of being. Religious emotion makes us feel that other kingdom to be close at hand, within our reach."[69]

On the other hand, love for one's enemies is not the only way this heightened expression of magnanimity occurs. Another is showing love "to anyone who is personally loathsome."[70] James observes that the annals of saintliness reveal a "curious mixture of motives" in this regard. The pure and simple motive of charity is one of these motives. Another is asceticism (which he will discuss in greater detail later). And a third is humility or the desire to disclaim any distinction between oneself and those who would normally be viewed as beneath oneself. James notes that all three were at work when Saint Francis of Assisi and Saint Ignatius Loyola exchanged their garments with those of filthy beggars, or when religious persons devote their lives to the care of those with leprosy or other especially unpleasant diseases. More extreme examples are the accounts of Saint Francis of Assisi kissing lepers and of saints who cleansed the sores and ulcers of their patients with their own tongues. James suggests that these and similar stories cause us "to admire and shudder at the same time."[71]

STRENGTH OF SOUL: EQUANIMITY, RESIGNATION, FORTITUDE, AND PATIENCE

James indicates that he will now speak about the fact that the faith-state that arouses human love also produces equanimity, resignation, fortitude, and patience, which he earlier identified as features of the *strength of soul*, the second of the four fruits of saintliness.[72]

James suggests that what someone has called "'a paradise of inward tranquility' seems to be faith's usual result; and it is easy, even without being religious one's self, to understand this."[73] He alludes to his earlier discussion of the sense of God's presence and to his reference there to "the unaccountable feeling of safety" that one may experience when one senses the presence of God. He adds, "And, indeed, how can it possibly fail to steady the nerves, to cool the fever, and appease the fret, if one be sensibly conscious that, no matter what one's difficulties for the moment may appear to be,

---

69. Ibid., 283–84.
70. Ibid., 284.
71. Ibid.
72. Ibid. Resignation has been added here to the three features of the strength of soul identified earlier (273).
73. Ibid., 285.

one's life as a whole is in the keeping of a power whom one can absolutely trust?"[74] For those who are deeply religious "the abandonment of self to this power is passionate." They not only *say* "God's will be done" but they *feel* it, and "the whole historic array of martyrs, missionaries, and religious reformers is there to prove the tranquil-mindedness, under naturally agitating or distressing circumstances, which self-surrender brings."[75]

Viewing this quality from a psychological perspective, James notes that the temper of tranquil-mindedness differs depending on whether the person is of somber or cheerful temperament. For the somber person it tends to take the form of resignation, and for the cheerful person it takes the form of joyous consent. He cites two examples of the former, Professor Jules Lagneau, "a venerated teacher of philosophy," and Blaise Pascal, a mathematician, physicist, and philosopher. Noting that Lagneau, who had recently died, was "a great invalid," James quotes the following from Lagneau's response shortly before his death to unnamed correspondents who had recently expressed their well-wishes:

> My life, for the success of which you send good wishes, will be what it is able to be. I ask nothing from it, I expect nothing from it. For long years now I exist, think, and act, and am worth what I am worth, only through the despair which is my sole strength and my sole foundation. May it preserve for me, even in these last trials to which I am coming, the courage to do without the desire of deliverance. I ask nothing more from the Source whence all strength cometh, and if that is granted, your wishes will have been accomplished.[76]

Lagneau's reference to "the Source whence all strength cometh" suggests that this response to his well-wishers may have been the source of James's term for this quality of saintliness: i.e., strength of soul. In any event, James

---

74. Ibid.
75. Ibid.
76. Ibid., 285. Lagneau's letter is quoted in the memorial issue of *Bulletin de l'Union pour l'Action Morale*, September, 1894. Lagneau was known for his reflective psychology. See Institut Alain, *La Psychologie Réflexive de Jules Lagneau*. James discusses reflex acts in his chapter on the functions of the brain in *The Principles of Psychology*. He gives this example: "If I stumble as I run, the sensation of falling provokes a movement of the hands towards the direction of the fall, the effect of which is to shield the body from too sudden a shock." He notes that the motion of the arms to break the shock may be called a reflex "since it occurs too quickly to be deliberately intended" (1:12–13). He also discusses semireflex actions: i.e., actions in which instinct and volition are involved on equal terms.

notes that there is something "pathetic and fatalistic about this, but the power of such a tone as a protection against outward shocks is manifest."[77]

Observing that Pascal shares Lagneau's "pessimistic natural temperament," James suggests that Pascal "expresses even more amply the temper of self-surrendering submissiveness."[78] He quotes the following from one of Pascal's prayers:

> I ask you neither for health nor for sickness, for life nor for death; but that you may dispose of my health and my sickness, my life and my death, for your glory, for my salvation, and for the use of your Church and of your saints, of which I would by your grace be one. You alone know what is expedient for me; you are the sovereign master; do with me according to your will. Give to me, or take away from me, only conform my will to yours. I know but one thing, Lord, that it is good to follow you, and bad to offend you. Apart from that, I know not what is good or bad in anything. I know not which is most profitable to me, health or sickness, wealth or poverty, nor anything else in the world. That discernment is beyond the power of men or angels, and is hidden among the secrets of your Providence, which I adore, but do not seek to fathom.[79]

James notes that there are those with "more optimistic temperaments" for whom the resignation is "less passive."[80] He cites the case of Madame Jeanne Marie Guyon, "a frail creature physically" but "of a happy native disposition," who "went through many perils with admirable serenity of soul.[81]

77. James, *The Varieties of Religious Experience*, 286.

78. Ibid.

79. Ibid. James is quoting here from Pascal's *Prières pour les Maladies*. The prayer is published in English translation in Pascal, *Thoughts, Letters, and Minor Works of Blaise Pascal* under the title "Prayer, To Ask of God the Proper Use of Sickness," 366–74. The quoted material is on pages 372–73. It is likely that Pascal was assisted in maintaining this spirit of resignation because, as James notes in his *Psychology: The Briefer Course*, he was one of several persons (John Wesley was another) who was said to have the capacity to become so deeply absorbed in a particular train of thought that they would be totally oblivious not only to ordinary sensations but also to the severest pain (90).

80. James, *The Varieties of Religious Experience*, 286.

81. Ibid. Madame Guyon was one of the early leaders of the Quietist movement in Catholicism. Born in Montargis, France, in 1648, she was married at the age of sixteen to thirty-eight-year-old Jacques Guyon, Twelve years later he died, leaving her with three children. Five years after his death she went to Switzerland to participate in the religious instruction of Huguenots who had recently been reconciled to the Catholic Church. This religious activity launched her on a course of travel, meditation, preaching, and writing that continued until her imprisonment in 1698. In her years of religious activity she became the subject of persistent and widespread rumors that she was guilty of

For example, Madame Guyon notes in her autobiography that when she was sent to prison for heresy, "some of my friends wept bitterly at the hearing of it, but such was my state of acquiescence and resignation that it failed to draw any tears from me . . . There appeared to be in me then, as I find it to be in me now, such an entire loss of what regards myself, than any of my own interests gave me little pain or pleasure; ever wanting to will a wish for myself only the very thing which God does."[82] Also, when she was sailing from Nice to Genoa, a storm kept her at sea for eleven days. She writes: "As the irritated waves dashed around us, I could not help experiencing a certain degree of satisfaction in my mind. I pleased myself with thinking that those mutinous billows, under the command of Him who does all things rightly, might probably furnish me with a watery grave. Perhaps I carried the point too far, in the pleasure which I took in thus seeing myself beaten and bandied by the swelling waters. Those who were with me took notice of my intrepidity."[83]

Noting that the "contempt of danger which religious enthusiasm produces may be even more buoyant still," James cites an episode in a recent autobiography by Frank Bullen titled *With Christ at Sea*, in which the author was on a ship in very bad weather. Bullen writes:

> Shortly after four bells we hauled down the flying-jib, and I sprang out astride the boom to furl it. I was sitting astride the boom when suddenly it gave way with me. The sail slipped through my fingers, and I fell backwards, hanging head downwards over the seething tumult of shining foam under the ship's bows, suspended by one foot. But I felt only high exultation in my certainty of eternal life. Although death was divided from

---

improper relations with her spiritual director and traveling companion, Fr. Francois La Combe. She claimed that the rumors were completely unfounded, but when he avoided her company because of the rumors, she pursued him from Switzerland to Italy and finally to Paris. In 1687 he was imprisoned in Paris for his alleged relations with her, and in 1688 she too was arrested. Through the offices of Madame de Maintenon. the mistress of Louis XIV, she was released and introduced into the royal circle. Her favor at court lasted until 1693 when her teachings aroused opposition from many within the church hierarchy. In 1694 she asked to be cleared of these unofficial charges of doctrinal deviance, and the following year a conference was convened to determine the orthodoxy of her views. Francois Fenelon, archbishop of Cambrai, defended her against the charges, but they lost their case, and she was arrested and imprisoned. In 1699 her quietist views were condemned by papal decree. She was released from prison in 1703 after renouncing her views and continued to write until her death in 1717. See Upham, *Life, Religious Opinions and Experience of Madame de La Mothe Guyon*; Guyon, *Autobiography of Madame Guyon*; and Capps and Capps, *The Religious Personality*, 127–35.

82. James, *The Varieties of Religious Experience*, 286–87.
83. Ibid., 287.

me by a hair's breadth, and I was acutely conscious of the fact, it gave me no sensation but joy. I suppose I could have hung there no longer than five seconds, but in that time I lived a whole age of delight. But my body asserted itself, and with a desperate gymnastic effort I regained the boom. How I furled the sail I don't know, but I sang at the utmost pitch of my voice praises to God that went pealing out over the dark waste of water.[84]

James turns next to martyrdom, noting that it is "the signal field of triumph for religious imperturbability."[85] He cites the case of a Huguenot woman, Blanche Gamond, who was persecuted under Louis XIV. She was severely whipped by six other women, each with a bunch of thick willow rods a yard long. As they struck her again and again, they exclaimed, "Pray now to your God." She later wrote:

> At this moment I received the greatest consolation that I can ever receive in my life, since I had the honor of being whipped for the name of Christ, and in addition of being crowned with his mercy and his consolations. Why can I not write down the inconceivable influences, consolations, and peace which I felt interiorly? To understand them one must have passed by the same trial; they were so great that I was ravished, for there where afflictions abound grace is given superabundantly. In vain the women cried, "We must double our blows; she does not feel them, for she neither speaks nor cries." And how should I have cried, since I was swooning with happiness within?[86]

In concluding his discussion of these qualities of the *strength of soul*, James observes that the "transition from tenseness, self-responsibility, and worry, to equanimity, receptivity, and peace, is the most wonderful of all those shiftings of inner equilibrium, those changes of the personal center of energy, which I have analyzed so often; and the chief wonder of it is that it so often comes about, not by doing, but by simply relaxing and throwing the burden down."[87] He suggests that "this abandonment of self-responsibility seems to be the fundamental act in specifically religious, as distinguished from moral practice," and he notes that this abandonment of self-responsibility "antedates theologies and is independent of philosophies," that, in fact,

---

84. Ibid., 288. See Bullen, *With Christ at Sea*.

85. James, *The Varieties of Religious Experience*, 288.

86. Ibid., 288–89. James is quoting here from Claparède and Goty's *Deux Héroines de la Foi*, 112.

87. James, *The Varieties of Religious Experience*, 289. Here he returns to the theme of relaxation that he introduced in his chapter on the religion of healthy-mindedness.

"mind-cure, theosophy, stoicism [and] ordinary neurological hygiene insist on it as emphatically as Christianity does, and it is capable of entering into closest marriage with every speculative creed."[88] Observing that Christians who have this capacity are "never anxious about the future, nor worry over the outcome of the day," he cites the example of Saint Catherine of Genoa, of whom it was said that "she took cognizance of things, only as they were presented to her in succession, *moment by moment*," for, to her, "the divine moment was the present moment."[89]

PURITY OF LIFE

At this point James takes up the third practical consequence of the fruits of saintliness, that of *purity*. Indicating that "the next religious symptom which I will note is what I have called Purity of Life," he observes that the saintly person "becomes exceedingly sensitive to inner inconsistency or discord, and mixture and confusion grow intolerable."[90] Whatever "taints the pure water of the soul" is repugnant, and along with "this exaltation of the moral sensibilities" there is "an ardor of sacrifice, for the beloved deity's sake, of everything unworthy of him."[91]

Noting that this purity is sometimes achieved in a single stroke while at other times it is more gradual, James cites a case of the more gradual form, that of Billy Bray, whom he introduced briefly in his lectures on conversion.[92] Bray tells about how he eventually conquered his love for

88. Ibid. He cites in this regard Dresser, *Living by the Spirit*; Call, *As a Matter of Course*; and Smith, *The Christian's Secret of a Happy Life*. James referred earlier to Dresser in his discussion of the mind-cure movement in his lecture on the religion of the healthy-minded, 96, 99. I also noted James's friendship with Annie Payson Call in the biographical sketch in chapter 1. See also my discussion of James's use of the books by Call and Smith in Capps, "Relaxed Bodies, Emancipated Minds, and Dominant Calm."

89. James, *The Varieties of Religious Experience*, 289. He is quoting here from Upham's *Life of Madame Catherine Adorna*. In the edition cited in the bibliography, quoted material is on 165–67 (italics original).

90. Ibid., 290.

91. Ibid. It is worth noting that James refers to purity of life as a "symptom." He also uses the word "symptom" in reference to asceticism (296). Although the word *symptom* has the connotation of a condition or manifestation of a disease or disorder it may also have a more neutral connotation, i.e., as any circumstance, event, or condition that accompanies something and indicates its existence or occurrence. See Agnes, *Webster's New World*, 1451. I believe that James is using it here in this more neutral sense, but his use of it alerts us to the fact that he believes that these two practical consequences of the inner condition of saintliness may take aberrant or pathological forms.

92. James, *The Varieties of Religious Experience*, 249, 256. His source for these accounts of Billy Bray, whom he identifies as "an excellent little illiterate English

tobacco. One evening he told a woman that he felt something inside telling him that tobacco was an idol, a lust, and she said that it was the Lord who was telling him this. He took his tobacco out of his pocket and threw it into the fire, and put the pipe under his foot and declared, "Ashes to ashes, dust to dust." However, the following day he had a toothache that was so painful that he did not know what to do. He thought the toothache was due to his having given up smoking, but he said to himself that he would never smoke again even if he lost every tooth he had. He also said "Lord, thou hast told us 'My yoke is easy and my burden is light,'" and when he said this, all the pain left him.[93] He has not smoked since.

In considering the ascetic forms that the impulse for purity of life may take, James focuses on the early Quakers, who battled against what they considered to be the worldliness and insincerity of the ecclesiastical Christianity of their day. Their founder, George Fox, was persuaded that such conventional customs as doffing one's hat and giving titles of respect were a lie and a sham, and his followers renounced them as sacrifices to truth. James cites Fox's account in his journal of the rage that the refusal to doff their hats to anyone provoked in "the priests, magistrates, professors, and people of all sorts" but "especially in priests and professors," and of "the blows, punchings, beatings, and imprisonments that we underwent for not putting off our hats to men!"[94]

James also cites the autobiography of Thomas Elwood, who was at one time a secretary to John Milton, noting that it offers "an exquisitely quaint and candid account of the trials he underwent both at home and abroad, in following Fox's canons of sincerity."[95] Elwood notes that by virtue of "the great goodness of God and a civil education," he had been spared the evils of common debauchery and profaneness, but "by the light of Christ" it was made manifest to him that he possessed other evils, "particularly those fruits and effects of pride that discover themselves in the vanity and superfluity of apparel; which I took too much delight in."[96] So he removed the "unnecessary trimmings" from his apparel. He also ceased to engage in the use of flattering titles and bowing the knee or body in salutation, noting that the latter is "one of the vain customs of the world, introduced by the spirit of this world, instead of the true honor which this is a false representation of, and used in deceit as a token of respect by persons one to another, who have no

---

evangelist," is F. W. Bourne's *The King's Son, a Memoir of Billy Bray*.

93. Ibid., 290–91. James is citing Matt 11:30.
94. Ibid., 292. See Fox, *Journal of George Fox*.
95. Ibid.
96. Ibid., 293. See Elwood, *The History of Thomas Elwood*, 32–34.

real respect one to another." Furthermore, this custom is an emblem of that divine honor that all who take upon themselves the Christian name "ought to pay to Almighty God" and "therefore should not be given to men."[97]

Finally, James quotes from the diary of the Quaker John Woolman, who tells about how he has at various times walked over ground where the dyes that are used in clothing have drained away, causing him to experience a longing "that people might come into cleanness of spirit, cleanness of person, and cleanness about their houses and garments."[98] The fact that dyes were invented partly to please the eyes and partly to hide dirt seems to serve as a metaphor for him of the tendency to hide one's unclean spirit rather than to purify it. Woolman goes on to tell about how his initial decision to cease wearing garments and hats that were dyed caused him to feel that he was setting himself apart from his beloved friends, so he delayed acting on his convictions for nine months, but then he attended a Quaker meeting during which "I was made willing to submit to what I apprehended was required of me."[99]

James suggests that a natural consequence of the "craving for moral consistency and purity" reflected in these personal accounts may well cause one to feel that the outer world is "too full of shocks to dwell in," and to conclude that the only way to unify one's life and keep one's soul unspotted is by withdrawing from it.[100] James cites in this connection Robert Louis Stevenson's observation that learning how to omit is the single most important art in writing and suggests that the law "which impels the artist to achieve harmony in his composition by simply dropping out whatever jars, or suggests a discord, rules also in the spiritual life," for when life is "full of disorder and slackness and vague superfluity," it "can no more have what we call character than literature can have under similar conditions."[101] And so, we have monasteries and communities of sympathetic devotees, and "in their changeless order, characterized by omissions quite as much as constituted by actions, the holy-minded person finds that inner smoothness and cleanness which it is torture to him to feel violated at every turn

---

97. James, *The Varieties of Religious Experience*, 293; see Elwood, *The History of Thomas Elwood* 32–34.

98. James, *The Varieties of Religious Experience*, 294–95. See Woolman, *Journal*.

99. Ibid., 295.

100. Ibid., 296.

101. Ibid. James does not cite his source for the Stevenson observation, but in *Essays in the Art of Writing*, published in 1905, Stevenson notes that "what to put in and what to leave out" is a question that continually arises for the writer, and he adds that "the sphinx that patrols the highways of executive art has no more unanswerable riddle to propound" (93).

by the discordancy and brutality of secular existence."[102] James concludes his discussion of purity by noting that it must be acknowledged that "the scrupulosity of purity may be carried to a fantastic extreme," and observes that it resembles asceticism, the topic to which he now wishes to turn.

ASCETICISM

James begins his consideration of asceticism with the observation that "the adjective 'ascetic' is applied to conduct originating on diverse psychological levels," so he will begin by noting that asceticism has various psychological progenitors. First, asceticism may be a mere expression of organic hardihood, of disgust with too much ease. Second, it may be the fruits of the love of purity as reflected in temperance in meat and drink, simplicity of apparel, and the nonpampering of the body. Third, it may be the fruits of love as reflected in sacrifices that one is happy to make to the Deity whom one acknowledges. Fourth, it may be due to pessimistic feelings about the self combined with theological beliefs concerning expiation; the devotee may feel that by doing penance he is freeing himself now or escaping from worse sufferings hereafter. Fifth, in psychopathic persons mortifications may have an irrational basis, an example of which is an obsession or fixed idea that must be worked off in order to get one's interior consciousness feeling right again. Sixth, ascetic exercises may be prompted by genuine perversions of one's physical sensibilities in which painful stimuli are actually felt as pleasures.[103]

It is apparent that the first form of asceticism is largely a matter of personal temperament; the second, third, and fourth forms are based on religious views and practices; and the fifth and sixth, which are also supported by religious views and practices, are related to pathological conditions, either psychological or physiological, or a combination of the two.[104]

102. James, *The Varieties of Religious Experience*, 298.
103. Ibid., 296–97.

104. The fourth ascetic expression might also reflect a pathological condition as it is due to pessimistic feelings about the self. But it appears from James's examples of this form of asceticism that these feelings are not psychopathological as such, although they could develop into a more psychopathological condition. James's own experience of melancholia (in the French Sufferer case) would be an example of such pessimistic feelings about the self, as he described himself as being "in this state of philosophic pessimism and general depression of spirits about my prospects," and his allusion to the mental patient indicates that he felt that he was in danger of becoming psychopathological (ibid., 160). It is noteworthy, however, that he did not have recourse to ascetic mortifications supported by theological beliefs about expiation but rather thought of reassuring Scripture texts.

James notes, however, that as he now proceeds "to give an instance under each of these heads," it will not be "easy to get them pure," for in cases of ascetic expression "several of the assigned motives usually work together."[105] He also indicates that before citing any examples of these various forms of asceticism, he needs to mention some general psychological principles that apply to all six of them. He especially has in mind here the fact that in the past century "a strange moral transformation" has occurred in the Western world, for "we no longer think that we are called on to face physical pain with equanimity," and "it is not expected of a man that he should either endure it or inflict much of it."[106] In fact, "the way our ancestors looked upon pain as an eternal ingredient of the world's order, and both caused and suffered it as a matter-of-course portion of their day's work fills us with amazement," and "we wonder that any human beings could have been so callous."[107]

The consequence of this historic change is that even in the Roman Catholic Church, "where ascetic discipline has such a fixed traditional prestige as a factor of merit," the more extreme forms of asceticism have "fallen into disuse and even discredit," and self-flagellation "arouses more wonder and fear than emulation."[108] Furthermore, to seek "the easy and pleasant seems instinctive," and "any tendency to pursue the hard and painful as such and for its own sake seems abnormal."[109] Nevertheless, "in moderate degrees it is natural and even usual in human nature to court the arduous," and "it is only the extreme manifestations of the tendency that can be regarded as a paradox."[110] James observes that the psychological reasons for this more moderate position are rather apparent. There are some men and women who "can live on smiles and the word 'yes' forever," but for others, the majority, "this is too tepid and relaxed a moral climate."[111] For them, "passive happiness is slack and insipid, and soon grows mawkish and intolerable" and a certain amount of "austerity and wintry negativity, some roughness, danger, stringency, and effort, some 'no! no!' must be mixed in, to produce the sense of an existence with character and texture and power."[112] James notes that the range of individual differences in this respect is enormous,

---

105. Ibid., 297.
106. Ibid.
107. Ibid., 297–98.
108. Ibid., 298.
109. Ibid.
110. Ibid.
111. Ibid., 298–99.
112. Ibid., 299.

"but whatever the mixture of yeses and noes may be, the person is infallibly aware when he has struck it in the right proportion *for him*. This, he feels, is my proper vocation, this is the *optimum,* the law, the life for me to live. Here I find the degree of equilibrium, safety, calm, and leisure which I need, or here I find the challenge, passion, fight, and hardship without which my soul expires. Every individual soul, in short, like every individual machine or organism, has its own best conditions of efficiency."[113] Even as a machine will run best under a certain steam-pressure or amperage, and an organism functions best under a certain diet, weight, or exercise, so with our souls: "Some are happiest in calm weather" while others "need the sense of tension, of strong volition, to make them feel alive and well."[114] For these latter souls, "whatever is gained from day to day must be paid for by sacrifice and inhibition, or else it comes too cheap and has no zest," and "when characters of this latter sort become religious, they are apt to turn the edge of their need for effort and negativity against their natural self; and the ascetic life gets evolved as a consequence."[115]

In light of this understanding of how the ascetic life appeals to some individuals and not to others, James proceeds to give examples of the six forms or expressions of asceticism. These examples include Thomas Carlyle's habit of beginning the day with a cold bath in a freezing Berlin winter, an example of ascetic expression #1 (organic hardihood, or disgust with too much ease); William Ellery Channing's incapacity for any form of self-indulgence, a combination of ascetic expression #2 (purity in the form of temperance) and ascetic expression #3 (the fruits of love reflected in sacrifices to God); the sacrificial restraints of John Cennick, the first Methodist lay preacher, as a spontaneous response to self-despair, a reflection of ascetic expression #4 (theological beliefs concerning expiation and penance to free himself now or from worse sufferings later); and the extreme forms of self-torture carried out by Henry Suso—a fourteenth-century German mystic—one of which involved an attempt to emulate the sorrows of his crucified Lord by lying down on a cross with thirty protruding iron needles and nails. These were a combination of ascetic expression #4 (theological beliefs concerning expiation and penance to free himself from worse sufferings later) and ascetic expression #5 (a psychopathological mortification that has an irrational basis).[116] James judges Suso's case to have been "distinctly pathological,"

113. Ibid.
114. Ibid.
115. Ibid.
116. Ibid., 308. The Carlyle example is from an unpublished lecture by a Professor Tyndall; the Channing example is from Channing's *Memoirs of William Ellery Channing*; the Cennick example is from Tyerman, *The Life and Times of the Rev. John Wesley*;

and what made it worse was the fact that Suso "did not seem to have had the alleviation, which some ascetics have enjoyed, of an alteration of sensibility capable of actually turning torture into a perverse kind of pleasure."[117] Thus, James cites the case of Marguerite Marie, the founder of the Sacred Heart order, as an example of ascetic expression #6, in which physical pain is experienced as pleasurable. Her biographer points out that "her love of pain and suffering was insatiable," and that "she said that she could cheerfully live till the day of judgment provided she might always have matter for suffering for God; but that to live a single day without suffering would be intolerable"[118]

The case of John Cennick is especially interesting, as it gives James an opportunity to comment on the therapeutic role that ascetic practices may play in an individual's struggle with pessimistic feelings about the self. In the wake of his experience of being convicted of sin, Cennick quit song-singing, card-playing, and going to the theater, and he began fasting, changed his diet, and prayed nine times a day. Finally, after two years of this new regime, he "found peace with God, and went on his way rejoicing."[119] James suggests that Cennick's asceticism initially took the form of self-mortification expressed in the impulse to expiate and do penance, but in the course of time it took "the form of loving sacrifice," and in this form "of spending all we have to show our devotion, ascetic discipline of the severest sort may be the fruit of highly optimistic religious feeling."[120] Here, then, James suggests that the fourth ascetic expression may not be subject to the usual critiques to which penitential actions have been subjected when they also reflect the third ascetic expression in which one is acting out of a genuine love for God.

The Virtue of Obedience

James concludes his discussion of asceticism by identifying three forms of self-mortification that have been recognized as indispensable to perfection in the "ecclesiastically consecrated character."[121] These are the chastity, obedience, and poverty that monks vow to observe.[122] James indicates that he

---

and the Suso example is from Suso's autobiography, the English version of which is titled *The Life of the Blessed Henry Suso, by Himself*.

117. James, *The Varieties of Religious Experience*, 310.

118. Ibid. See Bougaud, *Histoire de la Bienheureuse Marguerite Marie*, 265, 171.

119. Ibid., 302. The quotation is from Tyerman, *The Life and Times of the Rev. John Wesley*, 1:274.

120. Ibid., 302.

121. Ibid., 310.

122. Ibid.

wishes to make a few remarks about obedience and poverty. Jams does not explain why he does not wish to comment on chastity.

Regarding obedience James notes that the secular life of our twentieth century does not hold this virtue in high esteem, but "the duty of the individual to determine his own conduct and profit or suffer by the consequences seems, on the contrary, to be one of our more deeply rooted contemporary Protestant ideals."[123] This is so much the case "that it is difficult even imaginatively to comprehend how men possessed of an inner life of their own could ever have come to think the subjection of its will to that of other finite creatures recommendable."[124] James confesses that he himself finds such obedience to other human beings "something of a mystery" and yet "it evidently corresponds to a profound interior need of many persons, and we must do our best to understand it."[125] He suggests that obedience may serve various purposes. One is that it helps to maintain a firm ecclesiastical organization, which is the context in which obedience was originally declared to be a virtue. Another is that there are times in everyone's life when one can be better counseled by others than by one's self. The inability to decide is one of the commonest symptoms of fatigued nerves, and in these situations "friends who see our troubles more broadly, often see them more wisely than we do," so "it is frequently an act of excellent virtue to consult and obey a doctor, a partner, or a wife."[126]

Noting that these two forms of obedience (i.e., subjecting one's will to the authority of others and voluntarily seeking the counsel of others) are essentially prudential, he suggests that there is a third reason for idealizing obedience, one that is more directly related to the present study of the religious or spiritual life. James explains: "Obedience may spring from the general religious phenomenon of inner softening and self-surrender and throwing one's self on higher powers. So saving are these attitudes felt to be that in themselves, apart from utility, they become ideally consecrated; and in obeying a man whose fallibility we see through thoroughly, we, nevertheless, may feel much as we do when we resign our will to that of infinite wisdom. Add self-despair and the passion of self-crucifixion to this and obedience becomes an ascetic sacrifice, agreeable quite irrespective of whatever prudential uses it might have."[127]

123. Ibid., 310–11.
124. Ibid., 311.
125. Ibid.
126. Ibid.
127. Ibid.

James provides several illustrations of how obedience as an ascetic sacrifice is understood in Roman Catholic writings, and he notes that in Catholic discipline one obeys one's superior as a representative of Christ. He quotes passages from a biography of Ignatius Loyola and from a book on the practice of Christian perfection by Alfonso Rodriguez, a Jesuit priest, and notes that they make the point that in acting in obedience to one's superior, one saves oneself the trouble of having to determine whether or not one is following the will of God.[128] James concludes, however, with an example of the extravagance to which the virtue of obedience has been carried, that of Sister Marie Claire of Port-Royal Abbey being told by a new prelate who saw that she was tenderly attached to her Mother Superior that it would perhaps be better not to speak to the older woman again. The author of the history of Port Royal writes: "Marie Claire, greedy of obedience, took this inconsiderate word for an oracle of God, and from that day forward remained for several years without once speaking to her sister."[129] While James does not comment further on this example of obedience, he is clearly in sympathy with the author's view that obedience in this case was unfortunate.

The Virtue of Poverty

James turns next to the topic of poverty, noting that it has been viewed by all religions as "one adornment of a saintly life."[130] He suggests that since the instinct of ownership is fundamental in human nature, this is one more example of "the ascetic paradox."[131] And yet, "it appears no paradox at all, but perfectly reasonable, the moment one recollects how easily higher spiritual excitements hold lower instincts and impulses in check."[132] He quotes extensively from Alfonso Rodriguez's instructions for monks based on the text, "Blessed are the poor in spirit" (Matt 5:3). Rodriguez emphasizes that a monk's room may have no other furniture than a bed, a table, a bench and a candlestick and that it is not to be ornamented with pictures, armchairs, carpets, curtains, cabinets or bureaus. Nor is one allowed to have food in one's room, even for visitors, or keep a book in which to write one's thoughts. Furthermore, secular persons are not allowed to enter one's room, for, after

---

128. Ibid., 312–13; see Bartoli, *Histoire de Saint Ignace de Loyola d'après les Documents Originaux*; and Rodriguez, *Practique de la Perfection Chrétienne*.

129. James, *The Varieties of Religious Experience*, 314–15. The quotation is from Sainte-Beuve, *Port Royal*, 1:346.

130. Ibid., 315.

131. Ibid.

132. Ibid.

all, "we are all men, and if we were to receive people of the world into our rooms, we should not have the strength to remain within the bounds prescribed, but should at least wish to adorn them with some books to give the visitors a better opinion of our scholarship."[133]

James points out that Hindu fakirs, Buddhist monks, and Muslim dervishes unite with Jesuits and Franciscans in idealizing poverty as the loftiest individual state, and he suggests that it is worthwhile to examine the spiritual grounds for such a seemingly unnatural opinion. The first, which is common to human nature and requires no special religious rationale, is based on the opposition commonly drawn between those who *have* and those who *are*. Observing that we tend to glorify the soldier "who owns nothing but his bare life, and is willing to toss that up at any moment when the cause commands him," James suggests that the soldier is "the representative of unhampered freedom in ideal directions."[134] So too "the laborer who pays with his person day by day, and has no rights invested in the future, offers also much of this ideal detachment."[135] James adds that the loathing of "capital," which is reflected more and more among the laboring classes, "seems largely composed of this sound sentiment of antipathy for lives based on mere having"; he cites in this regard a poem by Edward Carpenter that makes the point that, as James puts it, "lives based on having are less free than lives based either on doing or on being."[136]

But beyond this ideal of being and doing there is an even more profound basis for the desire of *not* having, one that is related "to that fundamental mystery of religious experience, the satisfaction found in absolute surrender to the larger power."[137] Like the alcoholic or drug addict who wants to be weaned from his enemy but dares not face blank abstinence, and therefore hides supplies of it in his clothing and arranges secretly to have it smuggled in case of need, so money "is like the sleeping potion which the chronically wakeful person keeps beside his bed; he throws himself on God,

---

133. Ibid., 316–17. James is quoting here from Rodriguez, *Pratique de la Perfection Chrétienne*, part 3, treatise 3, chapters. 6–7.

134. James, *The Varieties of Religious Experience*, 318.

135. Ibid.

136. Ibid. See Carpenter, *Towards Democracy*, 362. James also relates the story of Saint Francis of Assisi, who refused a brother novice's request for a Psalter on grounds that he should not care for "owning books and knowledge, but care rather for works of goodness." When the novice returned a few weeks later to talk of his craving for a breviary, Francis said to him, "After you have got your Psalter you will crave a breviary; and after you have got your breviary you will sit in your stall like a grand prelate, and will say to your brother, 'Hand me my breviary'" (320). James is quoting here from Saint Francis's *Speculum Perfectionis*, 10.

137. James, *The Varieties of Religious Experience*, 320.

but *if* he should need the other help, there it will be also."¹³⁸ Thus, "really to give up anything on which we have relied, to give it up definitively, 'for good and all' and forever, signifies one of those radical alterations of character which came under our notice in the lectures on conversion."¹³⁹ When one embraces the virtue of poverty, "the inner man rolls over into an entirely different position of equilibrium, lives in a new center of energy from this time on, and the turning-point and hinge of all such operations seems usually to involve the sincere acceptance of certain nakednesses and destitutions."¹⁴⁰ Therefore, "throughout the annals of the saintly life, we find this ever-recurring note: Fling yourself upon God's providence without making any reserve whatever,—take no thought for the morrow,—sell all you have and give it to the poor,—only when the sacrifice is ruthless and reckless will the higher safety really arrive."¹⁴¹

James concludes his consideration of poverty by noting that there are other religious mysteries in the life of poverty besides the mystery of self-surrender. One is the mystery of veracity: Whoever first said "Naked I came into the world" possessed this mystery. Another is the mystery of democracy or the sentiment of equality before God of all his creatures. This sentiment "tends to nullify man's usual acquisitiveness" and "those who have it spurn dignities and honors, privileges and advantages."¹⁴² James notes that this is not exactly the sentiment of *humility*, although it comes close to it in

138. Ibid., 320–21.
139. Ibid., 321.
140. Ibid.
141. Ibid. James cites the case of Antoinette Bourignon, who asked her father permission to enter a cloister of the Carmelites. Her father refused, saying that he would not permit her to become a religious or give her any money to enter a convent. So she went to a monastery and offered to work there, expecting only that she would be provided subsistence, but the director told her they took no maids without money so that if she wanted entry to the monastery she would need to find a way to acquire the funds. Later, when her parents promised her to a rich French merchant, she left home at four in the morning, wearing only a habit and took one penny to buy bread for that day. But as she was going out she heard the voice of God saying to her, "Where is thy faith? In a penny?" She threw the penny away, begging God's pardon for her fault, saying, "No, Lord, my faith is not in a penny, but in thee alone." From then on she felt completely delivered from the heavy burden of the cares and good things of this world, and found her soul so satisfied that she no longer wished for anything on earth, resting entirely upon God, with only the fear that she might be discovered and be forced to return home, "for she felt already more content in this poverty than she had done for all her life in all the delights of the world" (321–23). The quotation is from George Garden, *An Apology for M. Antonia Bourignon*, 270. Garden, who was one of the ministers of St. Nicholas, the town parish of Aberdeen, Scotland, was deposed from the ministry because of his advocacy of Bourignonianism. See also her autobiography, *Light of the World*.

142. James, *The Varieties of Religious Experience*, 323–24.

practice, but of *humanity*, the refusal to enjoy anything that others do not share. He cites in this connection John Jay Chapman's reflections on Christ's saying to the young man who asked what he needed to do to have eternal life: "Sell all thou hast and follow me" (Matthew 19:21, KJV). Chapman notes that Christ may have meant that "if you love mankind absolutely you will as a result not care for any possessions whatever," and, if so, "this seems a very likely proposition."[143] Yet, Chapman adds, "It is one thing to believe that a proposition is probably true; it is another thing to see it as a fact. If you loved mankind as Christ loved them you would see his conclusion as a fact. It would be obvious. You would sell your goods, and they would be no loss to you."[144] Chapman goes on to observe that "there are in every generation persons who, beginning innocently, with no predetermined intention of becoming saints, find themselves drawn into the vortex by their interest in helping mankind, and by the understanding that comes from actually doing it. The abandonment of their old mode of life is like dust in the balance. It is done gradually, incidentally, imperceptibly. Thus the whole question of the abandonment of luxury is no question at all, but a mere incident to another question, namely, the degree to which we abandon ourselves to the remorseless logic of our love for others."[145] With this citation, James, in effect, affirms the form of ascetic expression that is the fruit of love—love for a Deity who has a profound love for all humanity.

CONCLUSION

This brings James to the concluding paragraph of his chapter on saintliness. He points out that "in all these matters of sentiment one must have 'been there' one's self in order to understand them."[146] He notes that no American can ever attain an understanding of a Briton toward his king or of a German toward his emperor, and neither can a Briton or German understand the peace of heart that an American experiences in having no king or Kaiser who stands between himself and the common God of all. If, therefore, "sentiments as simple as these are mysteries that one must receive

---

143. Ibid., 324.
144. Ibid.
145. Ibid. James is quoting here from Chapman's article in *The Political Nursery*, volume 4 (1900), page 2. *The Political Nursery* was a monthly journal that Chapman created in support of political reform. It appeared from March 1897 to January 1901 and was available to subscribers for one dollar a year. Among the issues he commented on were New York City politics, the Dreyfus case, and racial prejudice. See Simon, *William James Remembered*, 50.
146. James, *The Varieties of Religious Experience*, 325.

as gifts of birth, how much more is this the case with those subtler religious sentiments which we have been considering!"[147] Since we "can never fathom an emotion or divine its dictates by standing outside of it, the only sound plan, if we are ourselves outside the pale of such emotions, is to observe as well as we are able those who feel them, and to record faithfully what we observe; and this, I need hardly say, is what I have striven to do in these last two descriptive lectures."[148]

That he has succeeded in this objective seems patently obvious, so much so, in fact, that one cannot help but wonder whether the capacity to enter into the feelings of others as he has done here might itself be a form or expression of saintliness. In any event, his account in his essay "The Energies of Men" of a friend who is suffering from cancer is a beautiful example of how James could enter into the emotional world of another person, and this account is especially appropriate here because it concerns a friend of his who has exemplified to him what it means to be a living saint. James writes: "The most genuinely saintly person I have ever known is a friend of mine now suffering from cancer of the breast. I do not assume to judge of the wisdom or unwisdom of her disobedience to the doctors, and I cite her solely as an example of what ideas can do. Her ideas have kept her a practically well woman for months after she should have given up and gone to bed. They have annulled all pain and weakness and given her a cheerful active life, unusually beneficent to others to whom she has afforded help."[149] It is worth noting here that she has not chosen the path of obedience to her doctors. Although James does not explicitly say so, it is apparent from his reference to her saintly character that she has entrusted her life to God, the one whose wisdom is infinite.[150]

---

147. Ibid.
148. Ibid.
149. James, "The Energies of Men," in James, *Writings, 1902–1910*, 1238.
150. James, *The Varieties of Religious Experience*, 311.

8

The Prayerful Consciousness

As we saw in chapter 6 on the psychology of religious conversion, prayer often plays a major role in a religious conversion experience. There was the case of Henry Alline who paid no regard to what his father was praying during family prayers but instead prayed the words of Psalm 38. As he continued praying, a sense of God's redeeming love broke into his soul with such power that his soul seemed to be melted down with love.[1] There was also the case of David Brainerd, who came to realize that it was self-interest that had led him to pray and that he had never prayed from any respect to the glory of God. This realization led to a crisis in which he was unable to pray although he tried to do so for nearly a half hour. Then, suddenly, an unspeakable glory presented itself to him, and he experienced an inward apprehension of the spirit of God.[2]

In this chapter, I will focus on James's discussion of prayer in the nineteenth lecture of *The Varieties of Religious Experience*. This lecture, which is titled "Other Characteristics," follows his lecture on philosophy and precedes his lecture on general conclusions. The title of this lecture seems almost to imply, whether intended or not, that it is concerned with some aspects of religious experience that were not significant enough to discuss in the earlier chapters; and because this lecture comes so close to the end of the lecture series, the title gives the impression of being an effort to tie up a few loose ends. It might even serve a defensive purpose. If potential critics wanted to fault James for failing to deal with one or another feature

1. James, *The Varieties of Religious Experience*, 218.
2. Ibid., 213.

of religious experience that they considered important, he could rightfully claim that he at least made an effort to include it, and that he would have treated it at greater length had the lecture series been even more ambitious than it already was.

In any event, a lecture on "Other Characteristics" does not raise high expectations, and if one were informed of the title in advance, this might well be the lecture that one would be most tempted to miss. The preceding lecture on philosophy ends with the brief sentence, "In my next lecture I will try to complete my rough description of religious experience; and in the lecture after that, which is the last one, I will try my own hand at formulating conceptually the truth to which it is a witness."[3] Of the two, the final lecture—"Conclusions"—sounds considerably more important than the penultimate one—"Other Characteristics"—with its quite modest goal of trying "to complete my rough description of religious experience."[4] That the "Other Characteristics" lecture has received little comment in scholarly discussions of *The Varieties* indicates that it has, for the most part, been quickly skipped over by readers of *The Varieties*. Yet, for all its apparent insignificance in the lecture series as a whole, it is actually one of the most important, and largely because the central topic is that of prayer.

Before we consider what James has to say about prayer in this lecture, I would like to take note of his responses to James Bissett Pratt's questionnaire on the matter of prayer.[5] As we saw in chapter 2, Pratt distributed his questionnaire in 1904, two years after James's *The Varieties* was published. One of his questions concerned prayer and it consisted of two parts. The first part asked, "Do you pray, and if so, why? That is, is it purely from habit, and social custom, or do you really believe that God hears your prayers?" James's answer to this part of the question was brief: "I can't possibly pray—I feel foolish and artificial." The second part of Pratt's question asked, "Is prayer with you one-sided or two-sided—i.e., do you sometimes feel that in prayer you receive something—such as strength or the divine spirit—from God? Is it a real communion?"[6] Having answered the first part of the question in the negative, James did not write a response to the second part. This is the only question in the questionnaire that he left unanswered.

As we saw in chapter 2, Pratt also posed questions about the meaning of God for the respondent and about how the respondent experienced God. To the question "Is He a person?" James responded, "He must be cognizant

---

3. Ibid., 457.
4. Ibid.
5. James, *Writings, 1900–1910*, 1183–85.
6. Ibid., 1185.

and responsive in some way."⁷ To the question "How do you apprehend his relation to mankind and to you personally? If your position on any of these matters is uncertain, please state the fact," James responded, "Uncertain."⁸

James's negative answer to Pratt's question "Do you pray, and if so, why?" and his simple, one-word response—"Uncertain"—to the question about how God is apprehended prepare us for his discussion of prayer in *The Varieties*. At the very least, they suggest that prayer does not play a central role in James's own religious life, and that we might therefore expect that what he has to say about prayer is likely to be hedged with caution and reserve. On the other hand, these answers to Pratt's questionnaire are especially interesting in light of the fact that Pratt's manner of posing the question is quite compatible with James's own discussion of prayer in *The Varieties*. Given that his questionnaire was distributed just two years after *The Varieties* was published, we can well imagine that James's discussion of prayer in the "Other Characteristics" lecture was Pratt's primary source for his own questions on prayer.

THE USES OF RELIGION

James begins the lecture by noting that his long excursions through mysticism (lectures 16 and 17) and philosophy (lecture 18) now bring him back to where he had arrived at the conclusion of his lectures on saintliness (lectures 11–15). In his concluding lecture on the value of saintliness (lecture 15), he had noted that by abandoning theological criteria in favor of criteria derived from "practical common sense and the empirical method," he had been able to make a case for the uses of religion—to the individual who has religion and to this individual's usefulness to the world.⁹ He took particular note of the uses of such individuals to the "world's welfare" and observed that the great saints are immediate successes in this regard while the lesser saints are "at least heralds and harbingers, and they may be leavens also, of a better mundane order."¹⁰ On this basis, he had issued the invitation to "be saints, then, if we can, whether or not we succeed visibly and temporally," and he had added that "each of us must discover for himself the kind of religion and the amount of saintship which best comports with what he believes to be his powers and feels to be his truest mission and vocation."¹¹

7. Ibid., 1183.
8. Ibid., 1184.
9. James, *The Varieties of Religious Experience*, 377.
10. Ibid.
11. Ibid.

Thus, ultimately, the issue is not whether we are well- or ill-adapted to this world, but whether, in our exercise of the powers we possess, we have made our contribution toward "a better mundane order."[12]

James recognizes that there is at least a paradox and perhaps even an outright contradiction in this conclusion, for how is it that religion that "believes in two worlds and an invisible order" is here being "established by the adaptation of its fruits to this world's order alone?"[13] To address this paradox he devotes the next two lectures to mysticism and philosophy. Now, in lecture 19 he is back to the issue of the uses of religion. But whereas his lectures on the value of saintliness focused especially on the uses of the religious person to the world, he suggests that this lecture will be much more concerned with the uses of religion to the person who has it. It will address the question of what my religion does *for me*, and will therefore take on the question of whether, as he puts it in his final lecture ("Conclusions"), personal or "egoistic" religion is an inferior form of religion.[14] This penultimate lecture is therefore far more important than it might initially appear, for it addresses the question of whether religion that has its uses to the individual is less genuine or less true than religion—as reflected in the saintly character—that enables the individual to be of use to the world.

PRAYER AS THE SOUL AND ESSENCE OF RELIGION

After a relatively brief discussion of the role that the aesthetic life plays in determining the individual's choice of religion, James observes that "In most books on religion, three things are represented as its most essential elements," namely, "Sacrifice, Confession, and Prayer."[15] He gives only brief attention to sacrifice, noting that although sacrifices to God are omnipresent in primeval worship, ritual sacrifice has been eliminated from the major world religions (he cites Judaism, Islam and Buddhism) except that in Christianity the idea of sacrifice "is preserved in transfigured form in the mystery of Christ's atonement."[16] What these religions do is to "substitute offerings of the heart, renunciations of the inner self, for all these vain oblations."[17] James's comments on confession, which are equally brief, are concerned to make the point that confession, while not nearly as widespread as sacrifice

12. Ibid.
13. Ibid.
14. Ibid., 500.
15. Ibid., 462.
16. Ibid.
17. Ibid.

has been, "corresponds to a more inward and moral stage of sentiment," and "is part of the general system of purgation and cleansing which one feels one's self in need of, in order to be in right relations to one's deity."[18]

As James turns to the topic of prayer he says that his comments on this topic will be less brief. He begins with the observation that there has been much talk about prayer lately, "especially against prayers for better weather and for the recovery of sick people."[19] He agrees that prayer for better weather is of no avail, for "everyone now knows that droughts and storms follow from physical antecedents and that moral appeals cannot avert them," but prayer for the sick is a different matter, for "if any medical fact can be considered to stand firm, it is that in certain environments prayer may contribute to recovery, and should be encouraged as a therapeutic measure. Being a normal factor of moral health in the person, its omission would be deleterious."[20]

Thus, from the outset James makes clear to his audience that he is not an opponent of prayer, but that he believes prayer serves mainly the personal needs of individuals as it cannot directly influence the natural world. This does not mean, however, that prayer has no connection with the natural world, for, as he will go on to discuss, it directly influences our ability to respond to the world around us. For the moment, though, his point is that we should not join the scientific despisers of prayer, for it is a *medical* fact that prayer may contribute to the recovery of a patient. Furthermore, "petitional prayer is only one department of prayer," and when prayer is taken "in the wider sense as meaning every kind of inward communion or conversation with the power recognized as divine, we can easily see that scientific criticism leaves it untouched."[21]

James next makes the vivid and unequivocal statement that "Prayer in this wide sense is the very soul and essence of religion."[22] In support of this view he quotes the following statement on prayer by Auguste Sabatier, a liberal French theologian. Sabatier writes:

> Religion is an intercourse, a conscious and voluntary relation, entered into by a soul in distress with the mysterious power upon which it feels itself to depend, and upon which its fate is contingent. This intercourse with God is realized by prayer. Prayer is religion in act; that is, prayer is real religion. It is prayer

18. Ibid.
19. Ibid., 463.
20. Ibid.
21. Ibid., 464.
22. Ibid.

that distinguishes the religious phenomenon from such similar or neighboring phenomenon as purely moral or aesthetic sentiment. Religion is nothing if it be not the vital act by which the entire mind seeks to save itself by clinging to the principle from which it draws its life. This act is prayer, by which term I understand no vain exercise of words, no mere repetition of certain sacred formulae, but the very movement itself of the soul, putting itself in a personal relation of contact with the mysterious power of which it feels the presence,—it may be even before it has a name by which to call it. Wherever this interior prayer is lacking, there is no religion; wherever, on the other hand, this prayer rises and stirs the soul, even in the absence of forms or of doctrines, we have living religion.[23]

James comments: "It seems to me that the entire series of our lectures proves the truth of M. Sabatier's contention," for "the religious phenomenon, studied as an inner fact, and apart from ecclesiastical or theological complications, has shown itself to consist everywhere and at all its stages, in the consciousness which individuals have of an intercourse between themselves and higher powers with which they feel themselves to be related."[24]

James goes on to note that "this intercourse is realized at the time as being both active and mutual" and says that "if it be not effective; if it be not a give and take relation; if nothing be really transacted while it lasts; if the world is in no whit different for its having taken place; then prayer, taken in this wide meaning of a sense that *something is transacting*, is of course a feeling of what is illusory, and religion must on the whole be classed, not simply as containing elements of delusion,—these undoubtedly everywhere exist,—but as being rooted in delusion altogether, just as materialists and atheists have always said it was."[25] To be sure, if "direct experiences of prayer were ruled out as false witnesses, some inferential belief that the whole order of existence must have a divine cause" would undoubtedly remain, but this way of contemplating nature would reduce us to "the spectators' part at a play," whereas in experimental religion and the prayerful life we see ourselves as "active, and not in a play, but in a very serious reality."[26] He concludes, therefore, that the "genuineness of religion is thus indissolubly bound up with the question whether the prayerful consciousness be or be

---

23. Ibid.; Sabatier, *Esquisse d'une Philosophie de la Religion*, 24–26.
24. James, *The Varieties of Religious Experience*, 465.
25. Ibid.
26. Ibid., 465–66.

not deceitful," for the "conviction that something is genuinely transacted in this consciousness is the very core of living religion."[27]

As to what is transacted, "great differences of opinion have prevailed throughout human history," and he is quick to acknowledge that "the unseen powers" have been supposed to do things "which no enlightened man can nowadays believe in."[28] He even entertains the possibility that "the sphere of influence in prayer is subjective exclusively, and that what is immediately changed is only the mind of the praying person."[29] While his willingness to entertain this possibility may seem inconsistent with his assertion that in prayer "something is transacting," there is a difference between saying that "intercourse" takes place between the praying person and the higher power with which the person is related, and ascribing "influence" to this higher power. It is quite plausible that the "influence" that occurs in prayer is essentially that of a change in the mind of the praying person, and that this change need not be attributable to a direct "influence" exerted by the unseen power to whom the prayer is addressed.

James's earlier discussion in his lectures on conversion of posthypnotic suggestion is helpful here, for we need not assume that prayer must elicit a "suggestion," as it were, from the higher power in order to be considered a genuine transaction.[30] In fact, it is often the case that one is content with the thought—or belief—that God has "heard" one's prayer, and that no other evidence of the transaction is expected or required. Conversely, it is only in prayers of petition that the praying person seeks to exert influence on the higher or unseen power, and James has already noted that this is only one department of prayer. What ultimately matters, therefore, is not whether there is evidence of divine influence, but that through prayer "things which cannot be realized in any other manner come about: energy that but for prayer would be bound is by prayer set free and operates in some part, be it objective or subjective, of the world of facts."[31]

In support of his view that even if we are unable to determine whether some influence other than subjective is involved, this does not in itself invalidate prayer, James quotes from a letter written by Frederick Myers to a friend. Noting that prayer is the general name for the "attitude of open and earnest expectancy," Myers observes: "If we then ask to *whom* to pray, the answer (strangely enough) must be that *that* does not much matter. The

---

27. Ibid., 466.
28. Ibid.
29. Ibid.
30. Ibid., 234.
31. Ibid., 466.

prayer is not indeed a purely subjective thing;—it means a real increase in intensity of absorption of spiritual power or grace—but we do not know enough of what takes place in the spiritual world to know how the prayer operates;—who is cognizant of it, or through what channel the grace is given."[32] As a practical matter Myers suggests that we should "let children pray to Christ, who is at any rate the highest individual spirit of whom we have any knowledge," but "it would be rash to say that Christ himself *hears us*; while to say that *God* hears us is merely to restate the first principle,— that grace flows in from the infinite spiritual world."[33]

Thus, Myers contends that just because we do not know how the divine "influence" works does not mean that prayer is "a purely subjective thing."[34] But James is more cautious, proposing that the "question of the truth or falsehood of the belief that power is absorbed" be deferred until the next lecture.[35] In the meantime, he will focus for the remainder of the present lecture on "concrete examples" of the prayerful consciousness.

GOD AS A SUPERNATURAL CLERGYMAN

James's first concrete example is George Müller of Bristol, England, whose prayers in his view "were of the crassest petitional order."[36] Noting that Müller in his early years "resolved on taking certain Bible promises in literal sincerity and on letting himself be fed, not by his own worldly foresight but by the Lord's hand"[37] James tells about Müller's impressive achievements: "He had an extraordinarily active and successful career, among the fruits of which were the distribution of over two million copies of the Scripture text, in different languages; the equipment of several hundred missionaries; the circulation of more than a hundred and eleven million of scriptural books, pamphlets, and tracts; the building of five large orphanages, and the keeping and educating of thousands of orphans; finally, the establishment of schools in which over a hundred and twenty-one thousand youthful and adult pupils were taught."[38] In the course of this work he received and administered nearly a million and a half of pounds sterling, and traveled over

---

32. Ibid., 467. The very fact that James says that the friend "allows me to quote from it" leads one to suspect that the letter was written to James himself.
33. Ibid.
34. Ibid.
35. Ibid.
36. Ibid., 468.
37. Ibid.
38. Ibid. James states that his authority for these statistics is Warne, *George Müller*.

two hundred thousand miles of sea and land. During the sixty-eight years of his ministry, he never owned any property except his clothes, furniture and cash in hand; and at the age of eighty-six he left an estate worth only a hundred and sixty pounds.[39]

James notes that Müller's "method was to let his general wants be publicly known, but not to acquaint other people with the details of his temporary necessities."[40] For the relief of these "he prayed directly to the Lord, believing that sooner or later prayers are always answered if one has trust enough."[41] As Müller describes his prayers, "When I lose such a thing as a key, I ask the Lord to direct me to it, and I look for an answer to my prayer; when a person with whom I have made an appointment does not come, according to the fixed time, and I begin to be inconvenienced by it, I ask the Lord to be pleased to hasten him to me, and I look for an answer; when I do not understand a passage of the word of God, I lift up my heart to the Lord that he would be pleased by his Holy Spirit to instruct me, and I expect to be taught, though I do not fix the time when, and the manner how it should be."[42] Müller refused to borrow money but paid for everything in cash. This meant that he might not know from one day to the next whether he would be able to feed the children in his orphanage. Yet, he claimed that the money always arrived in the nick of time and no one went hungry. Once, when he received the sum he needed to carry on his work, he wrote in his diary: "It is impossible to describe my joy in God when I received this donation. I was neither excited nor surprised; for I *look out* for answers to my prayers. *I believe that God hears me*. Yet my heart was so full of joy that I could only *sit* before God, and admire him, like David in 2 Samuel vii. At last I cast myself flat down upon my face and burst forth in thanksgiving to God and in surrounding my heart afresh to him for his blessed service."[43]

James concludes that Müller "is a case extreme in every respect and in no respect more so than in the extraordinary narrowness of the man's intellectual horizon."[44] He explains: "His God was, as he often said, his business partner. He seems to have been for Müller little more than a sort of super-

---

39. James, *The Varieties of Religious Experience*, 468; see Warne, *George Müller*.

40. Ibid.

41. Ibid.

42. Ibid.; see Müller, *The Life of Trust*.

43. James, *The Varieties of Religious Experience*, 470; see Müller, *The Life of Trust*. As the money he received was a large sum earmarked for his building fund for a certain house, his reference to David is specifically to verse 18: "Then went King David in, and sat before the Lord, and he said, 'Who *am* I, O Lord God? And what *is* my house, that thou hast brought me hitherto?" (2 Samuel 7:18, KJV).

44. Ibid.

natural clergyman interested in the congregation of tradesmen and others in Bristol who were his saints, and in the orphanages and other enterprises, but unpossessed of any of those vaster and wilder and more ideal attributes with which the human imagination elsewhere has invested him."[45] In short, Müller "was absolutely unphilosophical. His intensely private and practical conception of his relations with the Deity continued the traditions of the most primitive thought. When we compare a mind like his with such a mind as, for example, Emerson's or Phillips Brooks's, we see the range which the religious consciousness covers."[46]

In a footnote to his observation that Müller's conception of his relations with the Deity was most primitive James provides an example of "an even more primitive style of religious thought"—that of Robert Lyde, an English sailor who as a prisoner on a French ship set upon the crew of seven Frenchmen, killed two, and made the others his prisoners, and brought home the ship. His account of this feat is replete with references to his prayers to God to help him, with each request resulting in his discovery of a weapon near at hand with which to assault an adversary.[47]

GOD AS GUIDING PRESENCE

James's next example of the "prayerful consciousness" is that of Karl Hilty, a professor of constitutional law at the University of Bern. James had previously cited Hilty's thoughts on the feelings of happiness that the near presence of God's spirit engenders, in his first lecture on the religion of healthy-mindedness; and in his first lecture on saintliness, James had noted Hilty's observation that when one willingly surrenders one's personal independence to God, one experiences "the disappearance of all *fear* from one's life" and an "indescribable and inexplicable feeling of an inner *security*."[48]

---

45. Ibid.
46. Ibid., 470–71. I will focus on Phillips Brooks in chapter 10.
47. Ibid., 471. James's source for Lyde's narrative is Arber, *An English Garner*, 440.
48. James, *The Varieties of Religious Experience*, 79, 275. These were references to Hilty's *Glück*, 18, 85. A professor of constitutional law at the University of Bern, Switzerland, Hilty had written a series of three small books on happiness in 1891, 1895, and 1898. James focuses on the third book here. An English text by Hilty titled *Happiness: Essays on the Meaning of Life* was published in 1903, one year following the publication of James's *The Varieties of Religious Experience*. It was translated by Francis G. Peabody, a professor in the Divinity School at Harvard; see Simon, *Genuine Reality*, 166. In his preface, Peabody indicates that this text consists of the first of Hilty's three books on happiness. See also Carlin and Capps, *100 Years of Happiness*, chapter 2.

Here, in his discussion of the prayerful consciousness, James presents Hilty as an example of those for whom "persistence in leaning on the Almighty for support and guidance brings with it proofs, palpable but much more subtle, of his presence and active influence."[49] Hilty notes, for example, that "one finds in this guided sort of life that books and words (and sometimes people) come to one's cognizance just at the very moment in which one needs them," or that "one glides over great dangers as if with shut eyes, remaining ignorant of what would have terrified one or led one astray, until the peril is past," and he suggests that this is "especially the case with temptations to vanity and sensuality" where "paths on which one ought not to wander are, as it were, hedged off with thorns."[50] On the other hand, there are situations in which "great obstacles are suddenly removed; that when the time has come for something, one suddenly receives a courage that until then was concealed, or discovers thoughts, talents, yea, even pieces of knowledge and insight, in one's self, of which it is impossible to say whence they come."[51] After citing other evidence of divine support and guidance, Hilty concludes that "with the consciousness of divine guidance, one sees many a thing in life quite differently from what would otherwise be possible."[52]

A TRANSFIGURED WORLD

James indicates that accounts such as Hilty's shade away into others "where the belief is not that particular events are tempered more favorably toward us by a superintending providence, as a reward for our reliance, but that by cultivating the continuous sense of our connection with the power that made things as they are, we are tempered more favorably toward their reception."[53] He describes the change that this form of the prayerful consciousness effects: "The outward face of nature need not alter, but the expressions of meaning in it alter. It was dead and is alive again. It is like the difference between looking on a person without love, or upon the same person with love. In the latter case intercourse springs into a new vitality."[54] And so, "when one's affections keep in touch with the divinity of the world's authorship, fear and agitation fall away; and in the equanimity that follows,

49. James, *The Varieties of Religious Experience*, 472.
50. Ibid.
51. Ibid.; see Hilty, *Glück*, part 3, 92ff.
52. James, *The Varieties of Religious Experience*, 473; see Hilty, *Glück*, part 3, 92ff.
53. Ibid., 474.
54. Ibid.

one finds in the hours, as they succeed each other, a series of purely benignant opportunities. It is as if all doors were opened, and all paths freshly smoothed. We meet a new world when we meet the old world in the spirit which this kind of prayer infuses."⁵⁵

James suggests that we find this spirit in Marcus Aurelius, in the Greek Stoic Epictetus, and in the mind-curers, transcendentalists, and so-called liberal Christians of his own day. In a footnote James quotes a passage from the writings of Epictetus, who discerns the providence of God in all the seemingly mundane processes of nature. Epictetus exclaims: "Good Heaven! Any one thing in the creation is sufficient to demonstrate a Providence to a humble and grateful mind. The mere possibility of producing milk from grass, cheese from milk, and wool from skins; who formed and planned it? Ought we not, whether we dig or plough or eat, to sing this hymn to God? Great is God, who has supplied us with these instruments to till the ground; great is God, who has given us hands and instruments of digestion; who has given us to grow insensibly and to breathe in sleep. These things we ought forever to celebrate."⁵⁶ Epictetus accuses those who do not sing this hymn to God of being blind and insensible, and therefore nominates himself to lead the singing: "For what else can I do, a lame old man, but sing hymns to God? Were I a nightingale, I would act the part of the nightingale; were I a swan, the part of a swan. But since I am a reasonable creature, it is my duty to praise God . . . and I call on you to join the same song."⁵⁷

James also cites a sermon by James Martineau titled "Help Thou Mine Unbelief" as an example of the spirit of "cultivating the continuous sense of our connection with the power that made things as they are."⁵⁸ Martineau points out that "the universe, open to the eye today, looks as it did a thousand years ago," and "we see what all our fathers saw," so "if we cannot find God in your house or in mine, upon the roadside or the margin of the sea; in the bursting seed or opening flower; in the day duty or the night musing; in the general laugh and the secret grief; in the procession of life, ever entering afresh, and solemnly passing by and dropping off; I do not think we should discern him any more on the grass of Eden, or beneath the moonlight of Gethsemane."⁵⁹ At the same time, "he who will but discern beneath the sun, as he rises any morning, the supporting finger of the Almighty, may recover the sweet and reverent surprise with which Adam gazed on the first dawn in

55. Ibid.
56. Ibid.; see Epictetus, *Works*, book 1, chapter 16.
57. James, *The Varieties of Religious Experience*, 474.
58. Ibid., 475.
59. Ibid.; Martineau, *Endeavors after a Christian Life*, 311.

Paradise. It is no outward change, no shifting in time or place; but only the loving meditation of the pure in heart, that can awaken the Eternal from the sleep within our souls: that can render him a reality again, and reassert for him once more his ancient name of 'the living God.'" 60

James observes that "when we see all things in God and refer all things to him, we read in common matters superior expressions of meaning" and the "deadness with which custom invests the familiar vanishes, and existence as a whole appears transfigured."61 He quotes from a letter from a friend who observed that when we try to sum up all the mercies and bounties we are privileged to have, we "realize that *we are actually killed with God's kindness*; that we are surrounded by bounties upon bounties, without which all would fall."62 The friend therefore asks: "Should we not love it; should we not feel buoyed up by the Eternal Arms?"63

SPIRITUAL ENERGY BECOMES ACTIVE

Following this reference to his friend's letter, James suggests that sometimes "this realization that facts are of divine sending, instead of being habitual, is casual, like a mystical experience."64 He cites an example from the Catholic philosopher Fr. Auguste Gratry, previously introduced in his chapter on the sick soul, who gives an account of an experience he had when he was in what James calls "his youthful melancholy period."65 Gratry writes:

> One day I had a moment of consolation, because I met with something which seemed to me ideally perfect. It was a poor drummer beating the tattoo in the streets of Paris. I walked behind him in returning to the school on the evening of a holiday. His drum gave out the tattoo in such a way that, at that moment at least, however peevish I were, I could find no pretext for fault-finding. It was impossible to conceive more nerve or spirit, better time or measure, more clearness or richness, than were in this drumming. Ideal desire could go no farther in that direction. I was enchanted and consoled; the perfection of this

---

60. James, *The Varieties of Religious Experience*, 475; Martineau, *Endeavors after a Christian Life*, 311.

61. Ibid., 475–76.

62. Ibid., 476.

63. Ibid. The "Eternal Arms" is a reference to Deuteronomy 33:27: "The eternal God is *thy* refuge, and underneath *are* the everlasting arms" (KJV).

64. Ibid.

65. Ibid.

wretched act did me good. Good is at least possible, I said, since the ideal can thus sometimes get embodied."[66]

James suggests that the main character in Etienne Pivert de Sénancour's novel *Obermann* experienced "a similar transient lifting of the veil."[67] It, too, happened on the streets of Paris, and the inspiration in this case was his coming across a flower—a yellow jonquil—blooming on a March day. He says that the flower "was the strongest expression of desire: it was the first perfume of the year. I felt all the happiness destined for man. This unutterable harmony of souls, the phantom of the ideal world, arose in me complete. I never felt anything so great or so instantaneous. I know not what shape, what analogy, what secret of relation it was that made me see in this flower a limitless beauty."[68] Sénancour goes on to declare that he will "never enclose in a conception this power, this immensity that nothing will express; this form that nothing will contain; this ideal of a better world which one feels, but which, it seems, nature has not made actual."[69]

James does not comment directly on these experiences, but he notes that in his previous lectures on conversion we heard "of the vivified face of the world as it may appear to converts after their awakening."[70] From such testimonies James draws this conclusion regarding the prayerful consciousness: "As a rule, religious persons generally assume that whatever natural factors connect themselves in any way with their destiny are significant of the divine purposes with them. Through prayer the purpose, often far from obvious, comes home to them, and if it be a 'trial,' strength to endure the trial is given."[71] Thus, "at all stages of the prayerful life we find the persuasion that in the process of communion energy from on high flows in to meet

66. Ibid.; Gratry, *Souvenirs de ma Jeunesse*, 122.

67. James, *The Varieties of Religious Experience*, 476; see Senacour, *Obermann*, letter 30.

68. James, *The Varieties of Religious Experience*, 477.

69. Ibid.

70. Ibid. He has reference here to his discussion of the feature of the state of assurance in which the world appears to undergo an objective change—manifesting uncommon newness and beauty—and to his contrast between this experience and "that dreadful unreality and strangeness in the appearance of the world, which is experienced by melancholy patients" (248). He also mentions in a footnote this reference to an earlier discussion of melancholy in his lecture on the sick soul, where he had noted that a relatively frequent change effected in a religious convert "is a transfiguration of the face of nature in his eyes," 151. Here too James contrasts this transformation with the case of melancholic patients who experience a change in the appearance of nature in the reverse direction. For them, "the world now looks remote, strange, sinister, uncanny. Its color is gone, its breath is cold, there is no speculation in the eyes it glares with" (151).

71. James, *The Varieties of Religious Experience*, 477.

demand, and becomes operative in the phenomenal world" and as long as this operativeness is considered to be real "it makes no essential difference whether its immediate effects be subjective or objective," for "the fundamental religious point is that in prayer, spiritual energy, which otherwise would slumber, does become active, and spiritual work of some kind is effected really."[72]

THE VIVIFIED FACE OF NATURE

The observation that spiritual energy becomes active in prayer concludes James's discussion of prayer.[73] However, he notes that he will return to the subject of prayer "as the core of religion" in his final lecture (lecture 20).[74] Before we turn to his final thoughts on prayer, I would like to draw some conclusions concerning the foregoing discussion of the prayerful consciousness by returning to his observation, expressed in his lectures on the sick soul (lectures 6–7), on conversion (lectures 9–10) and in the present lecture that the world can be experienced in two very different forms—either as a vivified and shining face or as a remote, strange, and sinister visage with glaring eyes.[75]

In his lectures on the sick soul, he noted that this very duality prompts the melancholic individual to ask, "If the natural world is so double-faced and unhomelike, what world, what thing is real?"[76] And thus: "An urgent wondering and *questioning* is set up, a poring theoretic activity, and in the desperate effort to get into right relations with the matter, the sufferer is often led to what becomes for him a satisfying religious solution."[77] As he undoubtedly has reference here to the "questioning mania" that he himself experienced when he was in the deeper throes of melancholia, it is likely that "the satisfying religious solution" will not occur until one has given up the theoretic activity itself. It is noteworthy therefore that in his portrayal of the prayerful consciousness, the effort seems much less theoretic, as if it were less a matter of conscious thought or active will and much more a matter of

72. Ibid.

73. In the final segment of the lecture he focuses on fact that the manifestations of the religious life "so frequently connect themselves with the subconscious part of our existence" (ibid., 477–78). Since we have discussed the role of the subconscious in the religious life in chapter 5, I will not discuss his further reflections on the subconscious in this lecture.

74. Ibid., 477.

75. Ibid., 151, 248.

76. Ibid., 152.

77. Ibid.

yielding to the sights and sounds around oneself. In effect, the energy comes from without, not from within, for "in the process of communion energy from on high flows in to meet demand, and becomes operative within the phenomenal world."[78] Whatever the ultimate source of the energy may be it is experienced in the prayerful consciousness as originating outside of the individual and as occurring in direct relation to the prayerful one's receptivity and yielding.

In light of the role that the prayerful consciousness plays in the transfiguration of the world around us, James's conclusion that through prayer the divine purpose, "often far from obvious, comes home to us," is especially noteworthy.[79] In fact, he uses a similar phrase in his answer to the final question in Pratt's questionnaire. The questionnaire asks: "What do you mean by a 'religious experience'?" James responded: "Any moment of life that brings the reality of spiritual things more 'home' to one."[80] The purpose of the prayerful consciousness, then, is not to effect an actual change in the natural world, for, as James makes clear in his discussion of petitional prayer, our prayers have no effect on droughts and storms. But as Auguste Sabatier expresses it, prayer is "the very movement itself of the soul putting itself in a personal relation of contact with the mysterious power of which it feels the presence," even perhaps "before it has a name by which to call it."[81]

Thus, the prayerful consciousness opens itself to the world that surrounds it and thereby to the unseen world to which the seen world is vivid testimony. In prayer understood in its widest sense as "inward communion," the spiritual world "comes home" to us. And for the one for whom the perception of the unseen world behind the seen world is not a habitual experience, it will be those experiences in which the natural world beckons oneself out of oneself—the drummer's tattoo, the yellow jonquil on a March day—that bring the unseen world home again. Thus, through the "vivified face of nature" the unseen world reveals its own benignant face. And this brings us to James's concluding reflections on prayer.

78. Ibid., 477.

79. Ibid.

80. James, *Writings, 1902–1910*, 1185.

81. James, *The Varieties of Religious Experience*, 464–65; Sabatier, *Esquisse d'une Philosophie de la Religion*.

THE PRAYERFUL CONSCIOUSNESS AND THE RELIGIOUS LIFE

In his lecture titled "The Reality of the Unseen" (lecture 3) James lamented the fact that "'science' in many minds is genuinely taking the place of a religion."[82] He noted that "laws of nature" are replacing the "feeling of objective presence" in the world, a presence that was only half-metaphoric, "just as even now we may speak of the smile of the morning, the kiss of the breeze, or the bite of the cold, without really meaning that these phenomena of nature actually wear a human face."[83] In a footnote to this passage he quoted Bernardin de St. Pierre's observation in his *Studies of Nature*: "Nature is always so interesting under whatever aspect she shows herself, that when it rains, I seem to see a beautiful woman weeping. She appears the more beautiful the more afflicted she is."[84] For religion, there is a certain "objective" truth in this view of nature as a beautiful woman weeping, a view that is not so much imposed upon nature as excited by it.

In his final lecture James returns to this conflict between a certain scientific view of the world and the religious view. He begins the lecture with an effort to summarize "in the broadest possible way the characteristics of the religious life" as these have emerged in the course of these lectures.[85] They include the following beliefs: (1) that the visible world is part of a more spiritual universe from which it draws its chief significance; (2) that union or harmonious relation with that higher universe is our true end; and (3) that prayer or inner communion with the spirit thereof—be that spirit "God" or "law"—is a process wherein work is really done, and spiritual energy flows in and produces effects, psychological or material, within the phenomenal world.[86] He adds that religion also includes the following psychological characteristics: (4) a new zest that adds itself like a gift to life and takes the form either of lyrical enchantment or of appeal to earnestness and heroism; and (5) an assurance of safety and a temper of peace, and, in relation to others, a preponderance of loving affections.[87]

This summary of the characteristics of the religious life indicates that prayer or inner communion is the means whereby one opens oneself to the

---

82. James, *The Varieties of Religious Experience*, 57.
83. Ibid., 58.
84. Ibid.; St. Pierre, *Studies in Nature*.
85. James, *The Varieties of Religious Experience*, 485.
86. Ibid.
87. Ibid., 485–86. The first of the two psychological effects is derived primarily from James's lectures on saintliness. The second, especially the assurance of safety and a temper of peace, is derived from his lectures on conversion.

unseen world and allows spiritual energy to make a difference in one's perception of—and receptivity to—the visible or phenomenal world.

In commenting on the central role that this accords prayer in the religious life, James asserts that the scientific attitude of the day is the greatest threat to religion because it takes the view that prayer is merely a "survival" from more primitive times when our ancestors believed that we could "coerce the spiritual powers" to "get them on our side," especially in "our dealings with the natural world."[88] While he shares the scientific community's critique of such efforts to coerce the spiritual powers, he distances himself from its insistence that we replace animistic views of the world as found in religion with science's "mathematical and mechanical modes of conception."[89] If science claims that animistic views of the natural world are mere "survivals" of a more primitive way of thinking, James cautions that the natural world possesses such "picturesquely striking" features that our ancestors would surely have viewed these "as the more promising avenue to the knowledge of Nature's life" than the "thin, pallid, uninteresting ideas" that "guide science's approach to nature."[90]

He observes that "it is still in these richer animistic and dramatic aspects that religion delights to dwell. It is the terror and beauty of phenomena, the 'promise' of the dawn and of the rainbow, the 'voice' of the thunder, the 'gentleness' of the summer rain, the 'sublimity' of the stars, and not the physical laws which these things follow, by which the religious mind still continues to be most impressed."[91] In effect, this scientific attitude and the melancholic mood share in common the sense that the natural world is dead and lifeless, and it is the religious temperament, with its perception of the "vivified face of nature," that experiences the world as receptively and responsively alive. The very fact that the scientific attitude shares the melancholic perception of the world as indifferent does not in itself invalidate science, but it surely calls into question its disparagement of religion. Thus, the prayerful consciousness, which is of critical importance to the religious perception of the natural world as transfigured, is not only the core of religion but also the basis for its claims against the scientific view that religion is a mere survival of more primitive ways of thinking and perceiving.

To be sure, the individual's perception of the phenomenal world is very much a subjective matter. For some, the world is warm and inviting; for

---

88. Ibid., 495.

89. Ibid., 496–97.

90. Ibid., 497. He cites in this regard concepts of weight, movement, velocity, direction, and position.

91. Ibid., 497–98.

others, it is cold and sinister. But there is an objective factor here as well, in that the world "out there" is not an undifferentiated mass but has features that stand out from the rest and that appear more "animated" than other features. For those who are religious, these are the very features of the world that have the sense and feel of divine presence. For them, the reality of God is perceptible behind the promise of the dawn, the voice of the thunder, the gentleness of the summer rain, the sublimity of the stars.[92]

CONCLUSION

In his discussion in *The Principles of Psychology* of the role that sense perceptions play in effecting belief, James observes: "No object which neither possesses [sensible] vividness in its own right nor is able to borrow it from anything else has a chance of making headway against vivid rivals, or of rousing in us that reaction in which belief consists. On the vivid objects we *pin*, as the saying goes, our faith in all the rest; and our belief returns instinctively even to those of them from which reflection has led it away."[93] To illustrate his point, he cites the role played by portraits or photographs of a dead or distant friend in enabling us to "realize" the person's existence. Indeed, "To many persons among us, photographs of lost ones seem to be fetishes" as the "mere materiality of the reminder is almost as important as its resemblance" to the loved one.[94] But what such portraits and photographs do is to heighten our awareness of the reality of the one who is no longer physically present. Also, the portrait and photograph testify to the objective reality of the one being portrayed.

James goes on to note that if portraits and photographs have such a powerful influence on our capacity to believe, so do words, but only if they are sensibly vivid. He says that "some persons, the present writer among the number, can hardly lecture without a blackboard: the abstract conceptions

---

92. In his Hibbert Lectures titled *A Pluralistic Universe*, delivered and published in 1909, the year of his death, James critiques the philosophical school of absolute idealism on much the same grounds that he critiques the scientific attitude, and he draws on the philosophical works of the German physicist-philosopher Gustav Theodor Fechner (1801–1887) in support of this critique. Fechner's significance for James is in the fact that the world he portrays is "thick," vivid and pulsating with life. While he has major reservations concerning Fechner's notion of "the earth soul" James is strongly supportive of his representation of earth in female form and, more particularly, as sympathetically disposed to us. For a brief discussion of James's endorsement of Fechner's views, see Capps, *At Home in the World*, 152–56.

93. James, *The Principles of Psychology*, 2:301–2.

94. Ibid., 304.

must be symbolized by letters, squares or circles, and the relations between them by lines. All this symbolism, linguistic, graphic, and dramatic, has other uses too, for it abridges thought and fixes terms. But one of its uses is surely to rouse the believing reaction and give to the ideas a more living reality."[95]

What James has given us in *The Varieties*, then, are word portraits that provide a vivid sense of their subjects' lives among us, so that we, in reading about their faith, may in a reflexive way have a faith of our own.[96] The book succeeds in this sense to the extent that its word portraits are vivid, thereby compelling our attention. Where there is such sensible vividness there will be living religion, for where sensibly vivid objects claim our attention, the reality of spiritual things is brought home to us. Religion dares to put a face on the visible world, and thereby, like portraiture, engenders belief in a reality that exists outside the work itself.

James concludes that three beliefs summarize in the broadest way the characteristics of the religious life. The first of these is that "the visible world

---

95. James, *The Varieties of Religious Experience*, 305. James confesses that he is not a very good "visualizer" himself. In his chapter on "Imagination" in his *The Principles of Psychology* he comments on persons who can give lifelike descriptions of what they have seen and then says in a footnote, "I am myself a good draughtsman, and have a very lively interest in pictures, statues, architecture and decoration, and a keen sensibility to artistic effects. But I am an extremely poor visualizer, and find myself unable to reproduce in my mind's eye pictures which I have most carefully examined" (2:53). In a later footnote in the same chapter he again confesses, "I am myself a very poor visualizer, and find that I can seldom call to mind even a single letter of the alphabet in purely retinal terms. I must trace the letter by running my mental eye over its contour in order that the image of it shall have any distinctness at all. On questioning a large number of people, mostly students, I find that perhaps half of them say they have no such difficulty in seeing letters mentally. Many affirm that they can see an entire word at once, especially a short one like 'dog,' with no such feeling of creating the letters successively by tracing them with the eye" (ibid., 2:61). James's confessions may indicate that he lacks the very ability that is necessary to "see" the phenomenal world, but they may just as well mean that his ability to see the phenomenal world is not in question, that what he cannot do is "see" *in here* (i.e., in his mind) the world out there. This means that he needs the visible world to stimulate thought and, conversely, he cannot think if, when he is in a melancholic mood, the phenomenal world offers no stimulation to thought. This would be consistent with his view that the natural world is necessary to make the spiritual or unseen world come alive and make its own reality felt. He would, I believe, be especially sympathetic with the views expressed by James Martineau in his sermon "Help Thou My Unbelief," quoted in *The Varieties of Religious Experience*, 475.

96. It is noteworthy in this regard that James includes himself in this collection of portraits. He is not, of course, front and center. In fact, he is there anonymously as the "French sufferer," a man who experiences the worst form of melancholy—that of panic fear—when he sees *himself*, potentially, in the black-haired youth with greenish skin whom he had witnessed in the asylum (James, *The Varieties of Religious Experience*, 160).

is part of a more spiritual universe from which it draws its chief significance"; the second is that "union or harmonious relation with that higher universe is our true end"; and the third is that "prayer or inner communion" with the spirit of this universe "is a process wherein work is really done, and spiritual energy flows in and produces effects, psychological or material, within the phenomenal world."[97] It may seem rather trite to suggest that James is proposing here that seeing is believing. But this, I believe, is precisely his point. If so, it is by means of the prayerful consciousness that our eyes are truly opened and we see that there is *more* to reality than meets the eye.[98]

---

97. James, *The Varieties of Religious Experience*, 485.

98. James suggests in his concluding lecture in *The Varieties of Religious Experience* that salvation arrives for a person when he "identifies his real being with the germinal high part of himself; and does so in the following way. *He becomes conscious that this higher part is conterminous and continuous with a MORE of the same quality, which is operative in the universe outside of him, and which he can keep in working touch with, and in a fashion get on board of and save himself when all his lower being has gone to pieces in the wreck*," (ibid., 508; italics original). I will return to this allusion to the "more" in chapter 11.

PART II

LIVING IN HOPE

9

A Troubled Man
The Case of Ansel Bourne

In this chapter I will focus on the American clergyman Ansel Bourne (1826–1910). He suffered from a serious mental illness—multiple personality disorder—and James attempted to help him by means of hypnosis. This case recalls our discussion in chapter 5 of the divided self and the process of unification. However, in Bourne's case this unification remained elusive. I will draw especially on Michael G. Kenny's study of Ansel Bourne supplemented by Eugene Taylor's reconstruction of James's Lowell lecture on multiple personality.[1]

In 1896 James delivered the Lowell Lectures on the theme of exceptional mental states at Huntington Hall in the Back Bay area of Boston. He was fifty years old at the time, and the Lowell Lectures, established in 1836, were ten years older. When he was asked to recommend a lecturer for the series, he did so, but he also volunteered himself as a possible future lecturer, suggesting that the purpose of his lectures would be "to bring together the newest insights in the field of suggestive therapeutics with those from psychotherapy, medicine, and psychology."[2] He would deal with subjects relating to mental illness but in such a way as to "shape our thoughts about them toward optimistic and hygienic conclusions."[3] James's goal would be to overcome the idea that mental illness or insanity is a taboo subject, one

---

1. Kenny, *The Passion of Ansel Bourne*; Taylor, *William James on Exceptional Mental States*, 73–92.
2. Taylor, *William James on Exceptional Mental States*, 5.
3. Ibid.

that is inappropriate for a popular public lecture series. His proposal was accepted and he was invited to give the lectures that very year, beginning in October and concluding in November.

The fourth lecture focused on multiple personality disorder,[4] and much of the lecture involved the presentation of cases of "alternating personality," a form of mental illness that had become more prominent in recent years.[5] Several of these cases involved "fugue" states, or the passage from one state of consciousness into another with complete loss of memory for the previous state. James presented three cases of "fugue" states that involved men who traveled long distances and had no recollection of having left home, of how they got to where they were going, or why they ended up there. He called this "ambulatory automatism," which distinguished it from automatic writing, an automatism that he had discussed in his second Lowell lecture on automatism.[6]

The first two of these cases were French patients who were presented in the writings of the French psychiatrists Philippe Tissié and Fulgence Raymond.[7] The third was that of the Reverend Ansel Bourne of Greene, Rhode Island. Michael Kenny notes that when James was informed of the case of Ansel Bourne by a member of the recently formed Society for Psychical Research, it occurred to him that it might be possible through hypnosis

---

4. The other lectures were on dreams and hypnotism, automatism, hysteria, demoniacal possession, witchcraft, degeneration, and genius.

5. The alternating personality was discussed in chapter 6 on the psychology of religious conversion.

6. As I noted in chapter 6, he also mentions automatic writing in *The Varieties of Religious Experience*. In his chapter on "The Reality of the Unseen" he notes that Theodor Flournoy has shared with him a testimony by a friend of his who has the gift of automatic or involuntary writing. This friend notes that whenever she practices automatic writing, it does not feel that what she writes is due to a subconscious self but rather to a foreign presence external to her body: "It is sometimes so definitely characterized that I could point to its exact position. This impression of presence is impossible to describe. It varies in intensity and clearness according to the personality from whom the writing professes to come. If it is someone whom I love, I feel it immediately, before any writing has come. My heart seems to recognize it" (62). In his "Other Characteristics" chapter James mentions a friend, "a first-rate psychologist" and "a subject of graphic automatism," who tells him that "the appearance of independent actuation in the movements of his arm, when he writes automatically, is so distinct that it obliges him to abandon a psychophysical theory which he had previously believed in, the theory, namely, that we have no feeling of the discharge downwards of our voluntary motor-centers. We must normally have such a feeling, he thinks, or the *sense of an absence* would not be so striking as it is in these experiences" (478–79). For him as for Flournoy's friend the movements of his arm are involuntary. James also cites a recent automatically written book by George A. Fuller titled *Wisdom of the Ages* (479).

7. Ian Hacking discusses both cases in *Mad Travelers*.

to recover Bourne's memory of the personality he had adopted during his fugue state. Having been exposed to hypnosis in his earlier days, Bourne was agreeable to this idea and was brought to Boston to begin a series of hypnotic sessions.[8] Born in 1826, he was sixty-four years old when he began the hypnotic sessions in 1890.

Because James's Lowell Lectures were not published, they have had to be reconstructed from James's notes.[9] But he included an account of the Bourne case in *The Principles of Psychology* in the section on alternating personality in his chapter on "The Consciousness of Self."[10] The following is the full verbatim account.

JAMES'S ACCOUNT OF BOURNE'S FUGUE STATE

The Reverend Ansel Bourne was brought up in the trade of a carpenter, but as a result of a sudden temporary loss of sight and hearing under very peculiar circumstances, he became converted from Atheism to Christianity just prior to turning thirty, and has since that time for the most part lived the life of an itinerant preacher. He has been subject to headaches and temporary fits of depression of spirits during most of his life, and has had a few fits of unconsciousness lasting an hour or less. He also has a region of somewhat diminished cutaneous sensibility on the left thigh. Otherwise his health is good and his muscular strength and endurance are excellent. He is of a firm and self-reliant disposition, a man whose yea is yea and his nay, nay; and his character for uprightness is such in the community that no person who knows him will for a moment admit the possibility of his case not being perfectly genuine.

On January 17, 1887, he drew 551 dollars from a bank in Providence with which to pay for a certain lot of land in Greene, paid certain bills, and got into a Pawtucket horse-car. This is the last incident which he remembers. He did not return home that day, and nothing was heard of him for two months. He was published in the papers as missing, and foul play being suspected the police sought in vain his whereabouts. On the morning of March 14, however, at Norristown, Pennsylvania, a man calling himself Albert John Brown, who had rented a small shop six weeks previously, stocked it with stationery, confectionary, fruit and small articles, and carried on his quiet trade without seeming to anyone unnatural or eccentric, woke up in a fright and called in the people of the house to tell him where he was.

8. Kenny, *The Passion of Ansel Bourne*, 68.
9. Taylor, *William James on Exceptional Mental States*.
10. James, *The Principles of Psychology*, 1:391–93.

He said that his name was Ansel Bourne, that he was entirely ignorant of Norristown, that he knew nothing of shop-keeping and that the last thing he remembered—it seemed only yesterday—was drawing the money from the bank, etc., in Providence. He would not believe that two months had elapsed.

The people of the house thought him insane; and so, at first, did Dr. Louis H. Read, whom they called in to see him. But on telegraphing to Providence, confirmatory messages came, and presently his nephew, Mr. Andrew Harris, arrived upon the scene, made everything straight, and took him home. He was very weak, having lost apparently over twenty pounds of flesh during his escapade, and had such a horror of the idea of the candy store that he refused to set foot in it again.

The first two weeks of the period remained unaccounted for, as he had no memory, after he had resumed his normal personality, of any part of the time, and no one who knew him seems to have seen him after he left home. The remarkable part of the change is, of course, the peculiar occupation which the so-called Brown indulged in. Mr. Bourne has never in his life had the slightest contact with trade. Brown was described by neighbors as taciturn, orderly in his habits, and in no way queer. He went to Philadelphia several times; replenished his stock; cooked for himself in the back shop, where he also slept; went regularly to church; and once at a prayer meeting made what was considered by the hearers a good address, in the course of which he related an incident that he had witnessed in his natural state of Bourne.

This was all that was known of the case until June, 1890, when I induced Mr. Bourne to submit to hypnotism so as to see whether, in the hypnotic trance, his "Brown" memory would not come back. It did so with surprising readiness; so much so indeed that it proved quite impossible to make him whilst in the hypnosis remember any of the facts of his normal life. He had heard of Ansel Bourne, but "didn't know as he had ever met the man."[11] When confronted with Mrs. Bourne he said that he had "never seen

---

11. Although, as James notes, Brown indicated that he had never heard of a man named Ansel Bourne, Michael G. Kenny, in *The Passion of Ansel Bourne*, indicates that Brown's memory contained facts that were also true of Bourne, such as the fact that "he recalled his birth date but said that he—Brown—had been born in New Hampshire, whereas on the same day Bourne had been born in New York" (ibid., 68). Kenny also notes that when James asked the hypnotically resurrected Brown persona what he had undergone back home Brown replied: "Passed though great deal of trouble . . . Losses of friends, losses of property . . . Trouble way back yonder. All mixed up, confused. Don't like to think about it." Also, in a later session when he was his Bourne personality, he was asked what was troubling him, and he responded, "Something I have been trying to get out for a long time—where I am and where I am going" (ibid., 78). Kenny's

the woman before," etc. On the other hand, he told of his peregrinations during the fortnight,[12] and gave all sorts of details about the Norristown episode. The whole thing was prosaic enough; and the Brown personality seems to be nothing but a rather shrunken, dejected, and amnesiac extract of Mr. Bourne himself. He gives no motive for the wandering except that there was "trouble back there" and he "wanted rest." During the trance he looks old, the corners of his mouth are drawn down, his voice is slow and weak, and he sits screening his eyes and trying vainly to remember what lay before and after the two months of the Brown experience. "I'm all hedged in," he says: "I can't get out at either end. I don't know what set me down in that Pawtucket horse-car, and I don't know how I ever left that store, or what became of it." His eyes are practically normal, and all his sensibilities (save for tardier response) about the same in hypnosis as in waking. I had hoped by suggestion, etc., to run the two personalities into one, and make the memories continuous, but no artifice would avail to accomplish this, and Mr. Bourne's skull today still covers two distinct personal selves.

The case (whether it contains an epileptic element or not) should apparently be classed as one of spontaneous hypnotic trance, persisting for two months. The peculiarity of it is that nothing else like it ever occurred in the man's life, and that no eccentricity of character came out. In most cases, the attacks recur, and the sensibilities and conduct markedly change.[13]

THE RESURRECTED SELF

While James was unsuccessful in reconciling the two personalities of Ansel Bourne, the A. J. Brown personality's observation under hypnosis that there

---

more expansive version of Bourne's responses is drawn from Richard Hodgson's article "A Case of Double Consciousness," which was originally presented to the Society for Psychical Research.

12. In a footnote James writes: "He had spent an afternoon in Boston, a night in New York, and afternoon in Newark, and ten days or more in Philadelphia, first in a certain hotel and next in a certain boarding-house, making no acquaintances, 'resting,' reading, and 'looking round.' I have unfortunately been unable to get independent corroboration of these details, as the hotel registers are destroyed, and the boarding-house named by him has been pulled down. He forgets the name of the two ladies who kept it" (James, *The Varieties of Religious Experience*, 392).

13. In a footnote James notes but rejects the theory that Ansel Bourne may have been engaging in an elaborate ruse. He writes: "The details of the case, it will be seen, are all *compatible* with simulation. I can only say of that, that no one who was examined Mr. Bourne (including Dr. Read, Dr. Weir Mitchell, Dr. Guy Hinsdale, and Mr. R. Hodgson) practically doubts his ingrained honesty, nor, so far as I can discover, do any of his personal acquaintances indulge in a skeptical view" (ibid., 393).

was "trouble back there" and he "needed rest" may provide the answer as to why the secondary personality emerged and why it took this particular form. Since Bourne was brought up to be a carpenter and worked in the carpentry trade before he became an itinerant preacher, contemporaries pointed out that he had some sort of identification with Jesus.[14] In effect, Jesus was his imitative example. Also, his conversion from atheism to Christianity resulted from his temporary loss of sight and hearing, the very sorts of symptoms with which Jesus's own contemporaries were afflicted and which he was successful in curing.[15]

Jesus too was an itinerant preacher. It is noteworthy therefore that the crisis that took Bourne eventually to Norristown was precipitated by the fact that he had remarried after his first wife's death in 1881, and his second wife insisted that he remain close to home. Consequently, he had resumed the carpenter's trade, and by 1887 he had money in the bank.[16] If, as James indicates, he took money out of the bank to purchase a lot, this would have been another, perhaps decisive step toward settling down for good. Thus his failure to carry through on this plan seems to indicate that his subconscious mind was determined to sabotage what his conscious mind was attempting to accomplish.

Michael Kenny notes in this connection that Richard Hodgson, who presented the case to the Boston chapter of the English Society for Psychical Research, felt that "a religious factor was also important in Bourne's 1887 transformation."[17] Hodgson suggested in his article "A Case of Double Consciousness" that when Bourne ceased his itinerant ministry "he became somewhat troubled, thinking that he was not as active in religious work as he should be. This thought that he was not 'on the path of duty' weighed on his mind, and he seems inclined to think that if he had been in active religious service, and therefore contented with his work, the experiences which he subsequently underwent would never have occurred."[18]

Kenny notes, however, that for Hodgson the question of how the enigmatic A. J. Brown, who did not differ in personality from Bourne himself, represented a solution to these difficulties remained a mystery, and Hodgson could only conclude that "taken altogether, the case is not a little

---

14. Kenny, *The Passion of Ansel Bourne*, 66.

15. See Capps, *Jesus the Village Psychiatrist*, 57–80. In the chapter on Jesus's healings of two blind men, I discuss the case of Ralph Waldo Emerson, who experienced temporary blindness when he was student at Harvard College (ibid., 63–68).

16. Kenny, *The Passion of Ansel Bourne*, 66.

17. Ibid., 78.

18. Ibid.

perplexing."[19] Presumably, if A. J. Brown had turned up in Norristown as an itinerant preacher, the case would not have been so perplexing. If he had done so, A. J. Brown would have been acting on the troubled thoughts of Ansel Bourne, who was feeling guilty over the fact that he was no longer engaged in ministry. But instead he rented a store and stocked it with stationery, confectionary, fruit, and small articles.

Perhaps, though, an important clue toward solving the mystery lies in the fact that although A. J. Brown and Ansel Bourne did not share the same birthplace, they had the same birthdate. Might A. J. Brown, then, have been that part of Ansel Bourne's character that life's circumstances did not allow to develop, the part of him that was neither the carpenter nor the itinerant preacher? And was his trip from Providence to Norristown—which included a stop in New York, his birthplace—an attempt to activate this part of himself?

James's essay "Great Men and Their Environment," which was originally a lecture for the Harvard Natural History Society in 1880 and published the same year in the *Atlantic Monthly*,[20] is especially relevant in this regard. Here James notes that what a person becomes in life may turn on some accidental circumstance so the course that one's life has taken could very easily have been otherwise. His illustration may have particular relevance to the life of Ansel Bourne: "Whether a young man enters business or the ministry may depend on a decision which has to be made before a certain day. He takes the place offered in the counting-house, and is *committed*. Little by little, the habits, the knowledge, of the other career, which once lay so near, cease to be reckoned even among his possibilities. At first, he may sometimes doubt whether the self he murdered in that decisive hour might not have been the better of the two; but with the years such questions themselves expire, and the old alternative *ego*, once so vivid, fades into something less substantial than a dream."[21]

Since Ansel Bourne had no prior experience as a tradesman, perhaps his A. J. Brown identity was "the old alternative ego" that had faded "into something less substantial than a dream." But dreams, after all, may continue to live in the subconscious mind and, as James suggests in *The Varieties*, conversions are typically the result of incursions or irruptions from the subconscious to the conscious mind. If the idea of becoming a tradesman was a buried dream of his, Bourne lived this dream under the name of A. J.

---

19. Ibid., 78–79.

20. James, *The Will to Believe and Other Essays in Popular Philosophy*, 216–54. Its title in the *Atlantic Monthly* was "Great Men, Great Ideas, and the Environment."

21. Ibid., 227.

Brown for several weeks and, in doing so, he proved that he had the makings of a successful tradesman. Then, however, his former identity returned and the A. J. Brown identity sank into oblivion. Because the two identities represented two very different life trajectories, it is not all that surprising that, as James put it, it was impossible to "run the two personalities into one."[22]

It may also be of some significance that James refers to A. J. Brown's small shop as a "candy store." This seemingly insignificant fact may suggest that Bourne's subconscious mind was attempting to help him escape from the bind that his adoption of Jesus as his imitative example had inadvertently gotten him into. Bourne's contemporaries had recognized that the fact that he was a carpenter by trade contributed greatly to his decision to become an itinerant preacher. In this regard, Jesus was his model and exemplar. But owing to his second wife's insistence that he settle down, he had resumed the carpenter's trade, something that Jesus, his model, would never have done. And herein lay the basis for guilt. Moreover, as A. J. Brown suggested under hypnosis, Ansel Bourne was "all mixed up" and "confused."

Perhaps, then, his subconscious mind was suggesting a way out of the bind he was in, advising him to do something different with his life, to become, as it were, the "candy man" who offers sweets to everyone, youngsters included. In any event, the "horror" that Ansel Bourne felt about "the idea of the candy store" and his absolute refusal "to set foot in it again"[23] reflects the degree to which this part of him could not be allowed to live. One cannot but wonder if the outcome may have been different had he viewed his A. J. Brown self as an attempt to embrace Jesus' calling upon adults to become like children (Matt 18:3).

THE POSSIBILITY OF SELF-RECONCILIATION

Whether or not the foregoing analysis illumines the mystery that Hodgson noted in his article, one thing is clear: James had good reason to hope that by means of hypnosis the two personalities could be reconciled to each other, for there was support for this very hope in another case of alternating personality that James presented in *The Principles of Psychology* and also in the Lowell Lectures.[24] This is the case of Mary Reynolds.[25]

22. James, *The Principles of Psychology*, 1:392.
23. Ibid., 1:391.
24. Ibid., 1:381–84; Taylor, *William James on Exceptional Mental States*, 77–78.
25. Taylor notes that James's source for the case of Mary Reynolds was Silas Weir Mitchell's "Mary Reynolds: A Case of Double Consciousness," published in 1888. Taylor adds that the case of Mary Reynolds was originally brought to light by Mitchell's

Mary Reynolds (1793–1854) was a melancholy young woman living in Meadville, Pennsylvania, who, for five weeks, was a completely different person: cheerful in the extreme, fearless, fond of practical jokes. Then she returned to her former self. These alternations from one state to another continued at intervals of varying lengths for fifteen or sixteen years, but they finally ceased when she was thirty-five or thirty-six years old. At this time her second state of cheerfulness and buoyancy became fully established. On the other hand, James notes that over time she changed from the "gay, hysterical, mischievous woman, fond of jests and subject to absurd beliefs or delusive convictions, to one retaining the joyousness and love of society, but sobered down to levels of practical usefulness."[26] Some members of her family spoke of this change as her third state. As James puts it, "She is described as becoming rational, industrious, and very cheerful, yet reasonably serious; possessed of a well-balanced temperament, and not having the slightest indication of an injured or disturbed mind. For some years she taught school, and in that capacity was both useful and acceptable, being a general favorite with old and young."[27]

That Ansel Bourne did not experience this transformation into a third state does not, of course, mean that his life was a failure. In fact, he must have experienced a great sense of relief when he realized that he was, quite literally, Bourne again. It's simply that one cannot help but wonder what might have happened had he been able to incorporate his A. J. Brown self into his Bourne-again self. As Michael Kenny puts it in the concluding sentence of his study of Ansel Bourne, "His intense preoccupied eyes look out from the old photographs as though he were trying—and failing—to remember something important."[28]

---

father, Dr. John Kearsley Mitchell, in the 1930s (*William James on Exceptional Mental States*, 77).

26. James, *The Principles of Psychology*, 1:383.
27. Ibid.
28. Kenny, *The Passion of Ansel Bourne*, 188.

10

A Spiritual Person
The Example of Phillips Brooks

As we saw in chapter 8, James began his discussion of the prayerful consciousness with the case of George Müller. He concluded that Müller's "intensely private and practical conception of his relations with the Deity continued the traditions of the most primitive human thought," and that when "we compare a mind like his with such a mind as, for example, Emerson's or Phillips Brooks's, we see the range which the religious consciousness covers."[1]

James's suggestion that the mind of Phillips Brooks warrants mention in the same context as that of Ralph Waldo Emerson is especially noteworthy for, unlike Emerson, Brooks did not have an international reputation as a scholar and writer. With the exception of his Beecher Lectures at Yale University, his published works consisted of sermons that he had preached as rector of Trinity Episcopal Church in Boston.[2] But James's allusion to the mind of Phillips Brooks suggests that he viewed Brooks as a person whose religious life deserves more than casual mention—that, in fact, Brooks may

---

1. James, *The Varieties of Religious Experience*, 471. Eugene Taylor also notes that Phillips Brooks was a charter member of the American branch of the English Society on Psychical Research that James inaugurated in 1884 (*William James on Exceptional Mental States*, 179).

2. Brooks, *The Light of the World, and Other Sermons*; Brooks, *Phillips Brooks: Selected Sermons*.

be especially exemplary of the characteristics of the religious life as he identifies them in the concluding lecture of *The Varieties*.[3]

James also referred to Brooks in his response to James Bissett Pratt's questionnaire on religion. As I noted in chapters 2 and 8, Pratt circulated a questionnaire in 1904 that consisted of ten questions about religion, and James was one of the respondents. Pratt asked the respondents what they meant by "spirituality" and to "describe a typical spiritual person." To the former question James wrote: "Susceptibility to ideals, but with a certain freedom to indulge in imagination about them. A certain amount of 'other-worldly' fancy. Otherwise, you have mere morality, or 'taste.'"[4] To the follow-up request for a description of a typical spiritual person he simply wrote: "Phillips Brooks." This, of course, was hardly a *description* of a typical spiritual person, but it was consistent with James's tendency, evident in *The Varieties of Religious Experience*, to draw attention to individual exemplars of various features and manifestations of the religious life.[5]

If James considered Brooks to be exemplary of a "spiritual person," what was it about Brooks that made him so? In a sense, James provides his own answer to this question by indicating what he means by *spirituality*: "Susceptibility to ideals but within a certain freedom to indulge in imagination about them" and "a certain amount of 'other-worldly' fancy." I suggest, however, that we can gain a more nuanced understanding of what makes Brooks a "spiritual person" by focusing on several of his sermons and his poem "O Little Town of Bethlehem." A short summary of his life will introduce the man who exemplified the spiritual person.[6]

THE LIFE OF PHILLIPS BROOKS

Phillips Brooks was born in Boston in 1835 and died there in 1893. He was the second of six sons. The family religious tradition was Congregationalism,

---

3. James, *The Varieties of Religious Experience*, 485–86. These five characteristics were presented in the section headed "The Prayerful Consciousness and the Religious Life" in chapter 8.

4. James, *Writings, 1902–1910*, 1185.

5. In *What Pragmatism Means* Pratt points out that for James the distinguishing feature of pragmatism among the philosophical schools is not that it is concerned with the practical (for other schools of thought can make this claim), but that it is concerned with the concrete and particular as opposed to the abstract and the general (85–86). Thus James's response to Pratt's request for a description of a spiritual person is a clear reflection of his pragmatism, and Pratt would have understood that this was the case.

6. My source for this brief biographical sketch is Raymond W. Albright's *Focus on Infinity: A Life of Phillips Brooks*.

but his mother and aunt were confirmed in the Episcopal Church when he was five years old. His father was confirmed seven years later. Dr. A. H. Vinton, the rector at St. Paul's Church in Boston, was his lifelong mentor. In his youth Brooks attended Boston Latin School and then entered Harvard College in 1851 at the age of sixteen.

After graduating from Harvard in 1855 Brooks taught at Boston Latin School but resigned before the year was out. Following several months of indecision, he enrolled at Virginia Theological Seminary in the fall of 1856. Brooks completed his seminary education three years later and considered three viable options: to become the assistant to Dr. Vinton, who had recently become rector of Holy Trinity Church in Philadelphia; to remain at Virginia Theological Seminary as head of its preparatory school and chapel assistant; or to become rector of the Church of the Advent in Philadelphia. He chose the latter. He remained at the Church of the Advent for two and a half years and then became rector of Holy Trinity Church, when Dr. Vinton moved to New York City. He stayed at Holy Trinity for seven years (1862–1869). In 1865, when he was twenty-nine years old, Brooks traveled to Europe, engaged in some brief theological study in Germany, enough to convince him that he lacked the necessary background and technical skills to be a scholar, then went to the Holy Land. Here he wrote the words to "O Little Town of Bethlehem," which was set to music by the organist at Holy Trinity, Lewis H. Redner.

In 1869 he accepted the position of Rector at Trinity Church in Boston. He remained at Trinity for twenty-two years. During his tenure at Trinity, a new church edifice was built, he became well known for his preaching, and he was heavily involved in ecumenical activities in Boston. In 1877 he was invited to give the Beecher Lectures at Yale University, which afforded the opportunity to reflect on his preaching principles. The same year Harvard University awarded him the Doctor of Divinity degree. In 1881 he was offered the position of preacher to Harvard University and a professorship in Christian morals. After much reflection he turned the offer down. In 1882 he asked the wardens and vestrymen of Trinity Church to grant him an extended vacation in order that he might regain his perspective on life.

On his return he remained at Trinity Church for eight more years and was then appointed Bishop of the Massachusetts Diocese in 1891. This appointment was controversial because many considered Brooks too liberal. In fact, several of his actions as rector of Trinity Church, such as presiding over the marriage of a couple despite the fact that the groom was not a member, had been censured by the previous bishop. Brooks died two years later (at age fifty-eight) of diphtheria, contracted when he visited a church one evening in his official role as bishop and was exposed to this highly contagious disease.

Brooks never married, so his only survivors were several brothers and their families. However, his death was a major event in Boston. Harvard students carried his body on their shoulders, and persons of all faiths felt the loss of his spiritual presence among them. Trinity Church stands in Copley Square, and on one side of this imposing edifice is a statue of Brooks by Augustus Saint-Gaudens. It portrays a large man (he was 6'4") with one hand upraised in a gesture of benediction and triumph. Jesus, a full head taller but considerably slimmer and clothed in a full length robe and hood, is standing immediately behind him and a cross looms behind them both. There is a pulpit to the left of Brooks and in front of Jesus, suggesting that Brooks's reputation was built on his preaching.

THE SERMONS: RESOURCES AND IDEALS

I would now like to turn to a brief discussion of Brooks's sermons. Given the vast number of sermons that he preached and the fact that many were published during his own lifetime this discussion will necessarily be selective. However, when one sits down to read his sermons, one can hardly escape the impression that a central—perhaps *the* central—theme in his sermons is that our problems and difficulties in life would seem more manageable if we would recognize our vast store of personal and spiritual resources. In failing to recognize that we already possess these resources, we allow our problems to immobilize us.

Thus, in "Visions and Tasks" Brooks discusses the role of vision in inspiring persons to carry out difficult tasks. Individuals who reach middle adulthood tend to lose their enthusiasm for the tasks they are responsible to perform:

> A man we see sometimes who, as he comes to middle-life, finds his immediate enthusiastic sight of ideal things grown dull; that is the almost necessary condition of his ripening life. He does not spring as quickly as he once did to seize each newly offered hope for man. A thousand disenchantments have made him serious and sober. He looks back, and the glow and sparkle which he once saw in life he sees no longer. He wonders at his recollection of himself, and asks how it is possible that life ever should have seemed to him as he remembers that it did seem.[7]

---

7. Brooks, *Phillips Brooks: Selected Sermons*, 141.

What can such a person do? What resources do persons in midlife already possess to bring them out of their dullness and disenchantment? For Brooks, the simple fact that they once had visions and dreams—which they now suspect are illusions—is the very resource that they may now draw upon in order to remain constant in their tasks. The very fact that life once seemed bright and filled with possibility is now their "most valued certainty." Therefore, one should "not part with that assurance for anything," for all the hard work that he "does now is done in the strength and light of that remembered enthusiasm," and "every day the dreams of his boyhood, which seem dead, are really the live inspirations of his life."[8] Thus, persons who are discouraged in middle life have the necessary resources to overcome their discouragement. The preacher's task is to direct their attention to the fact that they possess these resources.

In "The Egyptians Dead upon the Seashore" Brooks addresses the criticism that his continual emphasis on the resources available to persons to cope with the problems of temptation and sin is "the mere dream of an optimistic sermon."[9] In response, he appeals to his listeners to consult their own experience and ask whether "God has not sometimes given you the right to such a hope?"[10] As you look back over the past, are there not some real victories there? For example, "Are there not at least some temptations to which you yielded then to which you know you can never yield again? Are there not some meannesses which you once thought glorious which now you know are mean? Are there no places where you once stumbled where now you know you can walk firm?"[11]

Brooks goes on to say, however, that he is not appealing merely to human experience. His appeal is also to the Christian truth about humanity. When Christ takes hold of the natural person, "he quickens that struggle into life. No longer can that nature think itself doomed to evil. Intensely sensitive to feel the presence of evil as he never felt it before, the Christian man instantly and intensely knows that evil is a stranger and an intruder in his life. The wonder is not that it should one day be cast out: the wonder is that it should ever have come in."[12] Thus, Brooks contends that his appeal to the resources that an individual has for dealing with any problem is not mere optimism but is rooted in the conviction that the Christian faith has real, practical power. If the outcome were already assured, one would have

8. Ibid.
9. Ibid., 110.
10. Ibid., 111.
11. Ibid.
12. Ibid.

no need of hope. But hope is grounded in the assurance that Christ is a living resource and that through him there is victory over evil, whatever its form may be.

In short, Brooks affirms over and over again that we have not adequately understood the problems that beset us until we have taken account of the resources available to us for dealing with them. While we are inclined to recognize only the strength and tenacity of the problem or difficulty that we face, he bids us to pay attention to the greater strength we possess for overcoming it. As long as we look only at our limitations, our self-knowledge and our understanding of God are seriously distorted: How can you know "what lurking power lies packed away within the near-opened folds of this inactive life?" Have you ever dared to call yourself "the child of God and for one moment felt what that involves?"[13] He concludes: "There is nothing on earth more seemingly insignificant than men's judgment of their own moral and spiritual limitations."[14]

Other sermons could be cited in support of the claim that the central theme in Brooks's sermons is that we already have resources available to us which we fail to recognize. These two, however, make the point that some of these resources derive from who we are—or the persons we have been and are in the process of becoming—while others derive from the fact that we are the beneficiaries of the living Christ and are therefore not alone in the struggles of life. Thus, some resources are personal, and others are spiritual, but the very fact that we embrace—internalize—the spiritual ones makes it relatively pointless to try to differentiate the two kinds of resources.

William James cites Brooks's sermon "How to Be Abased" in "What Makes a Life Significant," one of three lectures that James delivered to students at women's colleges.[15] The citation occurs in the middle of a discussion of ideals. James asks what makes "morally exceptional individuals" different from the rest? His answer: "It can only have been this,—that their souls worked and endured in obedience to some inner *ideal*."[16] James acknowledges that "these ideals of other lives are among those secrets that we can almost never penetrate," although something about the person "may often tell us when they are there."[17] But to illustrate such an ideal he cites examples of persons who have embraced the ideal of voluntary poverty and notes that

---

13. Ibid., 114.
14. Ibid.
15. James, *Talks to Teachers*, 130–46.
16. Ibid., 140.
17. Ibid.

this is an ideal of which Phillips Brooks has "spoken so penetratingly."[18] An extended quotation from Brooks's sermon "How to Be Abased" follows.[19] A few sentences from this quotation provide a general sense of what Brooks has to say about this ideal:

> No life like poverty could so get one to the heart of things and make men know their meaning, could so let us feel life and the world with all the soft cushions stripped off and thrown away ... Poverty makes men come very near each other, and recognize each other's human hearts; and poverty, highest and best of all, demands and cries out for faith in God ... I know how superficial and unfeeling, how like mere mockery, words in praise of poverty may seem ... But I am sure that the poor man's dignity and freedom, his self-respect and energy, depend upon his cordial knowledge that his poverty is a true region and kind of life with its own chances of character, its own springs of happiness, and revelations of God.[20]

Following this citation from Brooks's sermon on the ideal of poverty, James asks:

> But what, exactly, do we mean by an ideal? Can we give no definite account of such a word? In a certain extent we can. An ideal, for instance, must be something intellectually conceived, something of which we are not unconscious, if we have it; and it must carry with it that sort of outlook, uplift, and brightness that go with all intellectual facts. Secondly, there must be *novelty* in an ideal—novelty at least for him whom the ideal grasps. Sodden routine for one person may be ideal novelty for another. This shows that there is nothing absolutely ideal; ideals are relative to the lives that entertain them.[21]

In the paragraphs of his lecture that follow these reflections on the nature of ideals, James emphasizes that ideals alone are not enough to make life significant, for ideals need to be coupled with an active will that seeks to

---

18. Ibid., 141. As we saw in chapter 7, James identifies voluntary poverty as one of the qualities of the saintly character.

19. Brooks's sermon "How to Be Abased" is one of twenty-one sermons in his *The Light of the World, and Other Sermons* (159–76), which was originally published in 1890. It follows "How to Abound," which was preached on the previous Sunday (141–58). The text for the two sermons is Paul's letter to the Philippians 4:12: "I know both how to be abased, and I know how to abound" (KJV). The NRSV translation is, "I know what it is to have little, and I know what it is to have plenty."

20. James, *Talks to Teachers*, 141.

21. Ibid., 142.

unite ideals with the real world so that progress occurs, for without a sense of progress life has little significance. Education is a means of multiplying our ideals and bringing new ones into view, but having a "stock of ideals" is not enough. In fact, in the abstract, "mere ideals are the cheapest things in life" and "everybody has them in some shape or other, personal or general, sound or mistaken, low or high," and some of the "most worthless sentimentalists and dreamers" possibly have them "on the most copious scale."[22] There must, therefore, be a fusion of ideals and "effort, courage, or endurance," for ideals are insufficient in themselves.[23]

IDEALS AND THE ACTIVE IMAGINATION

If the fusion of ideals and active will is essential to the sense that our lives have significance, James asks whether we possess an agency that inspires us to bring about this fusion of ideals and active effort, and he observes that intelligence is required to accomplish this fusion, especially for making judgments concerning the novelties in life that present themselves as ideals worthy of our commitment. But what is the source of this intelligence? I believe that James provides the answer when in his response to Pratt's questionnaire he describes spirituality as a "susceptibility to ideals, but with a certain freedom to indulge in imagination about them."[24] Imagination is the agency that we all possess—though in differing degrees—and it inspires us to make an ideal a living reality. And here Brooks's poem "O Little Town of Bethlehem" provides an excellent illustration of the use of imagination to activate one's ideals. As I noted earlier, he wrote this poem during his visit to the Holy Land in 1865. However, the Bethlehem that he imagines in his poem is not the city that he visited in 1865 but the little town of Bethlehem at the time of Jesus's birth. Here is the poem:

O Little Town of Bethlehem

O little town of Bethlehem,
How still we see thee lie!
Above thy deep and dreamless sleep
The silent stars go by;
Yet in thy dark streets shineth,
The everlasting Light;
The hopes and fears of all the years
Are met in thee tonight.

22. Ibid.
23. Ibid.
24. James, *Writings, 1902–1910*, 1185.

> For Christ is born of Mary;
> And gathered all above
> While mortals sleep, the angels keep
> Their watch of wondering love.
> O morning stars, together
> Proclaim the holy birth.
> And praises sing to God the King,
> And peace to men on earth.
>
> How silently, how silently,
> The wondrous Gift is given!
> So God imparts to human hearts
> The blessing of his heaven.
> No ear may hear his coming,
> But in this world of sin,
> Where meek souls will receive him still,
> The dear Christ enters in.
>
> O holy Child of Bethlehem,
> Descend to us, we pray;
> Cast out our sins, and enter in,
> Be born in us today.
> We hear the Christmas angels
> The great glad tidings tell;
> O come to us, abide with us,
> Our Lord Emmanuel![25]

    Here, Brooks emphasizes the sense of the stillness of the town and the silence of the gift that God has given. This gift does not appear with noisy fanfare but comes ever so silently. Moreover, all that we have hoped and all that we have feared converge on this quiet stable scene where a mother gives birth to a seemingly helpless child. Most important, the poem is a prayer—a prayer that this child who was born in Bethlehem will be "born in us today," and having been born in us, will continue to "abide with us." Thus the poem reflects the prayerful consciousness (as discussed in chapter 8) that enables the poet—and us—to imagine that the birth that occurred long ago in a little town in the Holy Land may occur again in our own hearts. As the "holy Child of Bethlehem" entered a world in which evil is omnipresent, so the "dear Christ" may enter into our hearts today and "cast out" the sin that impedes the realization of our inner ideals.

---

25. Ernest, *The Family Album of Favorite Poems*, 518.

BROOKS'S SPIRITUAL PRESENCE AND PHYSICAL STRENGTH

Aside from his poem "O Little Town of Bethlehem" Brooks was best known for his sermons. At the same time, those who heard him preach frequently commented on his spiritual presence and physical strength. Three months after his death on January 23, 1893, the *Harvard Graduates' Magazine* stated that "men listened, for the most part, not to the sermon, but to him," and added that he aimed "directly at the heart of his hearers," giving them not theology but "the presence of a strong, loving, aspiring, and believing soul."[26] If they responded to his strength of soul, a woman who occasionally attended services at Trinity Church in Boston had this to say shortly after his death about his physical endurance:

> I recall the curious feeling of physical exhaustion that came upon me as I left the church. It was like nothing so much as relaxation following a severe but victorious struggle in some athletic contest. And I remember wondering even then, 'If this so affects me, what must it be to him, and how can he bear it all?' It must have been this which finally wore him out, rather than the pressure of what most of us call work. When he was preaching he was pouring out strength as no other man could, as well as putting the power of his listeners to the utmost strain.[27]

In effect, he embodied his conviction that all individuals possess greater inner resources than they realize. As their minister, he saw his task to be that of encouraging his parishioners, by word and example, to recognize and utilize the vast store of personal and spiritual resources available to them. The statue of Brooks that stands outside Trinity Church today portrays the presence of a strong, loving, aspiring, believing soul, a man whose right arm is raised in a gesture of victory over the fears that reduce our ideals to empty words and phrases. But his imposing presence would not be that of a spiritual person were it not for the fact that another figure is standing behind him, and that this silent figure, who towers over him, is gazing out into the distance—where human hopes cancel human fears.

---

26. Townsend, *Manhood at Harvard*, 133.

27. Albright, *Focus on Infinity*, 392. In light of James's reflections on relaxation in his chapter on the religion of healthy-mindedness in *The Varieties of Religious Experience* and his lecture on "The Gospel of Relaxation" in *Talks to Teachers*, it is noteworthy that the listener suggested that the sense of relaxation that she experienced was due to the feeling that she had witnessed "a severe but victorious struggle."

11

THE LETTING LOOSE OF HOPE

THE PRECEDING CHAPTER ENDED with the suggestion that the future is the place where hopes cancel fears. In this concluding chapter I would like to expand on this suggestion by focusing on James's reflections on hope in *Pragmatism*.[1] As I will suggest near the end of this chapter, hope had for James a deeply personal significance and meaning. This focus on hope recalls our earlier reference in chapter 6 to James's view that the emotions characteristic of religious conversion are hope, happiness, security, and resolve. In effect, our discussion will suggest that hope is primary and that the other fruits are largely dependent on the fact that the religious life is grounded in and founded on the resource of hope.

THE PRAGMATIC METHOD

The context of James's reflections on hope is his discussion of the conflict that exists between philosophers who are rationalistically oriented and those who are empirically minded. His sympathies are clearly with the empirically minded philosophers, but he is concerned that empirical philosophy tends to turn "positive religious constructions out of doors."[2] One purpose of *Pragmatism* is to show that an empiricist philosophy can treat religious constructions as "cordially" as it treats facts. James suggests that pragmatism is the one empiricist philosophy that can and does treat

---

1. James, *Pragmatism*.
2. Ibid., 21.

religious constructions cordially, but it does so in a way that differs from theological and doctrinal claims and affirmations:

> Pragmatism represents a perfectly familiar attitude in philosophy, the empiricist attitude, but it represents it, as it seems to me, both in a more radical and in a less objectionable form than it has ever yet assumed. A pragmatist turns his back resolutely and once for all upon a lot of inveterate habits dear to professional philosophers. He turns away from abstraction and insufficiency, from verbal solutions, from bad *a priori* reasons, from fixed principles, closed systems, and pretended absolutes and origins. He turns towards concreteness and adequacy, towards facts, towards action and towards power. That means the empiricist temper regnant and the rationalist temper sincerely given up. It means the open air and possibilities of nature, as against dogma, artificiality, and the pretence of finality in truth.[3]

James notes, however, that pragmatism is a method only. It does not stand for any special or particular results but is instead an attitude of orientation: "An attitude of looking away from first things, principles, 'categories,' supposed necessities; and of looking towards last things, fruits, consequences, facts."[4]

To illustrate how the pragmatic method works, James addresses the current controversies between idealists (or rationalists) and materialists (or naturalists). He acknowledges that in provisionally taking the side of materialists he will seem to be contradicting his claim that he wants to treat religious constructions cordially, for whereas idealists usually make theistic claims, materialists see no reason for doing so, for they believe that "the laws of physical nature are what runs things."[5] In contrast, idealists believe that spirit exists independently of matter and that a higher spirit—the Absolute—is what ultimately runs things.

What is problematic about the idealists, however, is that they dismiss the claims of materialists by demeaning "matter" itself, viewing it as low, crass, and impure. In James's view this is both unfair and facile: "To anyone who has looked on the face of a dead child or parent the mere fact that matter *could* have taken for a time that precious form, ought to make matter sacred ever after. It makes no difference what the *principle* of life may be, material or immaterial, matter at any rate cooperates, lends itself to all life's

---

3. Ibid., 25.
4. Ibid., 27.
5. Ibid., 42. We may recall here his critique of the scientific attitude in the concluding lecture of *The Varieties of Religious Experience*. See chapter 8.

purposes. That beloved incarnation [of a child or parent] was among matter's possibilities."[6] Thus, the pragmatic method requires that we go further and ask the question: "What do we *mean* by matter? What practical difference can it make now that the world should be run by matter or by spirit? I think we find that the problem takes with this a rather different character."[7]

Applying the pragmatic criterion that an idea or viewpoint needs to make a practical difference, otherwise it is not worth our consideration, he goes on to note that as far as the *past* is concerned it makes no practical difference whether the world is the work of blind physical forces or of a divine spirit. Imagine that the world ends this very moment and therefore has no future whatsoever. In that case, would it matter whether the world was created by God or was the effect of physical forces only? James says no, as the two theories—that the world is the work of blind physical forces or the work of a divine spirit—would have exactly the same practical consequences. But both theories assume that the world does in fact have a *future*, that it has not completed itself. For the pragmatist, the issue is how the two theories conceive the future of the world, and in this regard there *is* a practical difference between them. Noting that we all know the picture of the last state of the universe, which evolutionary science foresees, he says that he cannot state it better than do the words of Arthur Balfour, who writes: "The energies of our system will decay, the glory of the sun will be dimmed, and the earth, tideless and inert, will no longer tolerate the [human] race which has for a moment disturbed its solitude. The uneasy consciousness which in this obscure corner has for a brief space broken the contented silence of the universe will be at rest. Matter will know itself no longer."[8]

For James, the appropriate objection to this view is that its vision of the future is hopeless in the ultimate sense. It is not, as James puts it, "a fulfiller of our remotest hopes."[9] In contrast,

> The notion of God guarantees an ideal order that shall be permanently preserved. A world without a God in it to say the last word, may indeed turn up or freeze, but we then think of him as still mindful of the old ideals and sure to bring them elsewhere to fruition; so that, where he is, tragedy is only provisional and partial, and shipwreck and dissolution not the absolutely final things. This need of an eternal moral order is one of the deepest needs of our breast. And those poets, like Dante and

---

6. James, *Pragmatism*, 43.
7. Ibid., 43–44.
8. Ibid. See Balfour, *The Foundations of Belief*, 30.
9. James, *Pragmatism*, 48.

Wordsworth, who live on the conviction of such an order, owe to that fact the extraordinary tonic and consoling power of their verse.[10]

Thus, the difference between the theistic and materialistic views is not in "hair-splitting abstractions about matters of inner essence, or about the metaphysical attributes of God" but in their very "different emotional and practical appeals," especially in their influence on "our concrete attitudes of hope and expectation."[11] Their practical difference lies in this fundamental fact: "Materialism means simply the denial that the moral order is eternal, and the cutting off of ultimate hopes; spiritualism means the affirmation of an eternal moral order and the letting loose of hope."[12]

THE AFFIRMATION OF AN ETERNAL MORAL ORDER

James anticipates the objection that these different prophecies of the world's future are about events so remote in time that practically speaking they mean nothing to a person of sane mind, that only insane persons concern themselves "about such chimeras as the latter end of the world."[13] But in his view this objection fails to do justice to human nature: "Religious melancholy is not disposed of by a single flourish of the word insanity."[14] Here, he implies that the religious melancholic is one who feels most deeply the sting of the materialistic worldview, and who has the deepest need for the theistic counterview that the world's future is one where the divine spirit has the final word. But the religious melancholic is only the more extreme case that proves a general fact about human nature, which is that we need to believe that the divine spirit plays an active role in the future outcome of our world. Without this assurance our conviction of an eternal moral order collapses, and life is then not worth living.

With this illustration of the pragmatic method James hopes to silence those who allege that his is a crassly utilitarian view of truth, as if truth is anything we want to believe in order to achieve immediate ends. While it is true that he is concerned about an idea's value for the here and now, this illustration makes the case for the practical differences resulting from our capacity to hope in the remote future of the world. Such hope directly affects

10. Ibid., 47. See Dante Alighieri, *The Divine Comedy*; and Wordsworth, *The Poetical Works of William Wordsworth*.
11. James, *Pragmatism*, 48–49.
12. Ibid., 49.
13. Ibid.
14. Ibid.

how we view our existence in the here and now. The practical difference between these two views of the world is that one inspires hope while the other invites despair.

James's illustration of the religious melancholic also enables him to challenge those who believe that only the insane are preoccupied with visions (delusions?) of the world's ultimate end. The religious melancholic is equally so preoccupied and is not in his judgment insane. On the contrary, those who have struggled with religious melancholy are philosophically deeper than those who settle easily into idealistic views of God and world. Their philosophical depth issues from the fact that they in a profoundly emotional way feel the sting of the materialistic view of the world's future. The materialist view is not unimaginable to them. As we have seen in previous chapters, they characteristically experience the world as dead and lifeless, as sinister and cold. Moreover, they may be extreme in their fear for the remote future of the world, but they are no different in kind from the vast majority of humans, who worry, at some level, about the ultimate fate of the world and what this means for their own everyday existence.

A religious melancholic himself, James had little patience with eternal optimists, but he could not accept the idea that materialists were right. As John Jay Chapman, who knew James well, said of him, "There was, in spite of his playfulness, a deep sadness about James. You felt that he had just stepped out of his sadness in order to meet you, and was to go back into it the moment you left him. It may be that sadness inheres in some kinds of profoundly religious characters,—in dedicated persons who have renounced all, and are constantly hoping, thinking, acting, and (in the typical case) praying for humanity."[15] In effect, Chapman suggests that sadness in the case of a dedicated person like James does not lead to despair, but contributes to a sense of hope and expectancy that leads to productive thinking and acting and also to the prayerful consciousness discussed in chapter 8. This allusion to the prayerful consciousness brings especially to mind James's formulation of the characteristics of the religious life in the concluding lecture of *The Varieties*.[16]

---

15. Simon, *William James Remembered*, 56.

16. These characteristics of the religious life are (1) "that the visible world is part of a more spiritual universe from which it draws its chief significance"; (2) "that union or harmonious relation with that higher universe is our true end; and (3) "that prayer or inner communion with the spirit thereof—be that spirit 'God' or 'law'—is a process wherein work is really done, and spiritual energy flows in and produces effects, psychological or material, within the phenomenal world"; and that religion includes these psychological characteristics: (4) "A new zest which adds itself like a gift to life, and takes the form either of lyrical enchantment or of appeal to earnestness and heroism"; and (5) "an assurance of safety and a temper of peace, and, in relation to others,

THE DEATH OF HERMAN

Although James had a general tendency toward sadness, I believe that there was an experience in his life that deeply influenced his refusal to accept the materialist view that, as Balfour puts it, "the energies of our system will decay, the glory of the sun will be dimmed, and the earth, tideless and inert, will no longer tolerate the [human] race which has for a moment disturbed its solitude."[17] This experience was the death of his son Herman, whom he affectionately called Humster.[18] William and Alice's third son, Herman died of bronchial pneumonia on July 9, 1885 (when James was forty-three years old). Herman was only eighteen months old. Alice had not been well following the birth of Herman. She had suffered from scarlet fever and whooping cough, the latter of which Herman also contracted. While Alice recovered from both afflictions, Herman's whooping cough developed complications and he came down with bronchial pneumonia. He suffered several convulsions, and finally, gasping for breath, he died on his mother's bed.

The next day William and Alice planned his funeral. They chose a small wicker basket as a coffin and lined it with soft flannel. They engaged the Unitarian minister Andrew Preston Peabody to conduct the service. The following day they took a buggy a few miles from Cambridge to Belmont, where, in the woods, they gathered birch branches and pine boughs, ferns, grasses, and wildflowers to cover the wicker coffin. They lay their dead child gently in the basket and arranged sprays of leaves at his head, grasses at his feet and flowers on his chest. Later, at the Cambridge Cemetery, the minister offered a prayer and closed the tiny coffin's lid. James wrote to an old family friend, "And there he lies, one more experience to bind me and Alice together, one more taste of the intolerable mysteriousness of this thing called existence."[19]

James himself noted that Alice's grief was visceral and intense, and Linda Simon points out that in his discussion of the instinct of parental love in *The Principles of Psychology*, which was published two years after Herman's death, James observed that "the passionate devotion of a mother—ill, herself, perhaps—to a sick or dying child is perhaps the most simply beautiful moral spectacle that human life affords."[20] Simon also notes that William's brother Henry immediately expressed his sympathy for William and,

---

a preponderance of loving affections" (James, *The Varieties of Religious Experience*, 485–86).

17. James, *Pragmatism*, 47.
18. Lewis, *The Jameses*, 382.
19. Simon, *Genuine Reality*, 197.
20. James, *The Principles of Psychology*, 2:440.

even more, for Alice because, as he put it, "Babies are soft memories and Alice will always throb to the vision of his little being." Simon adds: "That vision, Alice insisted, never left her, Always, she said, Herman was in her thoughts. 'I think of my little Herman—,' she told Elizabeth Evans, 'where is he now? He does not tell me. But I might as well have asked him, before he was born what his life in this world would be. How could he have conceived of sight and hearing and of moving about freely in this wonderful world? Had I tried to tell him, he would have shrunk back in terror and begged to stay safely in his mother's womb.'"[21]

Recalling Alice's response to James's father's death three years earlier, Simon suggests that "if Henry Sr.'s death had intimated for Alice the nearness of the spiritual world, Herman's death made belief in that world an urgent necessity for both William and Alice."[22] As Alice wrote to Elizabeth Evans, "I believe [in], I almost feel immortality, or peradventure something infinitely better, but life and immortality are surely calling to us all—and more than ever I want to listen."[23] Three days after Herman died, William James wrote to his cousin Kitty of his hope that Herman "is reserved for some still better chance" than the life he would have lived on earth, "and that we shall in some way come into his presence again."[24]

21. Simon, *Genuine Reality*. 198.

22. Ibid., 198. James was in London visiting his brother Henry when their father's death was imminent. Simon notes that his initial impulse was to return home immediately because, as he wrote to Alice, he wanted "to get to see him if possible before the end, & to let him see me and get a ray of pleasure from the thought that I had come." But on further reflection "he changed his mind: his father, after all, might not even recognize him; and his father's recognition was essential" (ibid., 179). There was also the issue of James's sister Alice, who felt that it would be much better if their brother Henry were to come to Boston to assist in the decisions relating to their father's death. Alice, James's wife, "was torn between urging William to return and fulfill his filial duty and stay away and acquiesce to his sister's wishes," but finally she decided that her sister-in-law was right. So she wrote William that "you could not be much comfort to that household now," especially because his father "has grown indifferent to things and people" (179).

23. Ibid., 198–99; see also Simon, *William James Remembered*, 62–63.

24. Simon, *Genuine Reality*, 199. Biographers note that a few months after Herman's death, William and Alice James became involved with a medium, Leonora Evelina Piper, who was twenty-six years old. They had previously gone to a materializing medium before Herman fell ill but had found this to be a rather unsatisfying experience. Materializing mediums claimed the ability to create visible and sometimes palpable manifestations of spirits, i.e., phantasms that caused tables to rise or spirits to rap. In contrast, Leonora Piper presented herself as a passive conduit whose body and voice were available to spirits of the dead, enabling them to send messages to the living. Simon notes that "Alice was desperate for a sign that Herman's spirit existed and was accessible to her," and that at one sitting Piper, who apparently knew nothing of the special burial that they had devised, described Herman, in Alice's own words,

The loss of little Herman reveals James's deep personal investment in his complaint that idealists in their desire to speak highly of spirit view material as crass and impure. To anyone who has ever looked on the face of a dead child "the mere fact that matter *could* have taken for a time that precious form, ought to make matter sacred ever after."[25] The loss of little Herman also gave James a strong personal motive for believing that the physical laws of nature do not have the final word. As he wrote to Elizabeth Evans, whose husband died the following year, "I can hardly express the sorrow I feel at your husband's being thus cut off almost before he had begun to show what was in him," and then he added, "The whole thing is one of those incomprehensible, seemingly wasteful acts of Providence, which, without seeing, we can only hope may someday be proved to spring from a rational ground."[26] A few weeks later he wrote to her, "I think the only thing we can do is to believe that the Good power does not appoint evil and pain of its own free will, but works under some dark and inscrutable limitations and that we by our patience and good will can somehow strengthen his hands."[27]

Thus, one who has suffered the premature death of his own child wants—needs—to believe that there is something more of human existence than the inexorable laws of nature. This something more is precisely what he needs to be able to affirm so as to hold on to the conviction that the world is run according to an eternal world order. Given his pragmatist orientation, James did not view such belief in merely intellectual terms. Rather, he emphasized its practical effects. In her unpublished memoir Elizabeth Evans observed that his letters to her offered "a glimpse into the philosophy which strengthened and deepened in Mr. James as his thought matured," and she briefly paraphrased several of his affirmations from his essay "Is Life Worth Living."[28] The relevant quotation from the essay itself is the following:

> I confess that I do not see why the very existence of an invisible world may not in part depend on the personal response

---

"with his hands full of daisies and other sweet nothings (from the point of view of science) which meant everything to me" (200). While they both suspected that Piper knew about family matters that emerged in these sittings and was therefore drawing on this independent knowledge, James noted that she mentioned some things that she could not have known about, such as her detailed description of the death throes of a cat that James had killed with ether, and that when she offered advice during their first visit on how to deal with the tantrums of their second child, she used his nursery name ("little Billy-boy"), which they did not use outside their family environment, 200.

25. James, *Pragmatism*, 43.
26. Simon, *William James Remembered*, 62.
27. Ibid., 63.
28. Ibid., 63–64.

> which any one of us may make to the religious appeal. God, in short, may draw vital strength and increase of very being from our fidelity. For my own part, I do not know what the sweat and blood and tragedy of this life mean, if they mean anything short of this. If this life be not a real fight, in which something is eternally gained for the universe by success, it is no better than a game of private theatricals from which one may withdraw at will. But it *feels* like a real fight,—as if there were something really wild in the universe which we, with all our idealities and faithfulnesses, are needed to redeem; and first of all to redeem our own hearts from atheisms and fears. For such a half-wild, half-saved universe our nature is adapted.[29]

Since we do not know for certain what vision of the world—the materialist or the theistic—will ultimately prove to have been the true one, what *feels* true is that it makes a practical difference in the ultimate outcome of things if we put our hearts and minds into assisting the divine spirit. By our patience and goodwill we may in fact strengthen *God's* hands.

GOD AS THE ETERNALLY HOPEFUL ONE

James concludes his discussion in *Pragmatism* of the materialist vs. theistic debate with the admission that "the issues of fact at stake in the debate are of course vaguely enough conceived by us at present. But spiritualistic faith in all its forms deals with a world of *promise,* while materialism's sun sets in a sea of disappointment."[30] Continuing, he bids his readers to

> remember what I said of the Absolute: it grants us moral holidays. Any religious view does this. It not only incites our more strenuous moments, but it also takes our joyous, careless, trustful moments, and it justifies them. It paints the grounds of justification vaguely enough, to be sure. The exact features of the saving future facts that our belief in God insures, will have to be ciphered out by the interminable methods of science: we can *study* God only by studying his Creation. But we can *enjoy* our God, if we have one, in advance of all that labor. I myself believe that the evidence for God lies primarily in inner personal experiences.[31]

---

29. James, *The Will to Believe and Other Essays in Popular Philosophy,* 61.
30. James, *Pragmatism,* 49.
31. Ibid.

Among these experiences, James, I believe, would encourage us to pay particular attention to our "trustful moments," moments in which we have the assurance that ours is a world of promise, one that justifies hope and expectancy. And then, fortified by hope and expectancy, we may *entrust* our lives to this world in the decisions and choices that we make. As he notes in his essay "Is Life Worth Living?":

> It is only by risking our persons from one hour to another that we live at all. And often enough our faith beforehand in an uncertified result *is the only thing that makes the result come true.* Suppose, for instance, that you are climbing a mountain, and have worked yourself into a position from which the only escape is by a terrible leap. Have faith that you can successfully make it, and your feet are nerved to its accomplishment. But mistrust yourself, and think of all the sweet things you have heard the scientists say of *maybes,* and you will hesitate so long that, at last, all unstrung and trembling, and launching yourself in a moment of despair, you roll into the abyss. In such a case (and it belongs to an enormous class), the part of wisdom as well as of courage is to *believe what is in the line of your needs*, for only by such belief is the need fulfilled. Refuse to believe, and you shall indeed be right, for you shall irretrievably perish. But believe, and again you shall be right, for you shall save yourself. You make one or the other of two possible universes true by your trust or mistrust,—both universes having been only *maybes,* in this particular, before you contributed your act.[32]

To this affirmation of personal risk I would want to add that the divine spirit was the original taker of risks, for, after all, the very fact that there *is* a world is due to the risk that God took in creating it. Moreover, because God took this risk, we may view God as the eternally hopeful One. The world is ultimately a self-projection of the divine spirit itself, and the very fact that the world has a future is because it is a projection of this spirit. That we exist at all, and that we may contemplate a future for ourselves, is ultimately because it is God's very nature to be hopeful. If we ask what generated this hope, we may surmise that God did not feel that his own existence was complete and therefore desired something *more.*[33] As James Weldon Johnson,

---

32. James, *The Will to Believe and Other Essays in Popular Philosophy,* 49.

33. See James's discussion of the "more" in the concluding chapter of *The Varieties of Religious Experience,* 508. Here he suggests that we may become aware of a "MORE" which is operative in the universe and coterminous with the germinal higher part of ourselves. I am taking the liberty here of suggesting that God also longed for a connection with something "more."

author of the poem "Creation," expresses it, "And God stepped out on space, and he looked around and said: 'I'm lonely—I'll make me a world.'"[34]

This decision carried great risks for God, for when hopes are let loose they take on a life of their own, having effects not originally intended. If, however, we view the world as originally the self-projection of the eternally hopeful One, we can be assured that when we look on the face of a dead child, we behold the face of God, and such beholdings will continue to sustain us until such time that the divine spirit looks upon our own lifeless frame and witnesses our final trustful moment.

---

34. Johnson, *God's Trombones*, 17.

References

Agnes, Michael, ed. *Webster's New World College Dictionary.* 4th ed. Foster City, CA: IDG, 2001.
Albright, Raymond W. *Focus on Infinity: A Life of Phillips Brooks.* New York: Macmillan, 1961.
Alighieri, Dante. *The Divine Comedy.* Translated by Charles Eliot Norton. Boston: Houghton Mifflin, 1891-92.
Alleine, Joseph. *The Solemn Warnings of the Dead; Or, an Admonition to Unconverted Sinners.* New York: Carlton & Phillips, 1855.
Allen, Gay Wilson. *William James: A Biography.* New York: Viking, 1967.
Alline, Henry. *The Life and Journal of the Rev. Mr. Henry Alline.* Early American Imprints, 2nd ser. Boston: Guilbert & Dean, 1806.
Allport, Gordon W. *The Use of Personal Documents in Psychological Science.* Social Science Research Council Bulletin 49. New York: Social Science Research Council, 1942.
American Psychiatric Association. *Diagnostic and Statistical Manual of Mental Disorders.* 4th ed. Washington DC: American Psychiatric Association, 2000.
———. *Diagnostic and Statistical Manual of Mental Disorders.* 5th ed. Arlington, VA: American Psychiatric Association, 2013.
Arber, Edward. *An English Garner: Ingatherings from Our History and Literature,* vol. 7. London: Constable, 1888.
Augustine, Saint. *The Confessions of St. Augustine.* Translated by John K. Ryan. New York: Doubleday, 1960.
Baker, Smith. "Etiological Significance of Heterogeneous Personality." *Journal of Nervous and Mental Diseases* 18 (1893) 664-74.
Balfour, Arthur James. *The Foundations of Belief.* New York: Longmans Green, 1895.
Barber, James David. *The Presidential Character: Predicting Performance in the White House.* 2nd ed. Englewood Cliffs, NJ: Prentice-Hall, 1977.
Bartoli, Daniello. *Histoire de St Ignace de Loyola d'après les Documents Originaux.* Bruges: Desclée, De Brouwer, 1893.
Beam, Alex. *Gracefully Insane: The Rise and Fall of America's Premier Mental Hospital.* New York: Public Affairs, 2001.
Berne, Eric. *Games People Play: The Psychology of Human Relationships.* New York: Grove, 1964.
———. *Transactional Analysis in Psychotherapy: A Systematic Individual and Social Psychiatry.* Evergreen Original. New York: Grove, 1961.

Besant, Annie. *Annie Basant: An Autobiography*. London: Fisher Unwin, 1893.

Binet, Alfred. *Alterations of Personality*. Translated by Helen Green Baldwin. New York: Appleton, 1896.

Binet-Sanglé, Charles. *La Folie de Jésus*. 3 vols. Paris: Maloine, 1908, 1910, 1912.

Blake, Robert R., and Jane S. Mouton. *The Managerial Grid: Key Orientations for Achieving Production through People*. Houston: Gulf, 1964.

Bougaud, Emile. *Histoire de la Bienheureuse Marguerite-Marie et des Origins de la Dévotion au Coeur de Jésus*. Paris: Paussielgue, 1894.

Bourignon, Antoinette. *Light of the World: A Most True Relation of a Pilgrimess Traveling towards Eternity*. London: Simpson & Low, 1863.

Bourne, Frederick W. *The King's Son; Or, A Memoir of Billy Bray*. New York: Ketcham, 1890.

Breuer, Josef, and Sigmund Freud. "The Psychical Mechanism of Hysterical Phenomena (Preliminary Communication)." In *Studies on Hysteria* by Josef Breuer and Sigmund Freud, 1-18. Edited and translated by James Strachey. New York: Basic Books, 1957.

Brooks, Phillips. *The Light of the World, and Other Sermons*. New York: Dutton, 1904.

———. *Selected Sermons*. Edited by William Scarlett. New York: Dutton, 1950.

Bullen, Frank T. *With Christ at Sea: A Religious Autobiography*. London: Hodder & Stoughton, 1900.

Bunyan, John. *Grace Abounding to the Chief of Sinners*. New York: Tiebout, 1797.

———. *Grace Abounding to the Chief of Sinners*. Edited by W. R. Owens. New York: Penguin, 1987.

———. *The Pilgrim's Progress*. New York: Washington Square, 1957.

Bussierre, Théodore Renouvard de. *The Conversion of Marie Alphonse Ratisbonne Followed By a Letter from M. A. Ratisbonne to M. Dufriche-Desgenettes*. London: Jones, 1842.

Call, Annie Payson. *As a Matter of Course*. 1874. Reprinted, Teddington, UK: The Echo Library, 2007.

———. *Power through Repose*. Boston: Roberts, 1891.

Capps, Donald. *At Home in the World: A Study in Psychoanalysis, Art, and Religion*. Eugene, OR: Cascade Books, 2013.

———. "Augustine's *Confessions*: The Story of a Divided Self and the Process of Its Unification." *Pastoral Psychology* 55 (2007) 551–69.

———. *The Child's Song: The Religious Abuse of Children*. Louisville: Westminster John Knox, 1995.

———. *Jesus the Village Psychiatrist*. Louisville: Westminster John Knox Press, 2008.

———. *Men and Their Religion: Honor, Hope, and Humor*. Harrisburg, PA: Trinity, 2002.

———. *Men, Religion, and Melancholia: James, Otto, Jung, and Erikson*. New Haven: Yale University Press, 1997.

———. "Relaxed Bodies, Emancipated Minds, and Dominant Calm." *Journal of Religion and Health* 48 (2009) 368–80.

———. *The Resourceful Self: And a Little Child Shall Lead Them*. Eugene, OR: Cascade Books, 2014.

———. "The 'Reversal of Generations' Phenomenon as Illustrated by the Lives of John Henry Newman and Abraham Lincoln." *Pastoral Psychology* 55 (2006) 3–25.

———. *A Time to Laugh: The Religion of Humor*. New York: Continuum, 2005.

———. "Was William James a Patient at McLean Hospital for the Mentally Ill?" *Pastoral Psychology* 56 (2008) 295–320.
———. *Young Clergy: A Biographical-Developmental Study*. New York: Routledge, 2005.
Capps, Donald, and Walter H. Capps, eds. *The Religious Personality*. Belmont, CA: Wadsworth, 1970.
Carlin, Nathan, and Donald Capps. *100 Years of Happiness: Insights and Findings from the Experts*. Santa Barbara: Praeger, 2012.
Carpenter, Edward. *Towards Democracy*. London: Unwin, 1892.
Channing, William Ellery. *Memoirs of William Ellery Channing*. 3 vols. Boston: American Unitarian Association, 1874.
Claparède, Théodore, and Jean-Francois Eduard Goty. *Deux Heroines de la Foi*. Paris: Sandoz, 1880.
Coe, George Albert. *The Spiritual Life: Studies in the Science of Religion*. New York: Eaton & Mains, 1900.
Daudet, Alphonse. *Notes sur la Vie*. Paris: Bibliothèque-Charpentier, 1899.
Doddridge, Philip. *Some Remarkable Passages in the Life of the Honourable Colonel James Gardiner*. Early American Imprints, 2nd ser. Boston: Lincoln & Edmands, 1811.
Dodds, E. R. "Augustine's *Confessions*: A Study in Spiritual Maladjustment." *Hibbert Journal* 26 (1927–28) 459–73.
Doody, John A., and John Immerwahr. "The Persistence of the Four Temperaments." *Soundings* 66 (1983) 348–59.
Dresser, Horatio W. *Living by the Spirit*. New York: Putnam, 1900.
———. *Voices of Freedom and Studies in the Philosophy of Individuality*. New York: Putnam, 1899.
Drummond, Henry. *Natural Law in the Spiritual World*. New York: Pott, 1890.
Dumas, Georges. *La Tristesse et le Joie*. Paris: Alcan, 1900.
Dwight, Sereno Edwards. *The Life of President Edwards*. New York: Carvill, 1830.
Eakin, Paul John. "Henry James and the Autobiographical Act." In *Fictions in Autobiography: Studies in the Art of Self-invention*, 56–125. Princeton: Princeton University Press, 1985.
Edwards, Jonathan. *Edwards on Revivals: Containing a Faithful Narrative of the Surprising Work of God in the Conversion of Many Hundred Souls in Northampton, Massachusetts, A. D. 1735*. New York: Dunning & Spalding, 1832.
Edwards, Jonathan, and Sereno Edwards Dwight. *Memoirs of the Rev. David Brainerd: Missionary to the Indians on the Borders of New-York, New-Jersey, and Pennsylvania; Chiefly Taken from His Diaries*. New Haven: Converse, 1822.
Ellis, Havelock. *Erotic Symbolism*. Philadelphia: Davis, 1914.
———. *The New Spirit*. London: Scott, 1891.
———. *Sex in Relation to Society*. Studies in the Psychology of Sex 6. Philadelphia: Davis, 1910.
———. *Sexual Inversion*. Philadelphia: Davis, 1901.
Ellwood, Thomas. *The History of Thomas Ellwood*. Morley's Universal Library 32. London: Routledge, 1886.
Emerson, Ralph Waldo. *Essays and Lectures*. Edited by Joel Porte. Library of America. New York: Literary Classics of the U.S., distributed by Viking, 1983.
———. *Miscellanies*. Boston: Houghton Mifflin, 1884.

———. *Lectures and Biographical Sketches*. Boston: Houghton Mifflin, 1891.
Epictetus. *The Works of Epictetus*. Translated by Thomas Wentworth Higginson. Boston: Little, Brown, 1890.
Erikson, Erik H. *Identity: Youth, and Crisis*. New York: Norton, 1968.
Ernest, P. Edward. *The Family Album of Favorite Poems*. New York: Putnam, 1959.
Fechner, Gustav Theodor. *Life after Death*. Translated by Mary C. Wadsworth. New York: Pantheon, 1943.
Feinstein, Howard M. *Becoming William James*. Ithaca: Cornell University Press, 1984.
Féré, Ch. *Sensation et Mouvement: Études Expérimentales de Psycho-mécanique*. Bibliothèque de philosophie contemporaine. Paris: Alcan, 1887.
Finney, Charles G. *Memoirs of C. G. F. Written by Himself*. New York: Barnes, 1876.
Fletcher, Horace. *Happiness as Found in Forethought minus Fearthought*. Menticulture 2. Chicago: Kindergarten Literature Company, 1898.
———. *Menticulture or the A-B-C of True Living*. Chicago: McClurg, 1896.
Foster, John. *Essays on Decision of Character*. Plainfield, NJ: Cushing, 1839.
Fox, George. *Journal of George Fox*. London: Richardson & Clark, 1765.
Francis, of Assisi, Saint. *Speculum Perfectionis*. Collection de documents pour l'histoire religieuse et littéraire du moyen âge 11. Edited by Pierre Sabatier. Paris: Fischbacher, 1898.
Freud, Sigmund. *An Autobiographical Study*. Translated by James Strachey. New York: Norton, 1952.
———. "Mourning and Melancholia." In *General Psychological Theory: Papers on Metapsychology*, by Sigmund Freud, 164–79. Edited by Philip Rieff. New York: Collier, 1963.
Fuller, George A. *Wisdom of the Ages: Revelations from Zertoulem, the Prophet of Tlaskanata*. Boston: Banner of Light, 1901.
Garden, George. *An Apology for M. Antonia Bourignon*. London: Brown, 1699.
Goddard, H. H. "The Effects of Mind on Body as Evidenced by Faith Cures." *American Journal of Psychology* 10 (1899) 431–502.
Gratry, Auguste. *Souvenirs de ma Jeunesse*. 4th ed. Paris: Douniol, 1876.
Greisinger, Wilhelm. *Mental Pathology and Therapeutics*. Translated by C. L. Robertson and J. Rutherford. 2nd ed. New Sydenham Society Series 33. London: New Sydenham Society, 1867.
Guyon, Jeanne Marie. *Autobiography of Madame Guyon*. 2 vols. Translated by Thomas Tyler Allen. London: Kegan Paul, 1897.
Habegger, Alfred. *The Father: A Life of Henry James, Sr.* Amherst: University of Massachusetts Press, 2001.
Hacking, Ian. *Mad Travelers: Reflections on the Reality of Transient Mental Illnesses*. Charlottesville: University Press of Virginia, 1998.
Harris, Thomas A. *I'm OK, You're OK: A Practical Guide to Transactional Analysis*. New York: Harper & Row, 1969.
Hillman, James. "Peaks and Vales: The Soul/Spirit Distinction as Basis for the Difference between Psychology and Spiritual Discipline." In *Puer Papers*, edited by James Hillman et al., 54–74. Irving, TX: Spring, 1979.
———. *Re-Visioning Psychology*. New York: Harper & Row, 1975.
Hilty, Karl. *Glück*. Fruenfeld: Huber, 1898.
———. *Happiness: Essays on the Meaning of Life*. Translated by Francis Greenwood Peabody. New York: Macmillan, 1903.

Hobbes, Thomas. *Leviathan, Or, the Matter, Force, and Power of a Commonwealth, Ecclesiastical amd Civil.* Morley's Universal Library 21. New York: Routledge, 1885.
Hodgson, Richard. "A Case of Double Consciousness." *Proceedings of the Society for Psychical Research* 7 (1891–92) 221–55.
Hodgson, Shadworth H. *The Theory of Practice: An Ethical Enquiry.* 2 vols. ATLA Monograph Preservation Program. London: Longmans, Green, Reader & Dyer, 1870.
Institute Alain. *La Psychologie Réflexive de Jules Lagneau.* Conference publication. Paris: La Menuiserie, 1995.
Jackson, Stanley W. *Melancholia and Depression: From Hippocratic Times to Modern Times.* New Haven: Yale University Press, 1986.
James, Henry, ed. *The Letters of William James.* Boston: Atlantic Monthly Press, 1920.
James, William. *A Pluralistic Universe.* A Bison Book. Lincoln: University of Nebraska Press, 1996.
———. *Essays in Radical Empiricism.* A Bison Book. Lincoln: University of Nebraska Press, 1996.
———. "Frederick Myers's Service to Psychology." *Proceedings of the English Society for Psychical Research* 17 (1901) 13–23.
———. *Human Immortality: Two Supposed Objections to the Doctrine.* Boston: Houghton Mifflin, 1898.
———, ed. *The Literary Remains of the Late Henry James.* Boston: Osgood, 1885.
———. *The Meaning of Truth.* In *Writings 1902–1910,* 821–978. Edited by Bruce Kuklick. Library of America 38. New York: Literary Classics of the United States, 1987.
———. *Pragmatism.* Great Books in Philosophy. Buffalo: Prometheus, 1991.
———. *The Principles of Psychology.* 2 vols. New York: Dover, 1950.
———. *Psychology: The Briefer Course.* Edited by Gordon Allport. 1991. Reprinted, Notre Dame: University of Notre Dame Press, 1985.
———. *The Selected Letters of William James.* Edited by Elizabeth Hardwick. New York: Doubleday Anchor, 1993.
———. "The Sentiment of Rationality." *Mind* 4 (1879) 317–46.
———. *Talks to Teachers on Psychology and to Students on Some of Life's Ideals.* Mineola, NY: Dover, 1962.
———. *The Varieties of Religion Experience.* Mineola, NY: Dover, 2002.
———. *The Will to Believe and Other Essays in Popular Philosophy.* New York: Dover, 1956.
———. "What Is an Emotion?" *Mind* 9 (1884) 188–205.
———. *Writings, 1902–1910.* Library of America 38. Edited by Bruce Kuklick. New York: Literary Classics of the United States, 1987.
Janet, Pierre. *État Mental des Hysteriques: les stigmates mentaux.* Paris: Rueff et cie, 1892.
Jastrow, Morris, Jr. "The Liver as the Seat of the Soul." In *Studies in the History of Religion.* Edited by David Gordon Lyon and George Foot Moore, 143–68. New York: Macmillan, 1912.
Johnson, James Weldon. *God's Trombones: Seven Negro Sermons in Verse.* 1927. New York: Penguin, 1990.
Jouffrey, T. S. *Mélanges Philosophiques.* Paris: Slatkine, 1979.

Kenny, Michael G. *The Passion of Ansel Bourne: Multiple Personality in American Culture.* Smithsonian Series in Ethnographic Inquiry. Washington DC: Smithsonian Institution Press, 1986.

Leuba, James. "A Study in the Psychology of Religious Phenomena." *American Journal of Psychology* 7 (1896) 309–85.

Lewis, R. W. B. *The Jameses: A Family Narrative.* New York: Farrar, Straus and Giroux, 1991.

Luther, Martin. *A Commentary upon the Epistle of Paul to the Galatians.* New York: Ezra Collier, 1844.

Marmontel, Jean Francois. *Memoirs of Jean Francois Marmontel.* Boston: Houghton, Osgood, 1878.

Martineau, James. *Endeavours after the Christian Life.* Making of America. Boston: American Unitarian Association, 1876.

Mattheissen, F. O. *The James Family.* New York: Knopf, 1947.

Menand, Louis. "William James and the Case of the Epileptic Patient." In *American Studies,* 3–30. New York: Farrar, Straus & Giroux, 2002.

Mill, John Stuart. *Autobiography.* New York: Holt, 1873.

Mitchell, Silas Weir. "Mary Reynolds: A Case of Double Consciousness." *Transactions of the College of Physicians and Surgeons,* April 4, 1888.

Molinos, Miguel. *The Spiritual Guide: Which Disentangles the Soul.* Glasgow: Thomson, 1885.

Monod, Adolphe. *Souvenirs de sa vie.* Paris: Fischbacher, 1885.

Müller, George. *The Life of Trust: Being a Narrative of the Lord's Dealings with George Müller.* New York: Crowell, 1898.

Murphy, Gardner, and Robert O. Ballou, eds. *William James on Psychical Research.* New York: Viking, 1960.

Myers, Gerald E. *William James: His Life and Thought.* New Haven: Yale University Press, 1986.

———, ed. *Self, Religion, and Metaphysics: Essays in Memory of James Bissett Pratt.* New York: Macmillan, 1961.

Newman, Francis William. *Phases of Faith, or, Passages from the History of My Creed.* New ed. London: Trűbner, 1881.

———. *The Soul: Its Sorrows and Its Aspirations.* 3rd ed. London: Trűbner, 1882.

Newman, John Henry. *Apologia Pro Vita Sua.* Garden City, NY: Doubleday, 1956.

Nisbet, John Ferguson. *The Insanity of Genius and the General Inequality of Human Faculty Physiologically Considered.* London: Ward & Downey, 1891.

Pascal, Blaise. *Thoughts, Letters and Minor Works.* The Harvard Classics 48. Edited by Charles W. Eliot. New York: Collier & Son, 1909.

Paulhan, Frédéric. *Les Caracteres,* Paris: Alcan, 1894.

Peirce, Charles S. *Selected Writings: Values in a Universe of Chance.* Edited by Philip P. Wiener. New York: Dover, 1958.

Perry, Ralph Barton. *The Thought and Character of William James.* Vanderbilt Library of American Philosophy. Nashville: Vanderbilt University Press, 1996.

Pratt, James Bissett. *Matter and Spirit: A Study of Mind and Body in Their Relation to the Spiritual Life.* New York: Macmillan, 1926.

———. *The Psychology of Religious Belief.* New York: Macmillan, 1907.

———. *The Religious Consciousness: A Psychological Study.* New York: Macmillan, 1920.

———. *What Pragmatism Means.* New York: Macmillan. 1909.
Prince, Morton. "Contributions to the Study of Hysteria and Hypnosis." *Proceedings of the English Society for Psychical Research* 14 (1899) 79–97.
Pruyser, Paul W. *The Play of the Imagination: Toward a Psychoanalysis of Culture.* New York: International Universities Press, 1983.
Ribot, Théodule. *The Psychology of the Emotions.* London: Scott, 1897.
Richardson, Robert D. *William James: In the Maelstrom of American Modernism.* Boston: Houghton Mifflin, 2006.
Robertson, Nan. *Getting Better: Inside Alcoholics Anonymous.* New York: Morrow, 1988.
Rodriguez, Alfonso, SJ. *Pratique de la Perfection Chrétienne.* Versailles: Lebel, 1813.
Rosenzweig, Saul. *The Historic Expedition to America (1909): Freud, Jung, and Hall the King-maker.* St. Louis: Rana House, 1994.
Roubinovitch, Jacques, and Edouard Toulouse. *Le Mélancolie.* Paris: Masson, 1897.
Rubin, Julius H. *Religious Melancholy and Protestant Experience in America.* Religion in America Series. New York: Oxford University Press, 1994.
Sabatier, Auguste. *Esquisse d'une Philosophie de la Religion.* 2nd ed. Paris: Fischbacher 1897.
Sainte-Beuve, Charles Augustin. *Port-Royal.* Bibliothèque de littérature. 7th ed. Paris: Hachette, 1922.
Selzer, Richard. *Mortal Lessons: Notes on the Art of Surgery.* A Touchstone Book. New York: Simon & Schuster, 1974.
Sénancour, Etienne Pivert de. *Obermann: Selections from Letters to a Friend.* Translated by Jessie Peabody Frothingham. Cambridge, MA: Riverside, 1901.
Simon, Linda. *Genuine Reality: A Life of William James.* New York: Harcourt Brace, 1998.
———, ed. *William James Remembered.* Lincoln: University of Nebraska Press, 1996.
Smith, Hannah Whitall. *The Christian's Secret of a Happy Life.* London: Longley, 1876.
Spinoza, Baruch. *The Philosophy of Spinoza: On God, On Man, and on Man's Well-Being.* Edited by Joseph Ratner. Dallas: Tudor, 2010. https://www.gutenberg.org/files/31205/31205-h/31205-h.htm.
Starbuck, Edwin Diller. *The Psychology of Religion: An Empirical Study of the Growth of Religious Consciousness.* New York: Scribner, 1899.
Stevenson, Robert Louis. *Essays in the Art of Writing.* London: Chatto & Windus, 1905.
St. Pierre, Jacques Henri Bernardin de. *Studies of Nature.* Translated by Henry Hunter. Philadelphia: Woodward, 1836.
Suso, Henry. *The Life of the Blessed Henry Suso, by Himself.* Translated by T. F. Knox. London: Burns, Lambert & Oates, 1865.
Taylor, Eugene. *William James on Exceptional Mental States: The 1896 Lowell Lectures.* New York: Scribner, 1983.
Thoreau, Henry David. *Walden.* 19th ed. Boston: Houghton, Mifflin, 1882.
Tolstoy, Leo. *A Confession and Other Religious Writings.* Translated by Jane Kentish. Hammondsworth, UK: Penguin, 1987.
———. *My Confession; and, The Spirit of Christ's Teaching.* New York: Crowell, 1887.
Townsend, Kim. *Manhood at Harvard: William James and Others.* New York: Norton, 1996.
Tyerman, Luke. *The Life and Times of the Rev. John Wesley.* 2nd ed. London: Hodder & Stougton, 1876.

Upham, Thomas Cogswell. *Life of Madame Catherine Adorna*. Boston: Waite, Pierce, 1845.

———. *Life, Religious Opinions and Experience of Madame de la Mothe Guyon*. New York: Harper & Brothers, 1849.

Voysey, Charles. *The Mystery of Pain and Death*. London: Williams & Norgate, 1892.

Warne, Frederick G. *George Müller: The Modern Apostle of Faith*. New York: Revell, 1898.

Whitman, Walt. *Selected Poems*. New York: Gramercy Books, 1992.

Wood, Henry. *Ideal Suggestion through Mental Photography: A Restorative System for Home and Private Use*. Boston: Lee & Shepard, 1899.

Woolman, John. *Journal*. New York: Collins, 1845.

Wordsworth, William. *The Poetical Works of William Wordsworth*. London: Nelson, 1865.

Wulff, David M. *Psychology of Religion: Classic and Contemporary*. 2nd ed. New York: Wiley, 1997.

Index of Names

Agnes, Michael, vii, 29, 61, 71, 77, 108, 154, 155, 171
Albright, Raymond W., 217, 225
Alighieri, Dante, 228–29
Alleine, Joseph, 138–39
Allen, Gay Wilson, 5, 77
Alline, Henry, 75–76, 81, 89, 101–3, 109, 126, 134–35, 144, 146, 184
Allport, Gordon W., 25
American Psychiatric Association, 140
Arber, Edward, 193
Aristotle, 120
Augustine, Saint, 96–100, 102–3, 109, 121, 123–24, 126

Baker, Smith, 94
Balfour, Arthur James, 228, 231
Ballou, Robert O., 141
Barber, James David, 61
Bartoli, Daniello, 179
Beam, Alex, 77
Berne, Eric, 61
Besant, Annie, 93
Binet, Alfred, 141–43
Binet-Sanglé, Charles, 29
Blake, Robert R., 61
Bougaud, Emile, 177
Bourignon, Antoinette, 181
Bourne, Frederick W., 172
Bowditch, Henry, 8
Bradley, Stephen H., 117–20, 146
Brainerd, David, 146
Breuer, Josef, 13, 109, 142–43
Brooks, Phillips, 193, 216–25

Brown, A. J., 211–15
Bullen, Frank T., 169–70
Bunyan, John, 71, 74–76, 79, 81, 86, 89, 111, 113–15, 126
Bussierre, Théodore Renouvard de, 136

Call, Annie Payson, 11–12, 171
Capps, Donald, 11–12, 20, 28, 43, 49, 82–83, 97, 100, 145, 165, 169, 171, 193, 202, 212
Capps, Walter H., 169
Carlin, Nathan, 193
Carpenter, Edward, 180
Channing, William Ellery, 176–77
Chapman, John Jay, 182, 230
Claparède, Théodore, 170
Coe, George Albert, 116, 145

Daudet, Alphonse, 92–93
Doddridge, Philip, 156–57
Dodds, E. R., 97
Doody, John A., 61
Dresser, Horatio W., 58, 171
Drummond, Henry, 136
Dumas, Georges, 72, 164
Dwight, Sereno Edwards, 132, 148–49

Eakin, Paul John, 39
Edwards, Jonathan, 132, 138–39, 148–49, 162
Edwards, Sarah, 162, 164–65
Eliot, Charles, 9–10, 12, 18–19
Ellis, Havelock, 46, 48
Elwood, Thomas, 172–73

245

246   Index of Names

Emerson, Ralph Waldo, 18, 33, 40, 92,
    129, 193, 212, 216
Epictetus, 195
Erikson, Erik H., 81, 83–84
Ernest, P. Edward, 224
Evans, Elizabeth, 232

Fechner, Gustav Theodor, 20, 202
Feinstein, Howard M., 5, 80–81
Fenollosa, Ernest Francisco, 110
Féré, Ch., 101
Ferenczi, Sandor, 13
Finney, Charles G., 149
Fletcher, Horace, 53, 109–11
Foster, John, 106–7
Fox, George, 26–28, 172
Francis, of Assisi, Saint, 28, 166, 180
Freud, Sigmund, ix, 13–14, 83, 109,
    142–43
Fuller, George A., 208

Garden, George, 181
Goddard, H. H., 57
Goethe, Johann Wolfgang von, 65
Goty, Jean-Francois Eduard, 170
Gratry, Auguste, 69–70, 196–97
Greisinger, Wilhelm, 68, 72
Guyon, Jacques, 168
Guyon, Jeanne Marie, 168–69

Habegger, Alfred, 5, 81
Hacking, Ian, 208
Hadley, S. H., 125–26, 156
Harris, Andrew, 210
Harris, Thomas A., 61
Hillman, James, 28
Hilty, Karl, 193–94
Hobbes, Thomas, 120
Hodgson, Richard, 11, 211–12, 214
Hodgson, Shadworth H., 129
Holmes, Oliver Wendell, Jr., 7
Holmes, Oliver Wendell, Sr., 7
Hume, David, 120

Ignatius Loyola, Saint, 166, 179
Institute Alain, 167

Jackson, Stanley W., 68

James, Alexander Robertson (Aleck)
    [son], 12
James, Alice [sister], 5, 8, 12
James, Alice Gibbens [wife], 9–11,
    16–19, 21, 85, 108, 231–33
James, Garth Wikinson (Wilky)
    [brother], 5–6, 10, 39
James, Henry [brother], 5–6, 39, 36,
    80, 81
James, Henry (Harry) [son], 11, 17,
    21, 36, 39, 80, 81
James, Henry, Sr. [father], 5, 10,
    80–82, 232
James, Herman (Humster) [son], xii,
    10, 231–32
James, Margaret Mary [daughter], 11
James, Mary Walsh [mother], 5, 80, 83
James, Robertson (Bob) [brother],
    5–6, 21, 39, 82
James, William, passim
James, William (Billy) [son], 11
Janet, Pierre, 13, 142–43
Jastrow, Morris, Jr.,
Johnson, James Weldon, 235–36
Jouffrey, T. S., 103–4, 123

Kenny, Michael G., 207–12, 215

Lagneau, Jules, 167
Leuba, James, 116, 124–27, 135,
    147–49
Lewis, R. W. B., 5, 77–78, 81, 84–85,
    218, 231
Loring, Katherine, 12
Luther, Martin, 18, 63, 65, 147
Lyde, Robert, 193

Marmontel, Jean Francois, 126
Martin, Lillian, 18
Martineau, James, 195–96, 203
Mason, R. Osgood, 143
Mattheissen, F. O., 81
Menand, Louis, 77
Mill, John Stuart, 126
Mitchell, John Kearsley, 215
Mitchell, Mary, 214–15
Mitchell, Silas Weir, 211, 214
Molinos, Miguel, 63

Index of Names

Monod, Adolphe, 146–47, 153
Mouton, Jane S., 61
Müller, George, 191–93, 216
Murphy, Gardner, 141
Myers, Frederick, 141–42, 190–91
Myers, Gerald E., 5

Newman, Francis William, 48–49
Newman, John Henry, 49
Nisbet, John Ferguson, 95

Palmer, George Herbert, ix–xi, 9–10, 21–22
Pascal, Blaise, 167–68
Paulhan, Frédéric, 93
Peabody, Andrew Preston, 231
Peabody, Francis G., 193
Peck, Mr., 149
Peirce, Charles Sanders, 15
Perry, Ralph Barton, 5, 18
Pilkington, J. G., 97
Piper, Leonora Evelina, 11, 232–33
Pratt, James Bissett, xi, 36–39, 83, 185–86, 199, 217, 223
Prince, Morton, 142–43
Pruyser, Paul W., 127
Pussey, Edward B., 97
Putnam, James, 43–45

Read, Louis H., 210–11
Reynolds, Mary, 214–15
Ribot, Théodule, 69, 120, 123
Richardson, Robert D., 5, 59, 67
Robertson, Nan, 59
Rodriguez, Alfonso, SJ, 179–80
Rosenzweig, Saul, 13
Roubinovitch, Jacques, 70
Royce, Josiah, 12
Rubin, Julius H., 85

Sabatier, Auguste, 188–89, 199

Sainte-Beuve, Charles Augustin, 155, 179
Selzer, Richard, 28
Sénancour, Etienne Pivert de, 197
Simon, Linda, 5, 22, 81–83, 182, 193, 231–32
Smith, Hannah Whitall, 171
Spinoza, Baruch, 62
Starbuck, Edwin Diller, 16, 49, 103–4, 109, 116, 124, 128–30, 133, 149–52, 157, 164
Starbuck, George, 39, 44
Stevenson, Robert Louis, 173
St. Pierre, Jacques Henri Bernardin de, 200
Suso, Henry, 176–77
Swedenborg, Emmanuel, 82, 84

Taylor, Eugene, 13–14, 141–43, 207, 209, 214, 216
Thoreau, Henry David, 161
Tolstoy, Leo, 71–76, 86, 105–6, 111–14, 126, 148
Toulouse, Edouard, 70
Townsend, Kim, 225
Tyerman, Luke, 177
Tyndall (Prof.), 177

Upham, Thomas Cogswell, 169, 171

Vinton, A. H., 218
Voysey, Charles, 161–62

Walsh, Hugh, 5
Warne, Frederick G., 191–92
Whitman, Walt, 50
Wilson, William Griffith (Bill W.), 59–60
Wood, Henry, 53
Woolman, John, 173
Wordsworth, William, 126, 229
Wulff, David M., 103–4

www.ingramcontent.com/pod-product-compliance
Lightning Source LLC
Chambersburg PA
CBHW031726230426
43669CB00007B/263